Martin Post

The Riverton Minister

Martin Post

The Riverton Minister

ISBN/EAN: 9783744790642

Printed in Europe, USA, Canada, Australia, Japan

Cover: Foto ©ninafisch / pixelio.de

More available books at **www.hansebooks.com**

THE

RIVERTON MINISTER,

—BY—

REV. MARTIN POST.

ATLANTA, GA.:
AMERICAN PUBLISHING AND ENGRAVING CO.
1897.

INTRODUCTORY NOTE.

This book contains a narrative drawn from life. Clothed somewhat in the garb of fiction, it is, so far as relates to the character, life-work and spirit of the Riverton Minister, fact. It is the story of a ministry which now is woven into the fabric of imperishable history; a ministry which was abundant in good that can never be lost or overestimated.

Obviously, any sketch of an individual, be the place he fills large or small as we measure, is at best but a fraction of his personal record and much more is it but a fraction of the record of his own times. But under the great law of compensation, while such a sketch loses of the general and cosmopolitan, it may gain in the local, personal and human. The writer has been compelled to exclude much material which, although highly important and often germane to this narrative, would, if adequately introduced, withdraw the focus from the one life opened to view in these pages and would multiply the pages into volumes.

May this tribute to a consecrated and beautiful life help to make other lives beautiful. M. P., Atlanta, Ga.

CHAPTER I.

Land of the West! Land of Promise! for four centuries the desire and hope of the under millions. The story of the thrill, the enterprise and daring evoked by that talismanic word, "The Great West," is already lapsing to the shadow land of tradition. Those annals of privation, exposure and brave achievement, of the leap from unbroken wilderness to giant Statehood, from scant subsistence to fabulous wealth,—the details of this heroic age of the Western Hemisphere must, like all things terrestrial, become "to dumb forgetfulness, a prey."

In this vast, and now reclaimed, interior of America, the van of the army of occupation halted for a day and garrisoned its forts, and on the morrow "folded its tents and stole away" before the drum beat of the irrepressible center and rear; still in quest of the Enchanted Land afar under the setting sun.

Thrice happy he who shall, even in humbler measure, aid these national chapters of heroic self denial and modest wealth, and often Christian devotement, and too often of unpublished greatness, to their deserved place in story and in song.

By the calendar it was the first day of winter in the year of our Lord, 1829, and by the geography it was on the banks of the

Pocanock River in the wilderness of the new State of Indiana. Here, as the day was nearly done, a solitary horseman rode up and halted. Evidently he had ridden hard. In truth, he had been in the saddle from daylight far into nightfall, for now almost six days: a new experience for John Goldwin.

He saw the smoke curling above the trees a mile below on the opposite bank, and had the comforting reflection that once there his journey would end. He gave the rein to his pony, and while pony stretched his neck and took breath, his rider gave loose rein to his thoughts.

The Pocanock waters cut their way through a dense wood, and the sun, fast disappearing behind the trees, was throwing his last javelins aslant the stream. The tall wild grass along the swales rasped its brittle blades with a crackling sound. Some of the forest leaves had forgotten to fall. A step in advance of the horseman a giant sycamore hung far over the brink. The current had eaten into the soil until the naked roots of the tree mutely appealed for protection against storm and stream. In that eloquent solitude relieved now by plunge of the wild duck, now by the plaintive voice of the mourning dove, now by the hoot of the solemn owl, nature seemed wholly uncognizant of man.

The solitude seemed to accord with our traveller's lone meditations. As he wiped his hat-stained forehead, he musingly reflected: "That sun is setting but mine is just rising. For me the day, sunlit or overcast, which I know not nor need to know, is but across this river. On its thither bank hope perches. Those colors of the gorgeous west—how deep and warm! How they grow! How they climb the sky! May I not read in them happy augeries? This I feel: that Love is there beckoning me and I follow."

In such mood was John Goldwin, when suddenly a rustle in the dense undergrowth at his right aroused him to recognize a hunter who stopped his horse beside him.

"Good evening stranger," said the son of Nimrod.

"Good evening;" replied John Goldwin, as he surveyed the hunter clad in a coon skin cap and brown "wamus" and linsey woolsey trousers, which were tucked into a pair of huge cowhide boots. A well worn leather pouch, a double barrel shot gun and a knife, sufficiently long and threatening, hanging from his belt completed his equipment. Sundry squirrel, duck and wild turkey hung from his saddle, front and rear.

"You seem to have had good success," said Goldwin as he cast his eye down upon the booty.

"Tol'able like," was the reply, "considerin' I've only be'n out since mornin'?"

"How far out have you been?"

"Out to Skunks Creek. I reckon that's right smart on to fifteen mile from here." Then surveying Mr. Goldwin's pony with an eye which took in his points at a glance, he said, "A good chunck of a pony, that. How far might you have travelled?"

"I left Madison on the Ohio river almost a week ago."

"I declare you've had a hard pull of it. It's middlin' tough at best, and on them that's used to it; and then this onsartin weather, mud, slush, ice and snow, beats all for bad trav'lin."

Having "spelled" their horses, they picked their way down to the water's brink. Little thought Goldwin as he feasted on the beauty of that river, how its liquid melodies were destined to flow into his life of battle and valorous achievement; little dream of the blessed human freightage it should one day convey to him.

"You are familiar with this ford; let me place myself under your leadership," said he.

"All right," said the hunter, "I reckon I ought'r know it. If I don't 'taint 'cause I hai'nt crossed it enough."

"Then you have lived in these parts for sometime?"

"Yes, its going on seven years since me and my woman and the children landed over there at Riverton."

"Indeed! Then you must be one of the founders of the settlement?"

"You're right there. When I put up my cabin, a Frenchman, old Dure, had a claim down at the Point and there was no other settler when I first set eyes on this neck of woods."

"Now, stranger," said the settler, let me advise you to hang that air pair of saddle bags across your shoulders, for now and then we step off into holes like and that pony of your'n haint no legs to speak of anyhow."

Mr. Goldwin, thanking him, accepted his thoughtful suggestion. When he emerged on the opposite bank, saving boots and leggins well splashed, he was none the worse for the fording. The frosty air of hastening nightfall soon stiffened their moist garments to ice, and moved them to quicken their pace. Threading the forest path which followed the winding of the stream, they soon stood on a gentle elevation and below them, picturesquely located at the juncture of the Rappilee and Pocanock rivers, lay the hamlet of Riverton.

Now our hunter never let an opportunity to gather news at first hand escape him, and he already opined that his companion was no ordinary visitor. So having exchanged names, he giving his as "Sam Drake," he said, "I'll 'low mebbe you're one of the Gov'm'nt Agents, or a land surveyor, or might be a school teacher?"

Goldwin answered evasively, reflecting that there was a sense in which he might be all of these.

"If you're a doctor you are wanted," said Drake, "for everybody at Riverton has the chattering shakes; mebbe you'll have them too. But I am not the man to scare you before hand. There's thistles everywhere, but mostly its green grass."

"Then," proceeded the speculative Sam, "I hav'nt seen a doctor since my sister took the fever and died down on White River."

Then Goldwin kindly drew from him the story of his only sister, the one pet lamb of the household, so amiable; loved by everybody; seemed like a white lily blooming in a desert. She had fallen a prey to one of those malignant fevers which were often so swift and fatal in the new settlements. Sam hurriedly brushed away a tear, but as he caught the eye of Mr. Goldwin, they both felt that mystic touch of nature which makes the whole world kin, and as Mr. Goldwin shook the rough hand of the hunter and parted, he thought that he already had one fast friend in Riverton.

Turning up to the tavern, the weary traveller passed over his pony to "Stubbs," the half breed hostler and servant of all work, and following the breezy landlord, Col. Grande, stepped within.

CHAPTER II.

Samuel Johnson loved to extol the old English tavern, but the Riverton hostlery constituted one of the distinct species, and, while plainly of the same genus, exhibited marked variations from the English type, with its sign of the Bull or Boar, or Sheep's-head, which looked stolidly on cavalier or round-head, churchman or dissenter for scores of generations. Here on the rim of civilization, was an instance of evolution modified by environment. Who at this intermediate stage saw the germs of a St. Dennis or Del Monte? Those pioneer "Travellers' Rests" already belong, like fossil enchronite or trilobite, to the curiosities exhumed from a by-gone age. Doubtless they knew the same genus homo that now careers over the earth; the same eating and drinking and quarreling and love making; the same lust of power and greed of gold; the same conflict of conscience and covetousness.

The Riverton tavern was a rough, two-story structure of unhewn logs, the interstices filled after the manner of what was known as "chinking and daubing," and the roof covered with "shakes," thin oak slits four or five feet long, which answered in lieu of shingles. These were held in place by long, heavy poles laid at regular intervals across them.

The apartments were at each end of the building, while a capacious drive way ran through its center, on the one side of which was a room extending over the width of the building, one end of which room served as kitchen and the remaining space, set off with three long tables, served as dining hall. On the other side of the central drive-way and landing place was a large room which answered the double purpose of office and general reception room, general gossip and news center for the settlement. It was flanked by a generous fireplace and graced with huge iron andirons, on which four and six foot logs were giving warmth and cheer, and fitfully decorating the sombre walls with an inimitable Rembrantesque play of dancing lights and shadows.

In one corner stood a rough semi-counter, semi-desk, rejoicing in the native wood colors, except as grease and rust had obscured them. Under this rustic counter were sundry kegs and a two gallon jug, while on the counter were ranged a pitcher and large glass and a half dozen small glasses, some of them nicked or cracked. The pitcher and large glass suggested water. The others somthing else;—what General Tupper not inaptly called, "the distilled juice of devils."

During the evening, as Goldwin observed, very many, and some more than once, drew up to the counter in quest of a little of this "inside matter."

A shelf, supported on two pegs driven into the wall behind the counter, was covered with tin candlesticks, each containing a small section of a tallow dip. The walls were unadorned save with a rifle and powder horn and an old shot-gun. and several attempts at art; such as a rude cut designed as a portrait of "Old Hickory," but dingy and dark and diabolical enough to have been the phiz of "Old Nick" himself. Yet do not prematurely decide as to the political bias of the place, for from the opposite wall, on one side of the door, "Harry Clay" looked down with a benignant smile and on the other "Daniel Webster" with his eternal frown.

Splint bottomed chairs and rough stools were scattered in front of the fire and several plank benches ranged against the wall and displayed divers attempts at wood carving and lettering with the irrepressible jack-knife.

Who shall record the political wisdom whittled out on this, the People's Bench? Cowper essayed to sing of the Sofa, and why not some favorite of the Muses attempt the annals and the honors of the puncheon slab bench which was so often consecrated by sprinkling with juices of the odorous weed. What debates it has sustained! What destinies have rested on it! What policies' have been carved upon it! What political slates here made or marred! Here the sacred Nine invite. Let some hitherto "mute inglorious" tune his lyre to "The Song of the People's Bench."

Back of this general reception room was a smaller apartment which seemed to be a universal stow-away. Here lay bits of harness, old saddles, coon skins, whip stalks, riding blankets, old tin horns, cups of wagon-grease and many other things which for the most part, had apparently quite outlived their usefulness, and were waiting burial or cremation.

Meanwhile John Goldwin joined the group about the fire; chatted and watched the steam rise from his boots, and hung fancies on the flame steeples which rose and fell on the maple and hickory logs until supper was announced and, presto, the scene shifted to the dining room.

We have hastened to describe this primitive hotel, for it very soon disappeared before the tidal wave from the East.

At the supper table Goldwin was half amused as he discovered eyes here and eyes there asking quite as plainly as any words could, "Who are you, young man? Whence and why did you come?" And during the evening, too, in the room of general rendezvous he was under the darts of these optical interrogation points. As the settlers dropped in at this news exchange, they quickly singled out the strangers, and John Goldwin was one of those whom having seen once, a second look was sure to be given him. Little surmised they how under that modest and seemingly unobservant aspect, this stranger was really observing and mentally digesting everything.

But our weary traveller soon found that even this ocular telegraphy could not keep his eyes open, and the landlord, or Col. Grande as he liked to be called, taking one of the tin candlesticks and Goldwin's saddle bags, piloted him up a ladder into the "loft," where were rows of beds or bunks extending the length of the building. A chintz of fantastic figures and colors partitioned the farther corner of this dormitory. Into this unique bed chamber this favored guest was ushered with an officiousness and flourish which would have done honor to the keeper of his majesty the King's bed-chamber.

Alone and free to roam in his thoughts, Goldwin almost forgot the present and was blind to surroundings, until the epitome of a candle flickered expiringly and recalled him to the immediate. The scene of the day, the resplendent sunset, the rock-bedded river with its cold splash and the strange faces illuminated by the great crackling fire logs, mingled with yesterdays and with the far away; the lake, the mountain, the New England home, dear mother and the boys, the old path to pasture, the rude school house, and the parsonage on the hillside where his heart had sought its Marian. As he turned on his pillow he spied through a crevice between the logs, a star. Was Marion, like that star, so brilliant, so cold, so far away? Goldwin, relaxed like a knight who had just laid off his armor, and soon was sleeping the sleep of the weary brave.

As he descended the primitive stairs the next morning, the first sight which met his eyes was two Indians, gashed and bloodstained, and lying in the heavy stupor which follows debauchery. Then as now, the white man's whisky was the red man's curse. Men passed in and out callous to the spectacle, or moved by it only to mirth or jest. Not so with this young stranger. On this, his first morning in Riverton, thus abruptly began his initiation into the infernal accompaniments of civilization. Do you wonder that with a heavy heart he walked out and under a morning sky which was the very embodiment of joy, said, "Can it be possible that the sun does not refuse to shine on such horrid scenes?"

CHAPTER III.

Heredity is a word to conjure with. We all like to trace the ancestral line and discover, or think we discover, the laws and the cause of this or that in the personages we are studying or commemorating. We say of A. as he becomes illustrious, "He comes of good stock," forgetful to say the same of B., his obscure and very indifferent brother. "Blood will tell," but so will some things else, and it were well for us amid our wise rules to leave abundant room for the play of environment, and above all, of will, human and divine. It may safely be taken for granted that the Goldwin genealogy is not conspicuously interesting to the general reader. Nor is it important to calculate just how many Welsh or Scottish or French or Dutch corpuscles swell the veins of the Goldwins. Suffice it for our purpose, that for a few moments we go back to Mr. John Goldwin's childhood and parental home.

Mrs. Sarah Hulburd Goldwin and her little family, having breakfasted, passed into the sitting room and she took down her Bible from the clock shelf for the customary morning worship. She took her favorite seat by the window which admitted the light directly upon the Scripture pages and where the rays seemed fondly to mingle their gleam with the silver which was cresting the waves of her dark hair. For a moment, her Bible unopened, she fed her spirit from the holy pages God had written in the scene without. It was a westward prospect; in the near foreground Lake Champlain; on the further shore the height where slumbered the ruins of Fort Ticonderoga, and in the distance, rising as guardian sentinels, the turrets and domes of the Adirondacks. "The strength of the hills is His," her soul whispered and reposed in the strength of the Eternal Love.

Beside her sat three boys, the manly and judicious John, the affectionate and alert Arthur, the rollicking little Thomas. One member of that group had passed into the long absence; yet, somewhat to the children and always to the mother, he was not absent. Three boys, a promise, a joy, a care, and now that she stood alone, a double solicitude. The high purpose of the father for their education now rested wholly upon her.

As she turned to her Bible, the eldest boy, John, the subject of this sketch, looked into her face with his wistful eyes and she said, "What is it John?"

For an instant the boy hesitated, then hitched his chair a little nearer and said, "Mother, can I ever go to college? I want to, oh so much!"

"Me, too," said Arthur.

"Me, too," said the roguish little mimic, Thomas.

For a moment Mrs. Goldwin did not reply. She was looking into the face of that dear husband. She was listening to his words in that last illness, words of sorrow that he could not live to aid her in endowing the precious boys with an education; words of faith that she should live to see their fond hopes fulfilled. Alone with her three children and with an income barely sufficient with strict frugality, to support them, how should the desire of the father and mother, yes, and as it now seemed of the children, be accomplished?

"Yes, John dear, I want you and your brothers to go to college. But it costs a good sum of money and means hard study."

"I know it does, mother," said John, "But I'll do all I can to help."

"Yes, my boy," she said, as she laid her hand on his shoulder, "I think you will. I know you want to be a good and useful man and I think some day you will go to college."

Then she read the 121st Psalm and she and John thought it must have been written expressly for them. They all knelt and so sweetly, tenderly and expectantly, the mother led her children to her Heavenly Father for help.

Education! How flippantly and assuredly and assumptively we talk of it! Fence off a little patch of our days, plant in it a few Greek and Latin and binomial roots and that is education! Put a fraction as equal to the whole! When you have discovered the boundary lines of being, then only may we essay to set bounds to education. So often the elements, so subtle and volatile, mockingly elude our proud analysis. The college—the joint hands of father and mother lay its corner stone. Mother is President of the Preparatory school. Home levels and squares and places the marble steps to the University of Life. Difficulty, privation, hardship, and self-sacrifice out of love to others are the invaluable corps of instructors.

Sometimes John would come from school saying, "Mother, my teacher says I am getting on first rate in Latin," and then he would declare that he was bound to push on and go to college. "College boys," he would say, "have any amount of fun, and I'm after the fun as well as the Latin and Greek." Then, young as he was, he would query over the ill-adjustments and ill-apportionments of life. "There's Uncle Phil," he would instance, "rich, plenty of money; could as well send his boys to college as not; but not one of them cares to study." Arthur, ever so much younger than they, almost always helps them out with their examples in arithmetic. "Mother," he would exclaim, "What's the reason things are so? Why don't we have money?" Hard question, who has fully answered it?

It happened one Saturday night after a day in the woods nutting that John, while Thomas and Arthur were rolling about in a frollic with dog Juno before the fire, related to his mother how they played court just for fun. "Arthur was arrested for stealing nuts and plead his own case. Uncle Phil's boys were jury and Thomas was clerk of the court and I was judge. I tell you Arthur defended himself well. But mother, Thomas whispered to him and gave him some of the smart things he said. Indeed, he did. He'll beat us all some day. And the judge, you know mother how sober and straight-faced he can be. He laid down the law to the jury good and strong." With boyish enthusiasm, John poured these things into the ready ears of the mother. Ambition, self-respect, family pride of the noble kind, warm the hearts of that little group. "Is this to my little lawyer boy?" thought the fond mother, as she looked into John's intelligent eyes? We shall see.

At that date Daniel Webster had furnished the school boys with scarcely any of his matchless declamations. But the eloquent peroration of his Plymouth address and later his plea in favor of the Greek Revolution, were circulating widely, and were eagerly caught up by these aspiring youth. Patrick Henry, however, was the favorite and his "Give me liberty or give me death," was detonated from rock to rock at almost any hour. The elaborate efforts, too, of Milton's "Moloch," or "Beelzebub" often held in awe the dumb stricken cows.

The neighbors were wont to say of John, "That boy has the stuff in him, solid all through." He was no premature old man. He was fond of boyish sports and not behind in Athletic contests. Nevertheless, when he slipped away from his comrades, they soon learned to suspect that he was hid away in some corner and lost in some book. That was hardly the day of town and school libraries. Books were few. Such as there were in the neighborhood were read and many of them reread by the meditative Vermont boy. But much of his thinking came not from books. Mountain, lake, cloud and sky have no scant share in the education of those whose minds are of the right fibre. As John plowed or sowed, or whetted his scythe, or pastured the cows, his patriotic soul would often roam away to the battles of Lake Champlain and Ticonderoga, and mountain and lake and defile came to be to him as brothers, living presences. Nature alike in her scenes of large peace, and in those of awful conflict, mingled with legend and tale of romance, and floated in memory and fancy, as cloud-play around the hills. The outer world, fashioned on rugged and ample scale, wrought a certain largeness and grandeur as well as tenacity, into the aspirations of the young Goldwins and entered the fabric of their thought in after years and under other skies, and afforded fitting symbols to body forth their spiritual interpretations.

Years passed. It was the last morning in June. The sunlight was glancing from green hillside and bare rock, and the lake was tossing back the dazzle of countless gems, while the sombre foliage of the oaks and pines was tremulous with the morning. Wagons rattling down the mountain roads, and clouds of dust hovering over those of the valley, betokened that the region was widely astir.

It was Commencement Day at Middleton College, Vermont. Fathers, mothers, sisters, brothers, sweethearts; care-visaged trustees and gay jesting schoolmates were crowding to the village church, eager to hear the young men who were bidding farewell to college days. In the graduating class was John Goldwin, while his brothers were approaching or crossing the thresholds of the college course. Between Arthur and Thomas sat the happy, justly proud mother. Had she not met Pres. B. that very morning and, busy as he was, had he not stopp d to press her hand and say, "Mrs. Goldwin, you are rich in your boys." Her heart was singing again that 121st Psalm, "My help cometh from the Lord who made heaven and earth," and she was living over again those mornings when college was far in the distance, invisible save to her radiant faith, and when she, with her little ones, went to the Divine Father for help.

John saw her as he rose to pronounce the valedictory and said to himself, "Mother never looked so beautiful as she does to-day." And there was another in that audience, Marian Braddock, whose eye seemed to him

to answer to his in that secret telegraphy
which mysteriously plays between souls
that are charged with the electric spark of
love. Secret, for as yet the connecting lines
had not ben seen by the world. By no form
of plighted words, indeed, had they themselves as yet recognized or sealed the bond.

"Fine fellow that Goldwin," said the
Chairman of the Board of Trustees, "somehow
I like him."

"You are right," said the President of the
College, "he is well poised, a clear thinker,
and touched with the gleam of the poetic;
just the one for solid results."

"By the way," rejoined the trustee, "when
I was in the legislature I knew his father,
Martin Goldwin, a young lawyer. He was
clerk of the upper house when he died, a man
of few words but prfect in his deeds."

"Now," added President B. "There is Belmar, one of Goldwin's classmates, quite
another type, brilliant, fascinating, but
pshaw! too many bridgeless gaps, too many
fields untilled."

Until his last year in college, John Goldwin
had in view, the profession of law. It was
natural that he should be attracted to the
path chosen by his revered father, and so,
without giving the subject as yet any very
serious thought, he had drifted into the
paternal preference. But he was not one
who could long be satisfied to drift. He was
maturing into one of those investigating and
unshackled minds which, welcoming the light

granted, must fearlessly think out its own schedule. During his last winter in college, the great question of existence met him and held him. Life was solemn, profound; of fathomless significance. He asked for light, and to him was fulfilled, "In Thy light shall we see light." He saw his personal Savior and humbly clasped him with every judgment and affection of his soul. He pursued his studies with the same, or if possible, even greater alacrity, but close observers saw that he was inspired with a new spirit and dwelt under a new, a boundless sky, resplendent with the love of his Divine Brother. Esteeming the claims of the profession of Law no less, he felt those of the Ministry more. So John Goldwin promptly turned his steps toward the New England Mecca of Theology in Massachusetts.

CHAPTER IV.

A light rap on the table and the buzz of voices suddenly ceased, and Rev. Dr. M. said, "The brethren will please come to order." Several theological students were about to be examined with a view to license and ordination for preaching the Gospel in the "far West."

"The Scribe will please call the roll." There was old Dr. C., his brown wig striving with only partial success to conceal his snowy locks. He was a little deaf and did not hear the thuds of his gold headed cane, as he vented his approval or disapproval.

Beside him was Bro. E., pastor at Waxham for fifty years, fresh from a tilt with his church, where certain young persons, sons of Belial, as he termed them, sought to bring the old Colony pulpit down a step or two towards the people. But Bro. E. said, "the nearer the sky the nearer heaven" and not an inch was it lowered.

Then there was Rev. Bro. D. His head was level; he looked on many sides of a question and always reached the charitable and wise conclusion.

And there was Dr. A., the guardian of Hyper Calvinism. His round face, square cornered brow and blinking eyes reminded the wags of an owl. The especial bulwark on which he perched was Adam's sin.

Close at hand was Dr. W., the famous logic chopper, hemming and clearing his throat for action. It was taken for granted that he knew all the ins and outs of foreknowledge, fore-ordination, predestination and precondemnation.

Dr. N. was the Apollos of the group, enkindling, ready, felicitous.

Bros. F. and H., and K., were examples of younger ministers, pastors of rural and village churches; practical, pushing out into unevalgelized districts; some of them fresh from blessed revivals, all of them so engrossed in fighting present sin that they quite neglected original sin

The little dapper man who sat near the Scribe was Dr. S., an indomitable stickler for technicalities. He could dance all day on some point of a pin precedent or punctilio.

Some minds are all angles and squares; no curves. Some are dry as last year's chips. Some are last year's bird's nests. Some are fountains sparkling in the sunlight. Some are ponds, green-scummed and stenchful. Some are elms, majestic, graceful and heavenward, and some are oaks, rough-barked, gnarly and immovable.

We must not forget to mention Dr. G., the *bete noir* of the student who was not well qualified in Hebrew. It was said that for forty five years he had never breakfasted until he had read a chapter in the original tongue of Moses and David.

The young theological students now took their places in front of the brethren, submitted their papers and replied to inquiries concerning their Christian experience, and their theological tenets. This new ministerial material seemed quite conformable to the traditional pattern. True, just the slightest ripple of expectancy passed over several faces at one stage of the catechizing. It was when Dr. A., bristling with texts from Paul, applied his peculiar probe.

"Mr. Goldwin," said he, "when you take up the work in the West, you expect to preach a stiff, uncompromising Calvinism, do you not?"

"Well—yes—and—no," replied the candidate, "I expect to preach just as stiff a Calvinism as the Bible gives me to preach; no more, no less; I intend to declare the whole counsel of God, as He gives me to see it."

With this unexpectedly shrewd and comprehensive reply, Dr. A. was obliged to seem satisfied.

The candidates having been examined, the Brethren voted "to be by themselves" for a few moments. Then ensued an interlocutory session.

"It does seem too bad to send young Goldwin out among the backwoodsmen," said the polished, scholarly and urbane Dr. B.

"Yes," replied Dr. M., "men of his scholarship and cultivated tastes must be quite out of place in the semi-barbarous wilds of the West."

"I don't know about that," said Bro. L., as he thought of his one brother, so studious and promising, who had gone out to Marietta, Ohio. "Let us," he continued, "remember that they who are penetrating to those unexplored regions are of our sons and brothers, and let us beware how we characterize them, lest we reflect damagingly upon ourselves."

Mr. H., a layman from Foxbury, was shuffling about nervously in his seat and finally broke out, "Paul, the scholar and poet of the Apostles, was not retained for the 'eligible pulpit' at Jerusalem, nor did he settle down with the Metropolitan church at Antioch, but pressed out far hence to the Gentiles, and found call for his best powers in the uttermost parts of the earth."

Likewise Rev. Father T., the Apostle John of the group, as he was sometimes called, said, "Brethren, if young Goldwin has it impressed upon him that he should go as a Missionary into our Western country, beware how you utter a word against it, lest you be found fighting against God."

So John Goldwin was ordained with due form and solemnity to the work of preaching the Gospel in the great North West Territory, much as now one is set apart to go to Alaska, or into the jungles of Central Africa.

The close of this day, so eventful in the life of John Goldwin, found him alone in his room reflecting and striving to grasp the reality. He was at last commissioned for his life-errand, and he was glad to be once more in the privacy of his own thoughts. He had struggled through one of the streams which mark a boundary and now was planting his feet on new territory. Or, he fancied himself like one crossing a series of mountains. He felt that he was now on the brow of the first range. He saw the long climb behind him; home, school-house, academy and seminary were behind him. He stood to-night on the first summit, professional life. He looked back at the plains and hills traversed and forward at the heights, still above him and to be scaled. He never felt more humble, never more thankful, never more hopeful.

And yet he was turning his face from what all were pronouncing a most rare and attractive opening. Prof. P. had asked him if he might recommend him to a church in Hartland, Maine, and Goldwin knew well that this Professor's recommendation was bout equivalent to securing for him the position. It was a coveted position. Hartland was a city noted for its natural beauty and its commercial advantage, and, what was more to John Goldwin, for its refinement and high bred intelligence. There he would have opportunity to pursue his studies and gratify his pure tastes; there he would be in the center of a large, appreciative, and inciting circle of kindred minds,

s... nded with abundant aids, with a pastor's library, maintained by an annual fund from the church. Prof. E. had said to Goldwin, "Better think carefully before declining such an opening."

He did think carefully, but he could not be blind to the fact that there were probably scores of desirable persons ready to fill the vacancy at Hartland, and he said, let me go where other ministers do not go. He heard a voice for him from the settlements multiplying and peopling as by magic in the West. It grew more distinct, daily more imperative. It was his duty to listen to it. He knew what he was declining. He was keenly alive to the inducements to accept the field which was already plowed and sown rather than that which was to be cleared of giant forests and stumps and only after many days or years of most arduous labor to be brought under the plow. Taste, culture, emolument, all the bent of his modest and scholarly nature, led one way; but he believed that duty and the denial of self for the sake of the Crucified, led another way.

One thought, however, troubled him, deterred him, sometimes, seemed about to turn the scale. The thought was of one whom he hoped to ally to himself in the dearest of earthly bonds. For her sake how he coveted the already producing field and the already provided home. The thought of exposure and discomfort, not for himself, that he could bear, but for one who had always been carefully shielded from hardship, disturbed him; tossed him as a lion his prey.

And yet, after all, he could not help saying, "Are not women also called to that higher privilege of forgetting self in the service of others? Is not their winning and purifying influence especially needed where there are so many infl ences toward savagery?" Goldwin had at first felt that he was being rent and torn between contesting forces, to neither of which he dared to surrender. But with such a man as he, this could not continue. Like the brave man that he was, he fought his way out. The smoke and dust fled. Sweet light came and he saw clearly the strong angel of Duty pointing him Westward.

To-night he saw that matchless angel, saw and wondered that he had not seen before that he was Love. Yes, he was sure that he had never felt stronger nor happier than to-night. His soul overflowed with thankfulness and he was girded with a degree of power unfelt before.

As he drew his chair up to the table and adjusted the shade of the lamp overhanging it, so as to focus the tempered light on himself and the unwritten page before him, all unconsciously, he presented a Rembrantesque study which would have been fortune and fame for any artist, had he succeeded in transferring it to canvas. That full and finely modeled brow, those clear, resolute, soulful eyes, that soft brown hair rolling back in waves, which the elfish light was sowing with shreds of gold—unique embodiment of manhood.

Then he wrote two letters; short but full of heart love. One to his dear mother. Well he knew that on that memorable day her thought and prayer had been for him. To her his first word was due. Another letter he wrote, sealed it and addressed it, "Miss Marian Braddock, Ryeburgh, Vermont." So the "day was done" and amid songs of peace he slept.

And in visions of the night he saw his brother Thomas in a vast and open-air amphitheatre delivering an oration, and an eagle sailing far above him, narrowed his circle more and more, till at last he perched just before the orator and listened spell bound. And his brother Arthur was sitting at a desk preparing an article for the Middleton Journal and a dove flecked with gold alighted upon his right shoulder. Then the scene of the night vision shifted John stood on the brow of a steep acclivity and beckoned to Marian to come to him. She advanced a few steps and then as he extended his hand to her, she turned and fled. Next he saw Marian in a sumptuous and brilliantly illuminated reception hall. Never did she appear more queenly and she wore a crown of gold inwrought with precious stones. But the crown broke in many segments, which, one after another, fell, crumbling, to the marble floor, and her marvelous beauty fell from her, as petals from the rose. He awoke in the first gray of dawn and the rain was dashing on the roof.

CHAPTER V.

A morning in October! Let the poets sing of it, but court the muses assiduously as they may, they never can rise to the height of the theme. Its thrill and aroma escape them. Out of the Night came clean Morning, clad in bridal robes fresh from the Sun's golden web.

John sprang up, singing, "To the Hills, to the Hills away." Now for home, sweet home, and that other home on the heights. The stage left at eight o'clock. Thrusting into his portmanteau little tokens of rememberance for mother and brothers, he hastened around to the village hotel, where "Jehu" held the reins and blew the horn. All was bustle and as usual, some were arriving at the last minute and there was rushing and elbowing, and now and then words escaping which we will not record. And there was the inevitable stout woman, with a flaming carpet sachel swelled to bursting, and two band boxes and an umbrella, and a small boy. Puffing and perspiring her way to the front she insisted upon riding on top. But the driver insisted that the upper seats were taken, and that the stage would be top heavy and finally had her squeezed into the inside back seat between two gentlemen whom she quite obscured.

Four horses, seven passengers on deck and ten in the cabin. Fare sir, please. All settled. Doors shut with a bang. All right. Go ahead, Jehu; go he does.

Nature was offering her best for the pleasure of the journey. Gold, and orange, and crimson had here and there crept into the foliage and were giving hint of gorgeous autumn. Orchards were radiant with red-cheeked apples, and the farm boys were running up ladders into the tree tops, plucking the mellow fruitage and storing away in barrels so much laughter and cheer for the open fireside and long winter evening. Off to the right and to the front, sunshine and shadow were chasing over the distant mountains and into the sky. Cattle and sheep peacefully grazed, or calves and colts capered, in the undulating pastures. Thrifty villages, and scattered along between, the hospitable barns and neat and comfortable homes, abodes of intelligent freemen, made John Goldwin proud to say, "This is my own, my native land."

The second morning out brought fresh horses and a change of driver, who was known along the road as Jack Barnett. Like John Goldwin, he sprang from a thrifty home in Vermont, and he and the young minister were once mates in the same district school.

In obedience to an aside suggestion from

Jack, Goldwin climbed up to a seat with him.

"Some good horse flesh you drive?"

"That I do," replied Jack, pleased to see that the young preacher observed his equine pets.

"So you know a good horse as well as a good sermon?"

"Yes, Jack; I believe I can see the good points in each."

Started now on his favorite theme, Jack straightening himself up, said, "from a small boy I was always fond of horses and not over fond of books; if I had studied them as eagerly as I did horses, I should have known something now. By the by, John, did you know how near I came once to going to college?"

"No," said John, looking eagerly at him. "Tell me how it was. I wish you had gone."

"So do I wish it now," rejoined Jack, "but you see, I was a boy, and boy like, when father offered to send me to college and give me a hundred dollars for each year I was there, or give me three hundred dollars cash, and 'Dick,' a splendid four year old colt, I foolishly chose the cash and Dick."

"Great mistake," said John, "a little compulsory education you needed just then."

Jack smiling, said, "Guess I did. My stars! If I had got the education I could have earned the three hundred dollars and the colt mighty quick."

"But then, " continued Goldwin, "I suppose you thought that the cash in hand would carry you a great deal farther than an education would."

"O, yes," said Jack; "how my sister did plead with me to go to college; told me I'd regret it all my life if I didn't. But I thought I knew all that was worth knowing. Good advice was thrown away on me. I tell you John, I've found out one thing;" emphasizing his words with his whip stalk, "it's brains that win. Why, there's Will Richards and Abe Williams, my boy mates; not as bright and quick to learn as I was, if I do say it, who went to college, got their conceit balls pricked, learned to use their brains on short notice; and now, oh, my! look where they are. I'm nowhere compared with them"

"Jack, you're orthodox on the college question."

"You better believe I am," cried Jack. "Experience, that dear schoolmaster, has taught me that it takes training, learning, to put value into a horse or a man. But so it goes," said he, as he drew himself up and cracked his long whip; "live and learn, you know."

"Yes," observed John, philosophically, "foresight is better than hindsight." Then pointing to the off leader, he added, "you believe in education for horses. There's one that needs a little."

"That's so," rejoined the driver, as he gave the delinquent a taste of the end of his lash; "he inclines to shirk; have to stimulate him occasionally. There's a deal of ˙uman na-

nature in horses; like men, they are about as selfish as they dare be."

"No, no;" stoutly protested the young minister, "I doubt that concerning horses and deny it concerning men. At any rate, the remark is to be classed among those which are too sweeping."

"Well now," answered Jack, "I am backed up pretty well, for the good Book says all men are liars. How is that for sweeping?"

"Ah, yes, David said that, but confessed that he said it in his haste," was the reply.

"Well, anyhow, " said Barnett, "look at these horses. There's that off leader, old lazy bones, that you've just admitted would throw all the work onto the others if he could."

"O, just give him a memento at the lash end of your whip; give him something to think about and he's all right. No very deep selfishness there," interposed Goldwin.

"There's his mate," pursued the driver, "a fiery fellow that needs watching; tough as whalebone; lots of service in him; but you never know when or where he'll break out in some nonsense; try to rush up a stone wall or down a precipice, fly the track, and of course, hurl everything to ruin. He's cranky. I call him my 'Radical.' "

"Crank is a more appropriate name," interposed Goldwin.

"And here," continued Jack, "is this nigh wheel horse. She's doing splendid work today. but she's just according to the company she's in. Put her alongside a young cut-up and she'd be as fractious as the devil. I call her my 'Turn-coat.'"

"Bravo," cried John, patting him on the back; "I'll have you appointed Professor of Philosophy—horse philosophy. But here's one more steed. Give him a character. I should guess he's the best horse in the team."

"You're right this time," answered Barnett. "He's your old reliable; wants none of your new fangled ways; knows the beaten track and keeps it right on to the day of judgment. I call him 'Old Conservative.'"

"Very good," retorted the young minister, but with a twinkle in his eye asked, "how about your theory? That horse character does not look selfish."

"But what," reasoned the driver, "if this horse concludes that good behavior generally secures good treatment; that steady, straight work is the better for himself in the long run? Then the motive with the horse, as with men, is selfishness after all."

"No, no;" interrupted Goldwin; "not selfishness but self-interest; quite a different thing and quite right, too Self-interest is regard for No. 1, so far as that does not interfere with No. 2 or any other number. That is natural and justifiable, and harnesses mankind together in harmony. But selfishness is all for No. 1, to the neglect or destruction of every other number. Self-interest accords with the Golden Rule: selfishness clashes with it. Self-interest is the pure brain feeding grain; selfishness is that grain turning sour and poisonous."

"Rotting into whiskey, I 'spose you mean," said Jack.

"That's about it, I guess," assented Goldwin.

"Well," said Jack, who in his heart was really pleased to see how his old acquaintance with a word poured daylight into the subject, "I see that you are professor of theology and I am only professor of horseology. But then, you know, every man has his price."

"No, I don't know that," said John Goldwin. "I know that it is said that every man can be bought if you will only come to his price; but I know that, like many another popular saying, it is too sweeping. Every man has his price—so the devil affirmed concerning Job, but Job was too much for him. And your own observation won't bear you out. You know, Jack, for example, that your good father and mother are not actuated by selfishess; far enough from it."

A tender look came over Barnett's bronzed face, as he thought of the dear old folks at home.

Now they were approaching a station, the last before climbing the mountain.

"Here I always bring out my Methodists," said Jack, with a mysterious air.

"All right," said the minister, "that will insure progress."

The coach dashed up to the village hotel,

its arrival the only sign of life in the sleepy hamlet. The small boy suddenly danced attendance, eyes and mouth open, watching every movement of the driver, doing him any little service as obseqiously as the Postmaster does for his Congressman, and aching for the day when he can take the driver's throne and whirl the long whip so adroitly as to behead a fly on the leader's flank.

"All aboard," shouted the driver, and started for a climb of seven miles. Mr. Goldwin observed:

"We have six horses now."

"Oh, yes," was the reply, "those fresh leaders I always put on for the climb. They're all go ahead, like to lead and they put new life into the other horses. They'll be tuckered out against we reach the summit and there they'll lay off. I call them my 'Methodists'."

The young minister laughed and said, "I am glad to see that the stage has a good strong Calvinistic break. But whew! How we have to take the dust. My eyes are full of it."

"Well, you know, its the man who carries the dust that fills the public eye," said philosophic Jack, as he skillfully trotted his team around a sharp curve.

Goldwin smiled at these grains of wisdom culled from the dust. From admiring the almost human sensitiveness of the faithful horses to the voice and hands of the driver, now, as the crest of the mountain was reached, he became absorbed in the resplendent vision, both the outward and the inward. For all he saw—the wide area of earth and sky—was canvas and palette for his mind-painting. The disappearing sun was casting cloud-deeps around his going, now moated and embattled castles of crimson, unfurling pendants of fire; now walls and towers and cities of purple and gold, whose reflected radiance lay aslant earth and sky, robing a world in softened light.

"What can equal this," exclaimed Goldwin, "Those sun-swathed clouds! They roll and billow magnificently. Sea of glory!"

"Well yes, now that you speak of it, that is a fine sight," said Jack, "I wonder I had not seen it before."

Forms and faces radiant with love, John Goldwin was seeing on that canvas. Mother and brothers and home, and that other face now never quite absent from his sight, were seen in every water drop and flower and cloud. He was indeed on the crest of the mountain.

CHAPTER VI.

Ryeburgh was a village clinging to a Vermont hillside, and like a sleepless sentinel on the outpost, was keeping watch over the low country and the placid Champlain; chiefly distinguished, however, to us and the young minister with whose history we are now concerned, because here lived Marian Braddock. Her father was then and for years had been the clergyman of the town. For years, too, he had been one of the trustees of Middleton College, and even little Ryeburgh could tell of ten or twelve students whom he had started in Latin and Greek and inspired with aspirations which, by dint of struggle and much self-help, carried them through the Middleton curriculum.

Marian was about four and twenty, tall, gracefully molded, with hair that was dark and eyes which were intensely dark, and a countenance beaming with intelligence and glowing with suppressed fire. There was that about her which drew attention. One upon meeting her would wish to study her; not so much, however, because of elicited affection, as by way of mental speculation.

She had a select class of twenty or more young ladies whom she instructed in French and also in History, English and American, and in general literature. Her pupils were gathered from a wider vicinage than little Ryeburgh, and while they respected and admired, could none of them really be said to love her. Yet there was always on the part of Miss Braddock amenity, dignity, perfection of manner and sparkling *naivete* which rendered her very attractive. There clung to her something of the freshness and piquancy of her mountain atmosphere, and with all, a certain bewitching flavor of originality and independence It is surely not surprising that Middleton students often competed for the privilege of sniffing the air of this rare mountain blossom. Mr. Goldwin, on arriving home, sought the first opportunity to call and pass an evening with Marian.

"Well, John," said she, "I suppose you are a bird feathered out, wings plumed, for they say you are now full fledged. Bird of Paradise, probably."

"O no, still bird of earth, and of humble feather and flight." Then he added more seriously, "Nevertheless, Marian, as soon as set free, I do 'Flee as a bird to your mountain.'"

"O then, jail bird escaped from prison!" Marian archly replied, "Complimentary to that Theological Seminary. One would suppose that to be a veritable Saint's Rest."

"Veritable gathering of the sons of God, Marian, but as of old, Satan came also among them."

"Then," she retorted, "it would appear

that you young theologians haven't exercised him. Hope you haven't been 'donning the livery of heaven' though."

"No, nothing more sacred than sober black broadcloth.

She smiling added, "After all, I guess you needed his Majesty to stir you up, for it must be very monotonous not to have a little spice of sin."

"They do say," returned John, "that the Devil is a profound theologian, and what's more than can be said of some theologians, strictly orthodox."

"Yes," said she, "no one quotes Scripture more aptly for his purpose than he does." Then turning to John, she added, "Well now, I suppose you feel as though you were shoved out mid-streams and must bear down on the oars."

"I must," said he, "as soon as I have secured a fellow passenger." His features lighted up, and fastening his earnest eyes upon her, he continued, "Marian, I have come here to this old mountain home to find my mate. As I wrote you I have chosen the West. Will you go with me?"

Marian's black eyes dropped for an instant. Then there was just the slightest curl to her lips as she turned to Goldwin and said, "Pardon me John, I don't want to wound your feelings, but I must frankly tell you that you ask too much of me. New England is our natural home and you are needed here."

At this a cloud passed over Goldwin's face. And Marian, who usually bore herself with that refined self-control and composure which is the instinct of good breeding, and could sit with feet still and hands carefully clasped in her lap and entertain her company delightfully, to-night, in spite of herself, gave unmistakable signs that a mental tempest was on. To-night she was unquiet. To-night she was half gesticulating, or suddenly starting in her chair.

Resuming, she said, "John, you have adopted such romantic notions; you have left this practical age and gone back into the dreams of knight-errantry."

"How so? Please offer some proof of your charge."

"Proof! When the way opened to that fine church at Hartland you should have entered in at once, taking it as the bidding of Providence, as I believe it was. So would anyone have done who was not afloat on romantic impracticable ideas; and if you had gone to Hartland, I would have been ready to go with you. There I could still pursue my studies in modern languages and literature: there I should find occasion to use all my acquirements and so would you. But of what avail all our acquisitions, if we are to spend our days among half breeds and Potawotomies? If worst comes to worst, I think I can be a martyr, but I shall have to say that I am hardly ready to go chasing after martyrdom in this style."

It was obvious that John Goldwin was taken quite unawares by this, Marian's declaration of independence. Was she to give him clear instance in proof of Jack Barnett's assertion that all the world are about as selfish as they dare to be?

He arose and paced the room for a moment—only a moment, and then, by a strong effort, resumed his wonted composure and turning to Marian, said, "You misunderstand me, and I must add, disappoint me. I have thought this all over many, many times. I know well the attractions of a settlement in one of the centers of New England's best culture. I am keenly alive to them; for your sake I covet them. Out of devotion to you, I had once almost turned from what I esteem to be my duty and accepted those attractions."

He paused a moment, but she not replying, in a deep voice he proceeded, "To-night, Marian, has been a revelation to me. You do not look at life from my point of view. The difference is radical."

"Yes," said Marian, "I think it is."

"After all," pursued Goldwin, "it is entirely according to one's view point. Motive makes or mars. To lead the scouts and station the picket guards of Christian civilization, to carry peace and love into the great army of occupation whose tents gleam far away toward the sunset, to establish along those streams and over those prairies the impregnable defenses of freedom, patriotism and Christian brotherhood—tell me, Marian, if it is the inviting field you seek, where is there more inviting than this? Does not the true soldier, if given him to choose, ask for the front, and where the fight is thickest? Let my torch flame where the darkness is deepest. To me that is the 'inviting field.' "

"Wild dream! Morbid, morbid preference!" she exclaimed, but he was not to be interrupted.

"Already," he continued, "there are dozens of good men eager for that church at Hartland. Let me not crowd them. Let me go where the harvest is whitening and the laborers are few. I go to share with the pioneer; to help him break the soil for Christian homes and institutions. I go to grow with the growth of villages, cities, and states. I go to do as God gives me strength, for the wilds of Ohio or Indiana or Illinois, what heroic men of God from Massachusetts and Connecticut did a hundred years ago for the wilds of Vermont. 'Chasing after martyrdom?' Not I. Nor am I chasing after personal ease, or gratification of my social and literary tastes and ambitions. If this come to me I shall be glad and thankful, but the voice of Him whose name is written forever in my heart bids me 'Away.' "

John in his fervor and self-forgetfulness stood before Marian pouring out these impassioned words, his face lighted with a power and gleam which amazed, for the moment, almost overcame her.

But as he sank into a chair, she resumed, "Really John, it seems to me such a waste of education and talent. Seems like polishing pearls to set in a plough handle, or bestowing rare carving upon an axe helve."

"But is it waste?" said Goldwin, "that is the very question. To seek to make the great West, now rioting in natural beauty, blossom with moral beauty—is personal sacrifice on our part to this end a waste? Do facts sustain your assumption? But, Marian, do you suppose I insist upon your accompanying me now?"

"O," said she, "you have no thought of being unreasonable. I am sure of that. Still I think I know you well enough to be also sure that the darkest place you can find is the one you will go into, and I feel I ought to tell you that such is not my mood. Frankly, I am not ambitious of self sepulchering."

John turned to her in silence, a silence burdened with pity and soft reproach, a silence which said, "I see it all now; now Marian, I understand you and I think you understand me, although I do not think you quite appreciate my motive. Your soul is tuned to another key than mine. On the major chords of life we cannot harmonize." Then slowly, very slowly, but decidedly he said audibly, "We must play our parts separately."

They sat looking into the fire. The hickory log had crumbled into a heap of ruddy coals and was giving its fierce but final throbs of heat. They watched as already those coals began to take on the darkness of dying. John saw in those cinders his hopes, but now so bright, turning to ashes. The old clock in the back hall deliberately spoke twelve times. Roused from his meditations, John rose up to go. Then with indescribably sad sincerity he turned his eloquent eyes upon Marian, took her hand and said, "Good bye, Marian, God be with you." She replied, with just the slightest tremor in her voice, "Good bye, John." Neither dared trust themselves to say more. For an instant they stood silent with clasped hands. Then John Goldwin went out into the night. Marian lingered on the threshold till he was hidden in the deepening shadow. "Noble soul!" was her thought as she turned from the chill of the night air to the waning fire, and bringing the several embers together, hovered over them, seeking for some time to marshal her conflicting thoughts. The occasional flicker of blue flame was so in keeping with the complexion of her reflections. The room, always heretofore attractive, seemed now oppressively empty, and the great clock annoyingly obtrusive. She heard distinctly, in the great silence, the slow, measured breathing of father and mother as they sweetly rested. It seemed to mock her restlessness. Goldwin was still before her. The spell of his noble presence was still upon her. But it was to her Goldwin radiant and transfigured.

She had forged, as she had complacently thought, a perfect chain of argument; she had tried every link and supposed it flawless; she had brought it forward so confidently for Goldwin to admire, and no magician's wand ever swept an obstacle aside as easily and majestically as he had this. She was mortified, half vexed with herself, now that she felt that what she had delighted to call the lustre of her position and vantage was only a self-illusion. What inward commotion more harassing than to be convinced against one's will?

Rising with forced resolution, Marian took a book from the table, an elegant volume of choice selections from the poets, in which was a card bearing the name of John Goldwin, and retiring to her own apartment, laid it beside a package of letters in her private drawer, closed the drawer and locked it. Then, betaking herself to her pillow, at last, in the first gray of morning, she fell into a troubled sleep.

CHAPTER VII.

The New World! Volumes in the word! With what exultation John Goldwin repeated them as he looked out from his window at Riverton, as he stood on "the hill" and followed with his eye the two rivers Pocanock and Rappilee disclosed here and there by rifts in the almost universal forests: as he paused here and there before some giant tree of immense girth, as he thought of the lumber and houses growing in such trees, and of the mills and factories latent in those rivers. He sought to conceive of that untraversed landscape, as it soon would be when transformed into the abode of thousands of happy homes, and of churches and schools and libraries, and halls of justice and of art, and the center of a population rivaling in numbers and affluence that of the Eastern coast. Here, he said, I surely have the field and no one has larger in area or in potential greatness. I build on no other man's foundation. Cut and carve as I may, I trespass on no one. A blank page and I am bidden to write. Enthusiasm, hope, imagination, have the freedom of the New World. If only I may instigate moral advances here on a scale commensurate with the commercial advantage and opportunity and the natural beauty and opulence of Riverton. His heart burned with holy chivalry.

Material was at hand, but it was largely raw material. The timber had braved all sorts of weather and was naturally gnarly and tough. Riverton was an Indian trading post, one of the points selected by the government from which to mete out annual, or semi-annual payments to the original tribes of the soil. Here the Indian commissioner and general paymaster, General Tupper, had his headquarters. At this date the settlement was largely composed of adventurers who were playing the game for sudden wealth. The superintendent, General Tupper, was renowned for his wisdom and fairness. Nevertheless, here, as a rule, it was the unscrupulous white man pitted against the childish red man. A community delirious with the fury of the gambler was not the most promising material out of which to frame stable Christian homes and model society. Children in such atmosphere inhaled lewdness and lawlessness. Money and self-indulgence were the thought; sensuality the pleasure.

We, who know it only through retrospect, easily magnify the romance of the pioneer life; but, to those who encountered the facts, life was not all romance. The only private house at which John Goldwin succeeded in securing boarding and lodging for the winter was in the cabin of John Dale, who had a large and increasing family. The easy going Pater

Familias was annoyingly disregardful of the proprieties of life; quite disdained pocket handkerchiefs so long as he possessed a shirt sleeve or coat-tail, and thought no spot too good for his generous distributions of tobacco juice.

One curtained corner of the large family room was Goldwin's bedroom and study. All varieties of life and how thin the partition between! The priesthood has often been injured by withdrawal from the world. This danger did not threaten this minister. Sitting room, dining room, bed room and kitchen were very conveniently accessible, since all were built on the great American principle of many in one. Many were the "asides" here in the homiletic drama, and the comedy of life was hard by on the same stage. Sometimes the sermon became too ethereal for earth, and taking on ascension robes, went up the capacious chimney, along with the smoke and with the incense of the crane and the dutch oven. This house which Goldwin and a few others occupied, was so constructed as to secure an abundance of ventilation, so that the family were not in bad odor. The winter blasts piped and whistled and roared and howled—kept a whole menagerie—under the loose floor and between the logs, and often a miniature snow drift came unsolicited through the chinks.

The menu of the Dale house grew less and less varied, more and more devoted to that which would "stay by one," until finally it recorded a steady diet of fried pork in the morning, roast or boiled pork at noon, and salt pork, or occasionally pork sausage, at night. Therefore swinish propensities were not unaccountable. Who can wonder that that which was called the light bread was not always worthy of that name; and the biscuit, often soggy, were often soaked with lard. This refectory was a severe trial to the sensitive stomach of a student, and not conducive to cheerful reflections. Winters are non productive, but this one produced for Goldwin a dyspepsia which was tenacious as life and relentless as death.

The young minister's library, at the best not large, having come as far as Buffalo. wintered there until navigation opened late in the Spring. Hence his reading, for the first five months in Riverton, was confined to his Bible and hymn book. Well could he write to his mother that never before had the old Bible been such a treasure to him.

Mrs. Dale, the presiding genius of the household, was a fair representative of the pioneer mother. How she was able to keep her family clad and fed will ever be a mystery, and ungracious beyond endurance would be he who should dwell upon any infelicities which would sometimes intrude into her department; the miracle was that there were not more. Few great commanders, whose renown has come down the ages, displayed more tact, ingenuity or generalship, or mastered greater difficulties than did Mrs. Elizabeth Dale. To say that she did what she could is to render but scant justice. Time would grow weary to enumerate how often she had to face the old problem, "how to make bricks without straw." The light of the rude cabin of the early settler, beckoning alike to rich and poor to share its slender store, was the patient, plucky, resourceful pioneer wife and mother.

At this time the only public building in the settlement was the school house. It was erected on the economical plan of serving also as a public hall, and was open to anything which called the people together. General Tupper, hitherto the guiding mind of the town, a man of large landed possessions centering at Riverton, and marked by a generous public spirit, had insisted that whatever else halted, education must not, and that a commodious school building must be at once erected. He donated to Riverton the grounds on which it stood, and also reserved a handsome site on a little eminence east of the town, on which it was designed that in a few years should be reared a County Academy.

Men and women came to the school house to "the preachin'," as they phrased it, in glorious freedom from the tyranny of fashion. They fostered home manufactures, and the styles were almost as many and individual as the persons. Young Goldwin met with all the respect, if not devoutness which could be expected; an admission of the claims of religion in general, coupled quite too often with an ignoring of them in particular. The ruling spirits of Riverton were on the whole rather proud to have a minister among them —"helped to give character and dignity to the town," "sort'o handy at a funeral," "seemed like it used to be back East or down in Virginy." "Old Nat. Hawkins" vowed he had no use for preachers; they wer'n't producers nohow, and for his part, he couldn't see what good such as he was to a town.

"He's only a boy; doesn't look a day over twenty," said "Tim" the blacksmith, disdainfully.

"Now, don't you fool yourself," interposed Sol Perkins, "them light complected fellers is mighty deceivin'; he's a heap nigher thirty than twenty."

"Well" replied Hawkins, as he assumed a very wise look, "all I have to say is that he'll get his eye-teeth cut if he squats in Riverton."

"That he will," echoed a dozen voices, accustomed to echo Hawkins.

At that Sam Drake slowly drew his pipe from his mouth and said, "I ca'culate you'll find that air man Goldwin is nobody's fool, if he is young like. I'll bet you'll find he's a good head on them shoulders of his'en."

"Well, now boys," said Daniel Pierpont, and they all turned attentive ears to this young lawyer and recent comer to Riverton, who had thus far kept silence; "I make no pretensions to religion, and count myself no better than you, but I believe in religion and I favor the preacher. I was brought up to good morals, if I have backslid a little, and I tell you I wouldn't bring up a family where there are no Sundays and no churches. Sam Drake is right; this man Goldwin looks like genuine stuff, and I say give him a chance. Condemn no man until you've given him a hearing."

"That's good law," chimed a chorus of voices.

"Them's my sentiments," declared Landlord Grande, who, now that Pierpont had spoken so decidedly, ventured to crawl out of his shell.

"Free country," said one; "a little religion won't hurt," said another; and so the conversation passed to other topics. During this canvass of the minister's merits, Stubbs the half-breed, although standing in the background, and preserving an appearance of stolid indifference, was listening with both ears and weighing every word.

CHAPTER VIII.

John Goldwin, from a boy, had loved to flee to his mother and speak his heart to her. Now, so far away from her, he beguiled many a tedious hour by writing to her. But mail carriage was not then an easy thing. Communication with the Eastern states was a matter of from two weeks to two months, according to the season of the year, and the condition of the roads, and of navigation. The latter was practically tied up for at least one fourth of the year. Letter postage was twenty-five cents. The following is one of the letters Goldwin posted to his mother during his first winter in Riverton.

My Dear Mother:

How I do appreciate you, now that there is half a continent between us. What would I not give to look at men and things here through your eyes, as well as my own. I need your sedate, careful and womanly reflections, cast in with my glowing, hopeful, youthful dreams. The two well mixed might compound something about right. An ounce of good mother instinct would outvalue a pound of man logic, and might throw a fender around the fires of my ardor, so that stern reality should not scatter them. Mother, how would a wife do for a fender?

Here everything is in the future tense—no past-perfect tense, no precedents in these wilds. And yet none of us are clear of the past; would that some I could name here were. Opinion is often but another way of speling prejudice or custom. One man wants everything as it used to be in "old Vermont," (which is not so bad, is it?) and another as in "old Virginia." Why not compromise on a course which follows neither of these guides? If we could only make this new world new indeed! If, quit of every relic of wrong, pure of ancient taint, we were plastic to the hand of reason! Why carry with us the *impedimenta* which have clogged the older communities? It would seem as though our opportunity, such as comes not again in an age, would tempt into larger purposes and lift us into a greater life. And I believe it will too. Mother, I tell you I have great faith in this young giant West. Providence has untold grandeur and leadership in store for her.

And yet, mother, it must be confessed that the people here are quite on other thoughts intent. To read their titles clear to mansions on earth is full enough. Gain is godliness Hospitable we are here, open-palmed, swift to resent an injury. Of the two species under the genus American, we have more of the Jamestown and less of the Plymouth.

Send us more Pilgrim Rock. No building material like that. Green Mountain rock'll do—chip of the old block—no discount on Vermont granite. Sometimes even a little of it does wonders.

Now, mother, don't for a moment suppose that I say these things, except in a whisper to you. Not I. I never draw comparisons here, nor say Plymouth Rock nor Pilgrim Fathers. I am alone. No one is unkind, and yet my very mission does hedge me off, and I find no one quite like-minded to whom I can open my deepest longings. On Sunday morning, while you and all the town are going to "the Center" to church, as I go to the school house to preach, I hear the sharp report of the rifle, and I see many strolling by the river with gun or fishing rod, and others indolently sitting on a log or stump, puffing tobacco smoke from their clay or corn cob pipe.

Have I told you of all the offices I fill in Riverton? I have as many titles as the Duke of Bedford. Some call me "the preacher" or "that preacher;" some, a little more deferential, term me "the minister." Good Mrs. Drake, or Mrs. Tupper, say "our minister." I am told that some call me "the boy preacher." On the other hand some call me "elder" though just why I can not say. One man whom I frequently meet, accosts me as "parson," and the old Frenchman, Dure, styles me "the priest." But if they will only give me a hearing, they may call me as they please.

One office which by common consent seems to fall to me is that of church janitor. On Sunday it is my fortune to carry the key of knowledge, and to unlock the school house. Then I light the fire, and remember that John Foster says that "genius is the capacity to light one's own fire." Then, too, I am "the sexton that tolls the bell." Thanks to General Tupper, we have a pretty good school house bell.

But the office which I assume with greatest fear and trembling is that of chorister. You will laugh, but the other day I was selected to "pitch the tune" at a funeral. So I started China, the only funeral tune I know, and you will say that I do not know that. What will you say then, when I tell you that I receive high compliments for my musical ability? At divine service I can discover but one hymn book, and that is my own. So I go at it Western fashion and "line out." Thanks to you, I learned at family prayers to sing several hymns, and I sing "Hebron and Greenville" and "Rock of Ages." Then I vary the next service by reversing the order of tunes. At first it was a solo, or at most a duet. This lining out process bothers me, and several times I should have been unhorsed completely if it had not been for Mother Smile, whose piping treble came just in time to save me from pitching pell mell into the ditch. These things do not always conduce to increase my devotional feeling. Nevertheless, a little singing does gratify the congregation and make it seem more church like. Besides, of late I have fallen upon better times, for the school teacher, Miss Emily Sherburne, a niece of Gen. Tupper, has come to my relief, and by a little previous consultation and concert of action in selecting the hymns, she is able to lead the singing quite well. Once in a while Mr. Drake attempts the bass, and so we are said to have very good singing.

By the way, this Miss Sherburne is a rare person. General Tupper was the means of prevailing upon her to accept the position of teacher, and fortunately, he has no sympathy with the common sentiment that almost anyone can teach the primary classes. So instead of having a coarse, masculine woman to cuff the children around and pound something into them, we have a true lady from Old Dominion, educated and possessed of that indescribable grace and finish of manners, which are the charm of the best families of Virginia.

But why is it, pray tell, that I receive no word from Thomas the Tutor, or Arthur the Sophomore? Remind them that they have a forlorn brother somewhere in the wilderness. I suppose Arthur is engrossed in strife for class honor, and Thomas, is he captured by some modern Helen or Dido? Does he ever run up to the parsonage at Ryeburgh?

Mother dear, write just as often as you can, but when you are too busy to epistleize me, make Thomas or Arthur your quill driver, so that I may hear the oftener.

Your always affectionate boy,

JOHN.

P. S. This morning I heard the first bird of Spring! Hurrah! I shed no tears over the dissolution of stern Winter. "Fly swiftly round ye wheels of Time, And bring the summer day." J. G.

The letter went on its way to Vermont. Nearly a month had gone by and brought the "boys," Arthur and Thomas, home for the Spring vacation. Arthur, although the older in years, was the younger of the two in college advancement, having been delayed by ill health. But not to be daunted by any difficulty, he entered Freshman as Thomas became Senior and now was in full Sophomore blossom, while Thomas was "the new Tutor."

It was one of those first warm days which signalize the flight of obstinate winter and tell of blessings near. Thomas, in morning negligee was half reclining on the old bench under the large cherry tree, which was sending out a few ventursome blossoms, white signals of an army soon peacefully to open its banners to the sun. In his hand was a volume of poetry, unopened, for he seemed preoccupied, carried captive by the scene before him, and the memories, home loves, and days and dreams of boyhood, which it precipitated upon him. Was it not vacation, and might he not relax his grasp, drop the oar, and drift or throw out the anchor wherever fancy and fond association beguiled him? John seemed once more by his side. Clad in mitten and muffler, they were shoveling snow together; or they were coasting; or they were making their way across the pasture, dinner basket in hand, to the school house; they were hauling and chopping wood; they were climbing the hills and gathering berries or nuts; they were improving a holiday in fishing and bathing; or they were stretched on the grass, planning and aspiring, and declaring what should be their future; or they were taking the dear mother in the dusk of evening for a row on the lake, and the moon was lifting above the hill and filling the hour with sweet enchantment, and they were gradually dropping into silence, while thought and fancy kept time to the silvery dip of the oars.

Abruptly Thomas was recalled from his reverie by Arthur's ringing voice, as ignoring gates and old paths, he cleared the fence at a bound and, exulting in freedom and hilarity, landed in the door way, shouting, "Mother, a letter from John!"

The mother, in these days, deep in no reveries, but in the prosy problem of refitting and renewing the wardrobe of the two collegians—garments in all stages of existence heaped before her for review—deputized her boys to answer the welcome words from John. Here are some extracts from Thomas' vacation letter:

"My Dear Hoosier Brother:

Here we are in this blessed harbor again, and it seems as though you must come in soon. I listen, expecting your footstep on the walk, or echoing on the stairs, or your voice as you rush in from the woodhouse. Here almost every sight and sound is associated with you. Of you we sing, *Quorum magna pars fui.* You are our good Aeneas or our wandering Ulysses; or rather our Nestor, so apt in counsel.

How many things I want to discuss with you—projected plans concerning my future! I am like one suddenly dropped down in a wilderness—a jungle. I must cut my way out. But which way leads out? Where lies the "open?" Strange that when we so yearn to know which way lies wisdom, there should be no answering voice. It is questioning the Sphinx. 'Dip into the future far as human eye can see,' and how much darkness mocks the

> 'spirit yearning in desire
> To follow knowledge, like a sinking star,
> Beyond the utmost bound of human thought.'

John, I am hungry for the Great West. Your descriptions and experiences fascinate me, capture me. The potentialities of our vast, undeveloped country, invite, inspire and amaze me as no romance can. I hear the mighty pulse beat of the millions. They are crowding toward the golden fields of the setting sun. I want to be in the thick of these continental destinies. John, would that I were standing by you on the outpost—freedom's utmost verge.

As tutor, I am often called to do double work; my own, and also to fill every chance vacancy. Then, too, I read law all that I can; sandwich Blackstone and Kent with Ovid and Homer, Livy and Xenophon. Judge Parsons offers to share his law office with me and holds out the alluring prospect of a partnership at no distant date. But I pant to push out. I want to be at the head of the procession. I want to be in at the birth of States and Empires. *Juniores ad labores.*

Some of the members of our college Faculty are grand souls. It is a privilege to have their society. They are cast in too large a mould to be mere routine and martinet drill masters. They look before and after, and live in deductions which are large, generous, cosmical. Going in one channel of instruction year after year, there is as you well understand, John, great peril of becoming prosaic, humdrum and pointless. This one and that one—who they are you can guess—are mediaeval, mouldy, and mossy. I shudder at the thought of fossilizing. I could settle down here into a permanent professorship;

and some of my colleagues think me odd and unwise because I do not seize the opportunity. But they work their work, I mine. I bear within me a noble discontent. I would cut loose from shore and turn my prow into the mysteries which 'gloom the dark broad seas.'

My dear brother, how different your intellectual pabulum from ours. We daily, amid the consecrated groves and shrines of the Muses, and you amid the corporeal, mundane and pragmatical, and hundreds of miles from a book! Woe to him who in your situation, has no mill and no grist of his own! I see no evidence that your grain is giving out. You delight in thinking and can whet your own sword and temper your own spear. No fear for you in the intellectual lists.

Here we roll along the college groove and life is almost too even, not to say monotonous. Last week brought a little variation from the old score; a party at the President's mansion. It was given by his lovely daughters in honor of the Misses Holdredge, two elegant ladies who are visiting them. By the way, Marian was down from Ryeburgh, graceful, self poised and queenly as ever. Her repartee outsparkles all. She is the star of the mountains. Nevertheless, I must be honest, old fellow, and say that when at rest and not rallied in animated conversation, she appeared just a little drooping. Was it only my fancy—I think not—that I detected a shade of sadness and disquietude clouding the sunshine of her features. Come sir, explain. Has that "first bird of Spring" whispered to her of that paragon of women, Emily Sherburne, with whom you 'act in concert?' Would she make a good 'fender?' Look out! Those Southern belles, I trow, are more fire than fender! Your circumstances are very fortunate for cultivating the musical art! Hope you will not be charmed into a duet which terminates in a long solo in the minor key.

Your idiosyncratic classmate, Belmar, sailed around among the guests at the party, as flashy and Frenchy as ever; but Marian seemed to be the orb which, more than any other, governed his eccentric revolutions. When he and Marian confronted, the scintillations of wit showered on us, and 'from peak to peak leaped the live thunder.'

But enough of this world for my unworldly *frater* Let me tell you, Arthur is developing superbly; finest rhetorician and belles letters scholar in his class; same say, in the Institution. It is whispered that he is a welcome caller on one of the President's daughters. Mother is the same ' perfect woman, nobly planned.' The years approach her very softly and only give her, if possible, a more lovely grace and dignity, and winsomeness. Such peerless examples of true man and woman as our father and mother! Legacy invaluable, isn't it? We will simply have to be good and useful. And how can any but the noblest woman of the race at all correspond with our ideal?

Well, good bye, old Pathfinder. Open a trail for the over-weighted millions into Liberty, Truth and Love. And may I soon be there to see it.

Your affectionate,
THOMAS."

CHAPTER IX.

It was more than twice a twelvemonth after Mr. Goldwin came to Riverton, that the events of this chapter occurred. Succeeding a winter memorable for its extreme rigor, Spring seemed to revive not only Nature but man. Riverton advanced by strides and leaps. The buzz of the two saw mills and the fires of the brick and lime kilns hardly ceased night nor day. The sound of the hammer and the ding of the trowel were heard on every hand. Things assumed more the air of permanence. More and better houses were appearing. Riverton was in the flood of the tide of immigration. Jack Barnett, with a wholesome faced Vermont girl as his bride, was among the arrivals. Stories of the Eldorado of the West had brought him on as far as Riverton, and what his own eyes beheld induced him to settle there.

As has already been intimated, Gen. Tupper could, with much propriety, be called the Major Domo of Riverton. He had the honor of being the first to represent his territorially large district in Congress. His residence, spacious and inviting for those early days, stood back from the road in a stately wood which had been sufficiently invaded by the axe to give the house a wide and magnificent view of the Pocanock river and its tree-clad islands.

It was a summer evening and the General and his family were gathered on the verandah. His family consisted of Mrs. Tupper, matronly and a little stately, two daughters, Isabel, the eldest, and Sibyl, a brusque girl of sixteen years; two sons, George, two years older than Sibyl, John four years younger; and the General's niece and general favorite, Miss Emily Sherburne. A special zest attended this informal family convention, from the fact that the General had that day returned from the State Whig Convention held at Indianapolis; he having had the honor of presiding over the sessions of that body.

The brightness lingered on the Western sky. An atmosphere of rest and caressing endearment settled with the shadows and starlight around the family circle. Supreme hour of the day, and made doubly so now by Gen. Tupper's recent absence. He was never happiest—never himself in totality, except in the unreserve and *abandon* of his home. In gown and slippers he settled into his easy chair on the verandah, Isabel beside him, resting her hand on his arm; Sibyl on the ottoman at his feet; John with his head in his mother's lap and George and Miss Emily sitting on the steps.

Gen. Tupper was commenting on the personnel of the Convention, introducing and shewdly characterizing the prominent actors, and marching them across the stage, to the delight of the little group, when the young ladies caught glimpses of the tall form of Mr. Pierpont, the popular young attorney, coming up the winding walk. Begging not to disturb a scene so idylic, at the earnest protestations of half a dozen voices that he was most welcome, a fact well attested by the heightened color in the faces of Isabel and Emily—he dropped down upon the steps beside George and Miss Sherburne. Young Pierpont, affable, diligent and devoted to his profession, was obtaining about all the legal business which youthful Riverton afforded. His calls at the Tuppers' had been somewhat frequent of late, and gave mutual pleasure.

"Now, father, do tell me," said Isabel, "was my special friend, 'the gentleman from Boone,' at the Convention?"

"Indeed he was, and he got in his old speech about the 'Great West,' but this time he had put on a portico or steeple."

"And lightning rod, father?" inquired George.

"Yes, indeed, lightning rod and weather vane. The gentleman from Boone never does anything by halves."

"American eagle on the tip of the rod, I suppose," said Pierpont.

"No, not exactly," said the General, "he had the 'bird' with one foot on the Alleghanies and one on the Rockies, and dipping his tail in Lake Superior and his proud beak in the Gulf of Mexico. We had the usual variety. There was the 'Pomatum' chap from Posey county, slick, sweet-scented, freshly groomed, every hair in its place. He kept at least one eye on the gallery and went out of his way a dozen times to flatter the ladies. And there was the tragico-comico youth, him of the start theatric, eyes 'in a fine frenzy rolling,' who shook his raven locks, got in something from Macbeth, whispered, and the next word threw his voice to the third heaven."

"Such fellows will buzz around a convention like moths around a candle," said Pierpont.

"Get their wings singed sometimes, too; don't they, Uncle?" said Emily.

"Indeed they do, Emily. Still, don't understand me to say that these 'small insects' constituted the convention. Not at all. Flies and mosquitoes don't make a world. The plain, sensible citizen was there, and in force too. When all is said, these shallow pates don't make so very much of a show; sometimes are allowed to fill a gap; kill time while the committees are out. When they gained the floor the benches would empty; delegates would go out, some to liquor up and some to do lobby work. Squire Service and I took turns in calling the boys to order, just as they got their wings spread; not talking to the question, etc. The old Squire—he's one of the solid ones. No fuss and feathers about him. When he began to run his hand through his hair and point that index finger at us, we listened.

General Tupper was always observing and much given to generalizing from what he observed; and the proceedings at the convention had thrown him into a moralizing mood. Said he, "As I sat there, ostensibly listening to the speeches—largely the old stuff—which simply meant, 'I'm your man to serve the party and serve the country, just nominate me, vote for me,' and as I studied faces and actions and saw all that was behind the scenes, I could'nt help echoing Solomon a little and inwardly exclaiming, 'Vanity of vanities!' "

"Now, Uncle, that is too gloomy—a veritable chapter in Lamentations! Don't you think so, Mr. Pierpont?" said Emily.

"Yes," replied Pierpont, "I submit that he is too lugubrious. Let there be light and then trust the sober second thought of the people. There's sublimity in the voice of the people. In any dire emergency their might is wholesome."

"O, I understand that," interposed the General, "but this swell and strut of the Lilliputians across the political boards; this lording and swelling; this jobbing and lick spittling—supreme selfishness—and all in the name of the dear people!"

"Husband, I guess the trouble is, you're not a politician," said Mrs. Tupper.

"No, in its common groveling signification, I surely am not, and hope I may never become a politician."

"Nevertheless, Uncle," said Emily, "give us free speech, free press, free discussion; that's the palladium of our liberties, as the stump speakers all say."

"That's our safety valve," added Isabel.

"Keep the windows open and the air stirring in Uncle Sam's house," chimed in Mrs. Tupper. "That will keep it wholesome."

"There, General," said the lawyer, "the ladies are against you; better gracefully surrender."

"Yes, Papa," said Sibyl, "for cousin Emily never'll give up."

"But, seriously," said Pierpont, "was it the State Convention, or the bad water and vile Johnny Cake you swallowed at Indianapolis to which we are indebted for this diatribe?"

The President of the Whig Convention laughed at this and added, "Our bill of fare was very low, except in price, and our beds like corduroy."

"Count only the bright days," counseled cheery Mrs. Tupper.

"Ho! Ho! Mother Sunlight! Good rule, I'll admit," said her husband.

At that moment John said in a loud whisper, "Look, cousin Emily, there's Mr. Goldwin." But Isabel had already discovered him and advanced to meet him.

"Welcome, a thousand welcomes, Mr. Goldwin," said the General, "sit down by me. I bespeak your assistance, for I am much beset. All are against me."

"No," said Isabel, "its the blue devils that have beset Papa. Do please, Mr. Goldwin, charm them away."

"O, height of presumption," he replied, "for me to attempt when you ladies have been baffled. Must I prove it true that 'Fools rush in where angels, etc?'"

"But, General Tupper, let me ask," said Pierpont, "are we to conclude that you regard the late convention as a dismal failure?"

"O, no; by no means," was the quick reply. "It was not disappointing, except to the unsuccessful office seekers, and we need shed no tears over them." Then turning to the minister, he explained, "I was about delivering a homily suggested by my experience in political life, when this assembly took up some 'aside' and quite swept me aside."

"Good! I am glad that you believe in preaching from experience," said Mr. Goldwin, "and I am sure you are entitled to the floor."

"Very well," continued the General, "now I rise to make an explanation."

"Explanations are always in order," said Pierpont.

"This convention," pursued the General,

"only set me to realizing afresh how we creatures of the hour exaggerate the small and minify the great."

"For instance, Papa," said thoughtful Isabel.

"For instance, so many talk of General Jackson as if the heavens hung on his nod; or of Henry Clay as though he carried the United States in his pockets."

"Like what was said of Calhoun," remarked Goldwin, "that when he took snuff all South Carolina sneezed."

"That's it, exactly," said General Tupper. "Why give Jackson's bank phobia all the importance it deserves; last winter's almost forgotten snow bank had infinitely more effect on the country."

"Papa," said Isabel, "you remind me of a very impressive picture Mr. Goldwin gave us last Sunday in his sermon on Providence."

"Do I? What was it daughter?"

"He showed us Napolean riding at the head of that choice army, half a million strong, against Russia, and his face flushed with assured victory, when he saw a snow flake fall on the flowing mane of his charger. The Cossacks could not rout that grand army, but the snow flakes could."

"Thank you, Miss Isabel," said Goldwin, "I am sure of at least one good listener, when you are at church."

"That you are," said the father, and then proceeded, "if, we the people, are finally routed it will be because we, like Napolean, forget to reckon in the Almighty."

"So you see a snow flake, do you Papa?" asked Isabel.

"My daughter, I do see a storm coming."

"From what direction?" queried the weather prophet, George.

"O, it's in the air, its everywhere," he replied, "but it started in the South."

"There it is, Uncle; after your old bugbear, the slave?" said Emily as she uneasily changed her posture. "You people of the North never will"—

"Now, my little Emily," interposed the Uncle, "I know it stirs your Virginia blood, but it's a fact, the slave is up. He's like cork, bobs up in our courts and platforms, and Congresses"—

"And churches, too," chimed in Goldwin.

"Sure enough," said the General; "fact is, the African is bound to trouble us until we cease troubling him."

"True," interposed Pierpont, "but how about the Missouri compromise, that thus far and no farther; that eternal settlement?"

"O, the slave owner never meant that should be more than a temporary stay of proceedings," answerd the General.

These words struck Emily as fire does tinder. Her cheek reddened and her eyes flashed. Goldwin and Pierpont saw the active volcano and inwardly pondered.

"Uncle, my dear Uncle!" she exclaimed,

"you grossly misrepresent my own loyal South; indeed, indeed you do. I can not listen to such imputations."

"Well, well Emily," said the General, "I never meant to kindle the Southern fire on my own hearth. The colored man has bobbed up here, hasn't he! But now, I haven't listened to Southern clans for nothing."

"Perhaps Jefferson saw the storm, too," said Goldwin, "when he said, 'I tremble for my country when I remember that God is just.'"

"Well, 'Mother of Pearl,'" said the General, rising and turning to Mrs. Tupper, "I don't know how it is with you, but I'm tired; suppose we withdraw and consign these young people to their own devices?"

In the seclusion of their own apartments, Mrs. Tupper, mother like, forecasting events, said half aloud and as if soliloquizing, "Yes, Pierpont and Emily, Mr. Goldwin and Isabel."

"What's that, mother? What's that?" exclaimed the General, affecting a whisper and imitating her suppressed voice. "Why not reverse that? Why not Goldwin and Emily, Pierpont and Isabel? One is just as likely as the other?"

"Well," said Mrs. Tupper, still absorbed in her own prophecies, "all the tongues in Riverton will be wagging."

"Fiddle sticks! Let them wag," said the husband.

"Couldn't be better mated," said Mrs. Tupper, continuing her monologue.

"Building air castles again, ar'n't you, mother dear. What a sky full you'll have with getting your four children married off."

"Ah! Mr. Goldwin; look out for jealous mothers in the camp," continued the same low prophetic voice.

"O, bosh!" exclaimed the father, "crossing imaginary bridges! Goldwin, rest assured, is no novice. Besides, I don't believe he cares for our girls beyond a pleasant acquaintance," and with that, the weary man was soon asleep.

Meanwhile the young people, left to their own devices, started for a stroll along the river to see the moon rise. Birds, however, promiscuously grouped, by unerring instinct, single out their mates. Soon it was Emily and Pierpont and Isabel and Goldwin; while George and Sibyl soon followed with light wraps for the ladies.

Sibyl, tossing back her beautiful head piece and turning up her bewitching lip in feigned disgust, declared in an undertone to George, "There's never a ghost of a chance for little me, when Emily and Isabel are around."

"Come, come now, Miss Disgruntle! Just drop all this and be my escort, and do yourself proud," interposed George, as he playfully took her arm. Then in a more serious tone: "Sibyl, go many a league and you'll not see two such fine couples as those just ahead of us. I just like to look at them."

"O," added Sibyl quickly and not to be outdone in admiration of the pairs, "I'll never dispute that; they are just splendid."

"By the bye, how are you and Mr. Goldwin getting on in Latin?" asked George.

"O, tip-top! Mr. Goldwin is grand. I do believe I shall learn to love Latin,"said Sibyl. I was dreadfully afraid he'd think me awfully dull, but Mama says that Mr. Goldwin declared the other day that I would make a fine Latin scholar. O, but didn't that do me good!"

"Does he weave in a lecture occasionally; tell you how to be good and all that?" asked George, with a shrewd, quizical look.

"Not a bit of it," replied Sibyl. "I'm awfully afraid he will talk good and pious to me. But, if he did but know it, he does it beautifully every day without saying a word."

"Mathematics always in preference to Latin for me," said George, "How goes your arithmetic?"

"O, Emily pushes me on so fast in that,and then every few days she takes me into the woods and shows me so many new things about the plants and bugs and birds. Its wonderful, George, how many things she sees in some little flower or even a feather. The other day we were over at the swamp and she showed me six varieties of willows, where my stupid eyes had seen but one. I'm getting such an appetite for study that I don't know how I can ever satisfy it in Riverton. Dear me! I'm afraid I'll know as much as Emily after a while, and then I s'pose I'll have to teach school till I'm as old and dry as that dead log over there."

George, as he looked into those deep, entrancing eyes, was pardonably sceptical of his sister's forecast of her future. Then he broke out, "Sib, do you know I'm going to be a soldier; not one of these common ones, but a commander. The other day I talked to Mr. Goldwin about going to West Point and he took occasion to say what I knew he had been watching to say, that he thought I ought to enlist in the Christian army first, and I guess he was about right, too. Mr. Goldwin is a man of peace, you know, but then he did promise to intercede with father to get me an appointment at West Point. Not that I am dying to save my country or any other country, but there's fight in me and there's glory in soldiering."

Sibyl was silent and when George waited for a response, she said, "O, George, you break my heart!"

Coming to a grassy level on the river bank, the party dropped down upon it. Mr. Pierpont, with his long legs dangling over the bank, insisted that he never before had realized the fascination of the scenery. Making due allowance for his open vision of the fascination at this blissful moment, the surroundings certainly were sufficiently captivating. The moon was beginning to sift its light through the tree tops. The Pocanock was swollen by the late rains much beyond its accustomed volume. Tall sycamores were dipping their branches to the water's edge, and wild blossoms and herbs and shrubs were lading the night with perfume. All felt the transport of the hour. Emily never seemed more bewitching and Pierpont was riding on seas of enchantment. Song followed song. Carols and serenades full of moonlight and memory of the tender passion, echoed from heart and voice.

As they were singing, two whisky-crazed Indians, in a canoe, paddled swiftly by, yelling and gesticulating fiercely—the one disillusionizing discord. Swiftly they passed from view behind the foliage which covered the river banks, leaving but a momentary ripple, like their race, vanishing from sight and memory. Emily and Sibyl were singing, "Flow Gently Sweet Afton," when there was a twang of a bow string and a whirr through the leaves, and an arrow flew just in front of Emily and struck Pierpont deep in the thigh. "My God!" he cried, "am I shot?" At the same instant, an Indian howl on the river told plainly whence the shot had come. Immediately all sprung to their feet—all except Pierpont who attempted to rise but fell back with a groan. Goldwin leaped to his side, and by his presence of mind, restored the others to some degree of self-possession, as he resolutely drew out the arrow, although he necessarily caused Pierpont to shriek with agony, and at once proceeded to bandage the ugly wound as far as he could with Emily's white shawl. Then bidding the ladies hasten to the house and dispatch a messenger with all speed for Dr. Bancroft, he and George converted themselves into crutches and followed with the wounded man between them, half hobbling and half carried. When at last they laid Pierpont upon a couch in the east room at the Tupper's, pale and weak from over exertion and loss of blood, he fainted. The Doctor, soon at hand, carefully examined the wound and dressed it.

Meanwhile the young ladies in the sitting room walked the floor in agony of suspense. The moments seemed hours. At last the Doctor appeared. "Ugly flesh wound," said he; "may be some abrasion of the bone, but unless blood poison sets in, give him time, and he will come out all right."

"Thank God," exclaimed Emily, and sank back exhausted into a chair.

"What a merciful Providence that it is no worse," said Isabel, as she met the Doctor's keen, but kind, eyes fastened intently upon her.

"Now, ladies," said he, "to your rooms at once. The patient is in good hands; Mr. Goldwin insists upon staying beside him till morning. Quiet and sleep are Mr. Pierpont's best nurses. Mr. Goldwin suggests Mr. Barnett, who he says is a born nurse, and I will send him around by daylight. Now off! Off!" said he, at the same time lifting his arms as though discharging a flock of birds. "Off to your nests,"and off the ladies went smiling in spite of their forebodings, and the abrupt Dr. Bancroft, as usual, had his own way.

CHAPTER X.

The name inscribed on the weather-worn tavern sign of Riverton was N. D. Grande, which, expressed in its entirety, was Nicholas Demmy Grande. The bearer of this name, whom as landlord we have already casually met, was tall, red-faced, scaly nosed, head inclined to baldness, and hair, though daily trained to conceal that baldness, daily standing in revolt against that concealment; eyes a dubious gray that easily took on any meaning to suit the color of the times; eyes and face that were not a reflection of personality, but of the people around him. His nostrils had a dry vacuous and distended appearance, which was said to come of inveterate snuff taking, and stunning volleys accompanied the flourish of his red silk handkerchief. Nicholas D. Grande, or N. D. Grande, for he disliked, and as far as posible, suppressed the Nicholas, was an undeniable example of audacious claims and of slender capital. His pretensions were as swelling as his resources were scant. He was always intriguing in politics, always soliciting of the dear people some office, always lonely unless training with the crowd, always pressing to the front, and, generally, only to be ordered to the rear.

Often he borrowed the minister's pony for his electioneering trips. When a boy in Kentucky, he had chanced to hear Henry Clay speak—a fact of which he was always telling. When anyone in the pulpit, on the stump, or at the bar, furnished a pleasing example of oratory, then N. D. was always 'strikingly reminded of Henry Clay.' Col. Grande, for such was the handle attached to his name, no one new exactly how or why, wore fine clothes for a pioneer, lost no opportunity to sample liquors, and sported a style which his means could ill support. Rumor intimated that, though he posed in daylight as an exemplar of good morals, his associations and connections were sometimes quite shady.

Mrs. Col. Grande, tall and starchy, head high, had aspirations to be the leader in the developing society of Riverton. To outshine by her gowns, and, upon occasions, with her cuisine, was her summit and crown. She was a regular attendant upon divine service: generally arrived a little late, and marched to a front seat with enough state to mark a dignitary. The Colonel graced the church services upon large occasions. Mrs. Grande had it as one of her laws, "always be loyal to your minister." Moreover, beside deference to the clergy from principle, she had very great personal esteem for Mr. Goldwin. While much of this world clung to her garments, she was probably no more egoistic than many others who were more skilled in donning the other-world livery.

Then there was the Dale family that we have met before—one of the first to arrive in Riverton. Socrates Dale differed from some of his neighbors, in that he was always happy; and yet this is not strange, for he was always about to become rich; always had some project or scheme which was about to be the lucky hit. No matter what his objective world was, subjectively, he was on the hill tops of delight. He could with the sublimest indifference, pass by innumerable collapsed balloons, and devote himself supremely to constructing another air ship, which, in turn, landed him in the mire. For instance, he spent much time and what money was at hand, inventing a stump jerker, but the cumbrous affair cost too much per jerk. He puzzled his brain, too, over the idea of perpetual motion, with a view to applying it to modes of transit. How much others profited by the suggestion in his ventures, it would be impossible to say, but they profited him nothing. Careless as the earlier Socrates about his personal appearance, he was as fond as Socrates of quizzing and philosophizing with his neighbors. He always had time to stop and tell a story, or discuss the latest turn in politics; could drop his scythe in the meadow and leave his grass unraked and uncocked in haying time, and go a fishing. Honest, easy jogging, good natured Uncle Soc! His religion, like his property, so far as he had any, was in his wife's name.

Mrs. Dale, as we have previously said, was, in many respects, a worthy example of a pioneer woman. People often wondered how such a model of enterprise and thrift came to mate herself with Soc. Dale. Their children did not exhaust the Scripture names, but, as Uncle Soc. said, "they came mighty close onto it." "Not much Scripture to them except the name," said he, "nevertheless, there's this good to be said of them, all but two or three take after their mother."

Not only weeds but also flowers will persist in growing along the dusty and well trodden roadside. The Drake family knew toil and exposure. And yet, sometimes, a choice flower lifts its modest cup amid nettles and dog fennel. Rachel, the oldest daughter of this household, had soft, wistful eyes, and sometimes that far away look, which betokened that she found worlds of higher thought and emotion hard by the humdrum present. The life which is dull prose to some, is unwritten poetry to others. Rachel read and reread everything she could lay hold of, which is not saying very much, and had her dreams, and fancies, and philosophizings, despite her hard hands, her plain wardrobe and slender purse.

Her father, Sam Drake, whom we early met, was quite a philosophizer in his way— mused on many a problem as he drove his team afield, or as he sat and smoked. Homespun philosophy wears well, and the Platos and Aristotles are not the only thinkers, nor is truth sought and found only in the classic "groves of the Academy."

Mrs. Drake's lineage—she was a Davenant—ran back through Kentucky to the Carolinas, and thence across the waves, to a sweet and cultivated home among the Hugenots. Her ancestral thread was silken, and, retraced, led into choice tapestry, and a touch of refinement and courtly breeding survived down to Sam Drake's home. There was something about that frontier fireside which seemed to say, toil and terrestial gain after all are not all; like a perfume in the night which told of the unseen, dew-besprent, fruits and flowers.

An old and well thumbed little volume. "The Lady of the Lake," a battered, coverless copy of "Ivanhoe," "Pilgrim's Progress," full of direful cuts meant to be illustrations, and Weims' "Life of Marion," heirlooms of two generations, had accompanied these wanderers through the defiles of the Blue Ridge and over Kentucky blue licks, and into Indiana forests.

Jonas Drake, a big strapping boy, was as yet lying fallow. He went to church regularly and as regularly nodded through most of the sermon. People thought his mind never rose above corn dodger and bacon. Little they knew of what sometimes ran in his head.

And a younger scion of the Drake family

tree was seven-year-old Waxie; barefooted, bare-headed, except nature's head dress of tufted flaxen curls. The terror of Sunday morning to her was that hair which must be unsnarled. The reconcilement to Sunday was her new shoes, which came forth to shine with every seventh sunrise; and she walked the floor for an hour before church time just to hear them squeak. What shoes carried more innocent pride down the aisle than Waxie's?

Over in the corner, in the old battered and scarred cradle which had come over the mountains from the Carolinas, which had nestled Drakes back in the mist of antiquity, which had been broken and tinkered times innumerable and was rocking still—in that cradle in the corner was just the darlingest, perfectest baby that ever was, the very image of its father, and the very picture of its mother.

And does that complete the list? Waxie will give us no rest unless we catalogue the great dog Mixer, who came into the world long before Waxie, over whom she had rolled and turned somersaults in the grass many a day; Mixer, always getting in the way, the pest and pet in the house, who, with his master, when both were younger, has started many a rabbit and treed many a coon, and received the blessing of many a polecat; battle-scarred veteran that has bayed moons without number and hidden many a bone, now a litle *blase*, and chiefly remembered by what he has done; happy be his dreams as he stretches before the fire, and peaceful his journey to the canine Sheol.

There's another birthday sacredly remembered in that house. And there's another date not a birthday; yes, a birthday, when the blessed messenger we call Death came and carried one to the immortal home. So many things dated from the day that "little sister Bessie" died. Mr. Goldwin so often and so closely communed with this househould that it seemed almost as though he too had known and loved and lost this little ministrant child. Little sister, always counted, always near. How the thought of her lingered about that house, and softened the heart and the voice, and dissillusionized the eyes, and anchored the other world close by this. The angel Death had blessed that home.

Is it by some subtle law of association that, having spoken of death, we proceed to speak of the Doctor? Not but that Dr. Bancroft was as successful as is ever granted to man to be in keeping Death at a distance; indeed, it was often said that Death fought shy of him. Lyman Litchfield Bancroft had, at this time, been a citizen of Riverton scarcely a year; and yet, educated, skillful and conscientiously devoted to his profession, he was already well known and well employed. He began life under the shadow of the Berkshire hills. He had married happily and settled in an eastern village, and for a year had known home joy as unalloyed as falls to mortals. Then death took his all and left him disconsolate. Fleeing the scenes which only fed his grief, he wandered well nigh aimlessly into the lone wilds of the West, solitude his preferred companion, and at length drew up at Riverton. Pleased with the location and promise of the town, and wisely concluding to seek "surcease of sorrow" in actively pursuing the duties of his profession, he opened there an office. Somewhat blunt and sans ceremony, but profoundly honest and kindly of heart, he swiftly secured confidence and friendship. Nothing was more abhorrent to him than the palaver and pretense, which are sometimes the chief reliance of aspirants to the healing art. He was like a big brother to those who came in contact with him. Although not open to the charge of being handsome, he came near being so when he smiled, and certainly was not called homely. His features, probably, could not be termed classical, but they did suggest benevolence and vigor.

Dr. Bancroft had a penchant for collecting samples of nature's handiwork. His office was an omnium gatherum, a curiosity shop; tables and shelves and books were loaded with flora and fauna, fossils, skulls and skeletons of man and beast, snakes pickled in alcohol, papers and books. Among the latter, aside from medical treatises, there were two volumes which bore evidence of frequent use, Shakespeare and the Bible. "So many books," said the Doctor, "are but triturations of these. Why not go to the fountain head?"

As a physician, Dr. Bancroft was not satisfied to deal with symptoms or effects simply, but sought for causes; considered in each case temperament, constitution, environment and heredity, and endeavored in arriving at deductions to include all the considerations and data, mental as well as physical. People said he not only looked into a case but looked through it. But, then as now, there were people enough who liked humbuggery, and in the next block was the office of a man who assumed to attach M. D. to his name, and in that office all manner of quackery and ill advised work was carried on.

Mr. Goldwin and Dr. Bancroft enjoyed rubbing their minds together, differ as they might in their opinions. Pastor and physician are by reason of their callings, granted the freedom of many homes, and are entrusted with the most sacred confidences; and Mr. Goldwin was gratified to be able to believe that such opportunities for good or ill fell into the hands of one who was both conscientious and capable. Both the men held uncompromising convictions of rectitude, and of hostility to the whole liquor business.

Said the Doctor, waxing warm on his favorite topic, "Mr. Goldwin, the simple fact is, we are under law; this universe is under the reign of law. There are my bird pets, my rabbits, my dog; they never eat too much, never expose themselves unnecessarily, wont even smell of whiskey or tobacco. I never have to doctor them; law abiding, every one of them. Everything is law abiding until we come to man. He's a glutton and a drunkard and a sensualist. Break every statute of nature, try to jump through a stone wall, of course get the worst of it, and then in his extremity, run for the doctor to patch him up! Nature is, indeed, marvelously patient and forbearing, but beyond a certain point, never forgives; simply lays on the penalty."

"You're orthodox there, Doctor. Law is law, and penalty deferred, is not, as we human fools so often suppose, penalty repealed. Only th's, Doctor: let us go beyond nature and say God. Law in nature, in man, or in the Bible is God expressing His will. Doesn't it thrill us, when we really think of it, that every physical pain or inconvenience is our Divine Lawgiver's voice to us, 'Take care; danger; stop; this way lies penalty?' Mount Sinai in every one of us! Every cell and tissue atremble with our Heavenly Father's voice."

"How true that is, Mr. Goldwin! I'll think of that. But now let me ask, didn't you at the funeral yesterday speak of the sudden death of Matilda Chase as occurring in the mysterious Providence of God?"

"Yes, Doctor, I think I did."

"Well, now, I am inclined to question the mysterious Providence in this case. Matilda Chase, under direction from her mother, exposed herself unwarrantably, took a heavy cold, and therefore, had lung fever and died. From the first it was evident to me that she had gone beyond the point where nature forgives, and that no human means could save her. Now where is the mysterious Providence? The simple fact is Matilda violated the law of life and had to take the penalty."

"Very true, Doctor, but whose laws? Who made them? Did not God know when he made those laws that they would be violated by thousands, and among the number this dear young girl? And in this view of the case is there not a very strict sense in which God is active in this and, indeed, in every event?"

"I see your point, Mr. Goldwin. That, too, will do to think about."

"Doctor, if I could not take this view of every event, I should be all at seas. God is not outwitted by his laws. No event is a discovery or a surprise to him. Knowing all, absolutely every event, he wisely framed his laws."

The Doctor replied thoughtfully, "The difference between us seems to be that in my reasoning, I have not been in the habit of placing God and the event so close together as you do."

"But," said Mr. Goldwin, "there are other truths side by side with these we have named. They go together, or in pairs, like Drake's oxen. God Sovereign, man free; there's a pair of truths. They are in blessed wedlock. Sheer nonsense to attempt to reason or to live without accepting them."

"Well, Doctor," added Mr. Goldwin, rising to go, "we have run into the mysteries of course; every great truth takes us into mystery. We little insects venture out and dip the tips of our tiny wings in the illimitable deep."

"And," retorted the Doctor, "are glad to return to solid land again."

"Now," said the Minister, "I must go and see what can be done for that frantic mother, Mrs. Chase." He found her raging and storming. Matilda was gone, and it was almost the first time in the life of that mother that she had not had her own way. She was, as the neighbors said, 'a little woman with a tremendously big will'; and with such fluency and vigor did she assert her will, that every member of her family had long since ceased to contend against it.

Mr. Goldwin asked very tenderly, in speaking of the dear daughter, "Don't you think that your loving Heavenly Father did the best he could do for Matilda and for you who are so sorely bereaved, when he took your dear girl to heaven?" At this Mrs. Chase grew more violent than ever and said God was cruel and heartless, a very demon; and then she rushed to her room and locked the door, and for two days was not seen by any member of her family. It was in this room, and at this time that the greatest battle of her life was fought. She at last submitted her will to God, and then there came quietness and peace. When she reappeared before the family she was a changed woman..

CHAPTER XI.

Sam Drake, as his family enlarged, enlarged and improved his dwelling. The original house germ, the log cabin, knew itself no more. Built on to, weather boarded, lathed and plastered, and dressed over with paint, cool in summer and warm in winter, it was, as the Riverton Journal, a weekly paper just gasping into a tentative life, expressed it, "the handsome and commodious residence of Mr. Samuel Drake."

Now, in lieu of Sam, it began to be more often, "Mr. Drake." Not that he, with his house, was altogether made over. "Advancing civilization" did rub off some of the burrs indigenous to the frontier, but some of them adhered to him through life. Happy, indeed, shall we be if nothing more deleterious than a few burrs cling to us, tenacious as existence. The most exacting critic could but perceive that mental and moral gain accrued to Drake as years accrued; but, like the most of us, his life smacked strongly of its early surroundings, as good wine does of its noble vintage. While no one in Riverton was more heartily respected and esteemed than was he, there was at the same time something so kind and human and unconventional about him, that to his old friends and neighbors, made ceremony and formal titles seem an intrusion.

A few survivors of the recently dense wood stood around the house, like protecting patriarchs. Jonas had painted the front fence, and Rachel had trained a few vines, and Waxie had her flower bed to which she was always transferring wild plants and mosses which she watered and watched and mourned for as they pined away under culture. So the Drake place was a household possession and a pride, and, in after days, a delightsome memory to all its inmates, and to the neighborhood a happy exponent of domestic progress. Mixer alone lifted his tail in protest. To him the times were out of joint; there seemed no rest for his dogship; the places in front of the fire and on the door mat which he had once known, now knew him no more. Disconsolately, he betook himself to an old box, which Jonas, in grateful appreciation of the Mixer of the past, bedded with straw and placed under the back door apple tree. Sociologically Mixer was of the *Laisser faire* persuasion.

Long years after this time, Sam Drake enjoyed telling the story of his first cabin in Riverton, "which," he said, "he felt very much stuck up about when it got floored with bass wood boards twelve inches wide." "But," he added, with a merry twinkle in his eye, "that he didn't feel quite so proud when he found those same bass wood boards shrunk one inch every year for thirteen years." This was more true than some of the pioneer yarns.

Word had gone out of "a quilting at Mrs. Drake's." Now, be it remembered, that a quilting meant that through the long winter evenings some tired fingers had been busy cutting calico into a thousand or more small bits, infinitesimal squares, parallelograms, pentagons, hexagons, octagons, ellipses, and the whole family of triangles, and then sewing them together into something having four rectangles and called a block.

With the coming of Spring, it may be presumed that enough blocks had been fashioned generously to cover a bed. Now with padding between the upper and under, and the whole stretched on four long strips of wood, was constituted the thing which called together the dames and damsels near and far. The finished quilt represented something near a million stitches, and it, along with the spinning wheel, indicated what was the pastime of our foremothers. Does this passion of our grandmothers for chopping calico into bits for the sake of sewing them together seem to the maiden about to step into the 20th century, just a little ludicrous? When another hundred years have passed, may not her fads appear quite as much open to criticism?

Moreover, another fact to be remembered,

Mrs. Drake was one of those whose cookery always turned out just right, and she was always well supported by her first lieutenant, Rachel. The sweetest, whitest bread, the yellowest butter, the creamiest milk; cakes and custards which were pronounced perfectly delicious; platters and platters of chipped beef and venison, cold chicken, and ham, jellies, apple butter, pumpkin butter, plum butter, peach butter, and all other butters;—you would have thought Mrs. Drake was commissary for a small army.

Beside this, Mrs. Drake, to grace the occasion, had brought out her new set of dark blue dishes, which Mrs. Smile especially admired because, as she said, "they wouldn't show dirt."

Two filled quilting frames are submissively waiting for the needles. The hour has come. Everything is ready, and now how still. It is the hush which comes just before the battle. Rachel is seated at the outlook beside the window which is screened by the sweet scented honeysuckle which her fingers have taught to climb.

Social life in Riverton was social. Civilization had not yet introduced cliques and sects. "My set" had not yet partitioned it off into petty pens. Some gossip at these informal gatherings? Yes, and so there is where men gather at the corner grocery, or sit around on store boxes. Yes, liberty is abused, nevertheless the cure for the abuse lies in liberty; true liberty which is the creature of benevolent law. Free speech for woman as well as man. Blessings on the old quiltings. They stitch society together in common sympathies and loving mutuality; fashion the individual pieces into a many colored fabric. Blessings on that which lifts the weary feet for a while out of the daily tread mills.

But silence! There's a footstep on the gravel walk. Rachel from behind her redoubt takes observations. "Dear me, mother, if it isn't Mrs. Grande. Comes early does'nt she? Early to quilting, late to church!"

Here it may be well to state that there was one thing which now preeminently tasked the female thought of Riverton, viz, selecting the Minister's wife. On wife abstract there was one mind; on the wife concrete there were many. Different mothers, different minds. As they come to the quilting let us do a little mind-reading.

But Mrs. Grande has no marriageable daughters. She's disinterested. Not too fast. She has a sister who has just been secured to teach the village school. She's a round, smooth body, with two little exact curls which danced up and down in front of each ear. Mrs. Grande thinks her sister, Marilla Dean, is the very one for Mr. Goldwin. Crow's feet already coming in sight? Never mind that. She's well preserved; no young girl, giddy and unripe; one of the dignified and steady kind. Mr. Goldwin has been invited to tea at Mrs. Grande's often of late.

Another step; quick and business like. That's Mrs. Dale. When she comes, work begins. She thinks her Deborah would make the Minister's clothes look so well; keep his linen immaculate, and his stand up collar of most approved uprightness; and she can get a good meal of victuals in less time and in better shape than any other girl in Riverton.

And there's Mrs. Smile, My! how she waddles! Carries a deal of the adipose. She knows half a score of Smiles, among whom Mr. Goldwin could not go amiss. But "in particular, there's tall Jemima Persimmons Smile. She is so economical like, has "faculty," can make a dollar go farther than anybody else; takes an old coat and turns it, and I declare, you'd think it brand new;" very important trait in a Minister's wife.

Hello! there they come, all in a bunch. Mrs. Jack Barnett still carrying the fresh, clear complexion of Vermont; Mrs. Nat Hawkins, public mourner, goes to all the funerals anywhere in reach, sits close to the mourners and watches them, and then runs in "just a minute" at all the neighbors, and in her own dramatic way, tells them how the "mourners took on;" Mrs. Sol Perkins, too, and the blacksmith's wife, Mrs. Tim Jones; and Mrs. Enos Martyn, the merchant's wife, and others, some of them young friends of Rachel, an introduction to whom now in the general hubbub, would only be confusing. It is safe to say that these all have considered the preacher, if not his preaching, and have "an idea" just where he would do well to mate.

Mrs. Drake, good discreet soul, she's far enough from ever lisping a word, but that does not preclude her from thinking down deep in her heart that Rachel would exactly fill the place, for everybody likes her, and she has such nice ways, and she kind of naturally takes to religion.

Now all the small change of personal salutations and domestic inquiries has gone around, and all have got down to business. Buzz, buzz! The sound of many voices and the needles flying in and out.

"Wa'n't that just awful about Mr. Pierpont," said Mrs. Smile, as she straightened up to thread her needle. "Reach that spool, will you, Mrs. Perkins? Why they say he isn't expected to live."

"O! not so bad as that, I guess," interposed Mrs. Barnett, as she gave her needle an energetic pull. "The Doctor thinks he'll be around in a few weeks."

"Dr. Bancroft's a splendid physician,— couldn't have a better," said little Mrs. Martyn; "but how did it happen anyhow? I have heard so many reports I don't know what to believe."

Then each gave her own version of the catastrophe, all coming at last to the important facts, and all coupling Mr. Goldwin with Isabel in the moonlight stroll.

Meanwhile Mrs. Dale and Mrs. Grande

have their heads pretty close together as they are finishing off one corner of the quilt.

"Well," said Mrs. Dale, 'if he wants Isabel Tupper, it's a good thing, her father has the money to set her up, or else I'm thinking, Mr. Goldwin would find her an expensive luxury."

"Yes, indeed," said Mrs. Grande, "Father Tupper 'd have to set her up and buy her a piano. I think it would be a very poor match, myself."

"What's that?" said Mrs. Barnett, whose needle was overtaking Mrs. Grande, and who knew a little rumor of Mr. Goldwin's Vermont attachment. "Don't concern yourselves about Mr. Goldwin. I think you're all on the wrong trail."

"Do you? Do you?" said several voices at once.

"Yes, I know you are."

"O! Mrs. Barnett, who is she? Where does she live? Whom does she look like? When will he bring her here?" All showed these questions in their eager faces, but it took Mrs. Hawkins to ask them.

"Well, now, I've got into it, haven't I," exclaimed Mrs. Barnett, laughing and coloring deeply; "I'll stop right here; and remember I may be on the wrong trail."

For a moment the buzz died away; an ominous silence; evidently several thought that Mrs. Barnett had put a different aspect on affairs. Then Mr. Pierpont and Miss

Sherburne were discussed, as they rolled up a completed half yard of a quilt.

But Mrs. Drake, who had done some thinking and thus far had said little, and who generally made a point when she tried; evidently felt that the last word had not been spoken in regard to her pastor's case. So she opened her mind with a sedateness which at once gained attention.

"Now," said she, "it seems to me there are plenty of girls right here in Riverton, who can bake and brew, wash and iron, mend and make over, and who can hold their tongues and their tempers, and on the whole are pretty good Christians."

"Yes, yes, Mrs. Drake; you're right this time," broke in Mrs. Grande, Mrs. Hawkins and several others.

"But, don't be so fast, hear me through," continued Mrs. Drake, straightening herself up; "this and much more our Minister will want in a wife, unless I'm greatly mistaken."

"Isabel Tupper, or Miss Sherburne do you mean?" squeaked Mrs. Smile. At the mention of these names, Mrs. Col. Grande clouded and glowered, and clapped her hand to her heart as if taken with a sudden pain. If anything has a keener edge than jealousy, what is it?

But Mrs. Drake was not to be turned aside. "Some one," she persisted, "who is educated and able to enter into a Minister's thoughts and plans, and trials, too; some one to whom we can look up; and that fruit doesn't grow on every tree."

"I agree with you, Mrs. Drake," said the decided Mrs. Dale.

"And, still further," continued Mrs. Drake, "I believe our pastor can be trusted to do the wise thing."

"That he can," chimed in Mrs. Barnett; "I think we need concern ourselves only about our part of the work; rest assured, Mr. Goldwin will prove equal to his."

And so the pastor's wife was dropped. Not even Mrs. Hawkins had a word to add. Conscience did a little wholesome picking all around.

Then another topic which had been broached of late; the building of a Meeting House. All declared themselves tired of the school house, but some said, "We are too poor;" some, "the time hasn't come for that," or, "better wait till we decently support our Minister." But Mrs. Drake and Mrs. Dale were of other mind. "Build a church," said they, "and that will help the Minister, help everything good."

"Well let's do something, now," said Mrs. Barnett. Up spoke little Mrs. Martyn, "The only way to do something is to do it. I'll tell you, let's organize right here a church furnishing society, and if the men will build the church, we ladies will furnish it."

The suggestion carried with everyone. "That's it, say we do," came from half a dozen voices at once. Before the ladies went home from that quilting, Riverton had a Ladies' Church Aid Society, with Mrs. Drake as President and Mrs. Grande as Vice-President, and an Executive Committee with Mrs. Tupper and Mrs. Dale and Mrs. Barnett on it, and Mrs. Martyn as Secretary and Treasurer.

This action laid the first stone, and greatly encouraged Mr. Goldwin, who, if the truth were known, had suggested to several that the ladies take the initiative toward the new church. Again, blessings on the old quiltings.

CHAPTER XII.

A few hours after the ugly arrow had torn the flesh of Daniel Pierpont, quiet resumed place in the Tupper home, if not in the Tupper hearts. Emily alone in her room, letting her wealth of hair fall in freedom on her shoulders, seated herself at the open window, and, as the cooling breeze soothed her hot brow, sought to bring her mind, as a wildly driven bark, once more into port. The midnight had brought clouds, but between the rifts were the stars, and they talked to her. At that moment it was the stars and not the clouds which had a language. Was it real or was all a dream?

Of one thing Emily thought she was sure. She more than fancied she had seen that night in Pierpont's eye a light responsive, which was real; which was love. That last look he gave her, even in the midst of suffering and anxious foreboding, so soulful and tender; it must have been meant for her alone. She was sipping the first drops of a new delight. And yet was she sure? Not a word had he spoken. 'Twas the delicious pantomime of love. She could not be mistaken. She surrendered to the triumphant passion of her soul.

Meanwhile in a room below Pierpont had fallen into a stupor from which he aroused only to lapse into it again. Goldwin, left in charge of the sick man for the night, settled in the great chair by his bedside, with his limbs resting on a chair in front of him, and composed himself to thought, but not to slumber. What word had this strange night for him? He accepted no Turkish philosophy of fate. What doors did that arrow open through which he might bring help to these lives? Little did the people of Riverton realize how the young Minister yearned over them. Each person in thought many times he had weighed, and asked entrance in behalf of the truth to his heart. With more than a mother's tenderness and tenacity he hungered for the better things for these growing homes. His burthen of responsibility weighed heavily, and often he famished for more companionship in carrying it.

Sometimes faith came gushing from the rock, and gurgling by the wayside; sometimes it came only by hard pumping from a deeply buried spring. He was in the main cheerful, hopeful; but he was subject to the adulations of the human.

His little church, originally constituted with the apostolic number, twelve members, was now increased to twenty one. He scoured the territory widely around Riverton, preaching in private houses and from house to house, sowing beside all waters and, while he did not conform to the injunction, "salute no one by the way," he easily and literally observed another; "carry neither purse nor scrip."

Riverton all the while was crystalizing into what is called advanced civilization. Some who never take kindly to this advance, and are always hanging on the debatable margin where every man does that which is right in his own eyes, had "moved on." The town was beginning to have a personality; becoming an autonomy. It might be said that it had passed its first stage of fermentation, and had its first skimming. There were likely to be some dregs, and the final precipitate was problematical. Mr. Goldwin felt that there was but one reagent which could volatilize every unwholesome atom.

For the young minister, snatched from books and schools and erudition and set down in the all but inviolate wilderness, the change was novel, and adventure relieved many an otherwise tedious day. One evening he went out six miles to preach. The one family room had been seated with slabs stretched from bed to chair and from chair to chest, while two barrels, on which two tallow dips were persuaded to stand in their own strength and grease, served as candle sticks. The services had commenced, and Mr. Goldwin was getting under full canvas, when lo! a sudden reef! The man of the house undertook to give light by snuffing the long and curling wick and snuffed out one, and upsetting, put out the other. That darkness could be felt. Those were not quite the days of Lucifer matches. A touching appeal, a cry of "O mercy!" and the very stout old lady went shuffling about, and at last, by some mysterious fiat there was light. But in or out of the darkness, the preacher continued remarking and the thread of his discourse successfully unwound. This rural family counted themselves fortunate above many of their neighbors, in that they were able to ride to Riverton to church. For they had a very primitive ox cart which gee—woh—hawed up to the school house door of a Lord's day.

At the time that Mr. Goldwin was focalizing the Christian forces for organizing a church, he set out on his pony to notify a family which was living twelve miles from Riverton. A solitary ride; but solitude in the wood was not loneliness to Mr. Goldwin. Then he especially realized a Great Companionship, and a certain high composure and upper atmosphere stole thence into his ministries.

He was not long out when a sudden spurt of snow concealed the trail, and as the darkness drew on, the studious pastor awoke from sermon meditations to the consideration of that which was more immediate, and by way of a personal application, exclaimed, "Really, I do believe I'm lost!"

After wandering long, trying supposed paths to find them all bringing up nowhere, and concluding that night wherein all the beasts of the forest do creep forth, had voices conducive to feelings quite other than poetic, he dropped the reins on pony's neck and surrendered, and was brought, almost by a bee line, to a spot where were a few winking embers and a lone Indian. After encouraging the fire, minister and Redman sat down by it, and Mr. Goldwin attempted some of the Indian's provender; but the ashes and soot and long hairs were too much for his hunger, and the food was returned with thanks. So Redman crawled under his blanket and white man lay down under the shelter of a log with his feet to the fire, and, with one eye on his room-mate, watched for the morning. As there was no whiskey in camp the danger was not imminent. There was not even "baccer" enough to fill the pipe of peace! In the morning, Mr. Goldwin sought to shed light on his companion's theology. But such a look of derision and scorn of the "White Man's Great Spirit!" And with far too much reason.

Then, as now, Cupid assailed men and women. The minister, in his official capacity was called to a farm house some four miles from town. When he arrived at the house where the wedding was to be solemnized, to his surprise the duet had grown to a quartet, the party of the second part naively confessing "that times were a little close and he reckoned the job could be done cheaper if the parson said the word for all four at once." Mr. Goldwin literally smiled on the nuptial combine; and the story went with many a loud smile around Riverton. "Sharpest dodge yet on the preacher," said Hawkins, chucking Drake under the ribs. Drake shrugged his shoulders, and said, "rather a gouge game." Yet it was really planned in all simplicity and good intent.

But a wedding which left a still deeper impression on the young clergyman, was one which he attended after facing a sleety gale for nine miles. The happy couple were Dutch. The road being almost impassible, so that journeying with speed was impossible, the parson became chilled through. His good humor was just a little strained. But, once within, the huge fires of hickory and of hospitality soon put warmth in the blood, and the sight of tables apparently more than covered with every imaginable edible compound known to the English or Dutch cuisine filled all the near horizon with hope soon lost in glad fruition.

When the marriage and the feast were ended and Mr. Goldwin was about to leave, Hans and his Gretchen, hand in hand, followed him out to his horse. The blossoming bride pressed upon Mr. Goldwin a little package containing samples from the table, requesting him to carry it to his wife. At the same time Hans, taking out his leathern purse, inquired, "Vell vot's te tamage?" On being told that he was the better judge as to that, Hans, his sunflower face expanding with a broad generosity, handed over fifty cents, and with Gretchen squeezing his hand, said, "you did it tight parson. I wood hef geefen vun tollar than not hef it done."

Samuel Drake and John Barnett were chosen to office in the little church. It is an interesting fact that Stubbs, the half breed, of whom mention has been made, was the fruit first to ripen under the ministry of Mr. Goldwin. Stubbs was a man of all work, sometimes employed at the hotel, sometimes gardening for General Tupper, sometimes engaged elsewhere. Industrious and willing, and quick to catch a suggestion, he was called a handy person to have around. On the Indian side, tall, straight as an arrow, well knit and lithe as a fox; his features and mental cast bespoke the Caucassian side of his lineage. He was one of the few more fortunate and promising waifs of the West.

From that first day when Mr. Goldwin dismounted at the tavern and passed over his pony to Stubbs care, Stubbs had observed the minister closely. Supposed to see little and think less, he really saw everything and said nothing.

After a time he stepped in occasionally to church; at first rather timidly, and dropping down close by the door. Then he grew a little bolder and of winter Sunday mornings, he would happen in and lend a hand in kindling the fire and arranging the benches.

On one of these early Sabbaths in Riverton, the congregation had assembled and the discourse was well begun, when suddenly loud shouts without, many voices in the street, and three deer rush by, hotly pursued by dogs and several mounted hunters. In less than thirty seconds, Mr. Goldwin was addressing chiefly empty seats. But he was agreeably surprised to see that Stubbs, with all his instincts for the chase, obeyed a higher instinct and sat quietly facing him, as though nothing unusual had occurred.

When the little group of twelve gathered to constitute the first church of Riverton, Stubbs was one of the twelve. By odd hours with Mr. Goldwin he learned to read, and with a delight almost pathetic, he learned to scrawl his own name. He had always been called simply Stubbs; but when he came to be baptized, he chose to prefix it with the name Christian; so it was henceforth Christian Stubbs.

Mr. Goldwin was hardly, in all respects, an orator. Pompous declamation and studied contrivances of speech were never his care. Affection and cant he despised. If an earnestness, directness and sincerity which won attention and wrought conviction are oratory, then he was an orator. Clinging to his tenets, he was charitable toward those who differed from him. Also, while, exalting the spiritual, he did not forget the physical. Abundant exercise in the fresh air put strength and warmth into his thinking and red corpuscles not only in his blood but into his theology.

The day the church was born the school house was packed, and Mr. Goldwin, quite equal to the occasion, preached on the place and mission of the church, and produced a deep impression. Pierpont said that, take it all in all, it was the most powerful discourse he ever heard; and Col. Grande at the close stood on the school house steps, flourished his red handkerchief, blew his trumpet and said to nearly every passer out, "Mr. Goldwin to-day strikingly reminded me of Henry Clay."

These are a few of the incidents when Riverton and its young clergyman began to make history. To-night as Mr. Goldwin watched in that silent home of Gen. Tupper, he found himself repeatedly reviewing his part and his responsibility in that history; yet repeatedly returning to the bedside and its unquiet slumberer. For just now his special concern was for Pierpont. Not so much for his physical recovery; he expected that. His heart went out for this young chivalric and studious lawyer. With him he had much in common. Warm friendship conspired with Christian love in longing to see the character and influence of Pierpont keyed to the highest ideals. This man and many others stood near—stood within the outer court. For the thousandth time Goldwin asked himself, "How can I persuade them to cross the threshold and reverentially stand within the great Temple?"

Plans, hopes, memories, prayers—until, with the sweet notes of the first bird of morning stilling his spirit, he forgot all in a few moments of rest.

CHAPTER XIII.

Of course the Pierpont injury soon had all Riverton by the ears. Reports travelled and grew until some had it that the injured man would not live through the day. At this stage of uncertainty and alarm Dr. Bancroft appeared on the street and was the target of eager questioners.

"No, he is not dead nor dying," said the doctor. "May outlive all of us."

"What! is'nt he dangerously wounded?" said Hawkins, who was mouthpiece for the bystanders.

"The wound requires careful watching—may take a dangerous turn."

"I understand an Indian shot him," said Hawkins.

"Your understanding is at fault," said he imperturbable doctor.

"What do you mean? Wasn't Pierpont shot," asked several voices, and the eager faces crowded closer about the doctor.

"Certainly he was shot, but it wasn't an Indian that shot the arrow."

"Wasn't it? We heard it was"

"No, that's a mistake. It wasn't an Indian."

"Who in the deuce was it then?" inquired Hawkins. "Some white rascal?"

"I can't say, Hawkins; although I have my suspicions. I only know that the man who sold to the Indian the liquor is the man who shot the arrow."

Hawkins slunk away and ere long stealthily slipped into O'Flannigans. No whiskey bitters prescribed by Dr. Bancroft for his patients.

Mr. Goldwin found himself quite exhausted with the night of anxeity and watching, and with rehearsing the story of the tragedy to many eager questioners. So after dinner he quietly slipped out and chose a path which ran to north and east of the town and which soon concealed him in the forest's welcome solitude. Here lying down and looking up into the tree tops, and watching the gray squirrels spring from branch to branch, pausing occasionally to gaze at him so saucily; or listening to the chipmunk and the mourning dove, and now and then the whirr of a partridge, Mr. Goldwin fell asleep. At last the slant rays of sunshine creeping under the boughs and into his face, aroused him, and he resumed his stroll till he came to the bank of the Rappilee.

Here he stumbled on Jonas Drake, indulging his love of the lone woods and streams, and of fishing.

"Ah, Jonas, is it you?"

"Yes sir, it's myself I believe, Mr. Goldwin."

"What luck?" said Mr. Goldwin, as he

picked his way from rock to rock to the fisherman's side.

"O, moderate; more nibble than catch so far. Here I have an extra tackle, and I have a plenty of minnows, won't you try your luck?"

"That I will, with great pleasure," said Mr. Goldwin, and immediately begun to unwind the line and bait the hook. Soon he felt the fish biting tentatively and forthwith he forgot all his cares. After they had made quite a "catch," and Jonas had a glorious string of Gogolies, Bass, and Cat Fish; they set their fish poles, and sat down on the bank. Mr. Goldwin said, as he lifted his hat and wiped his face, "I'm feeling fifty per cent. better than I did two hours ago. Jonas, I'm glad I crossed your path to-day." The boy eyed him with real satisfaction.

Then, as they lay back on the grass, Mr. Goldwin told some fish stories of Lake Champlain and his college days. Jonas was a silent boy, and of a rather heavy cast of countenance, and, as is sometimes the lot of such boys, was called by many dull and inert. But he had his thoughts; and a few, such for instance as his mother and sister, knew it. "College!" In his mind he had often questioned concerning that unknown world, and, now that Mr. Goldwin had spoken the word, he had discovered the key to one of those quiet cells in Jonas' mind. His natural reserve was fast dissolving before Mr. Goldwin's frank, kindly way, which, while it gave the boy a feeling of freedom, gave him also a feeling of self respect. Turning a more eager look to Mr. Goldwin, he said, "College, what do you think of it any way?"

"Its value to a man, do you mean?"

"Yes, that's about it. Of course I know its thought to be about the thing for a preacher or lawyer, or a rich man's son; but does college pay the common man and the poor boy?"

"Indeed, it does, Jonas. I was far from being a rich man's son." And then Mr. Goldwin gave a rapid sketch of his early life, his father's early death, his mother's frugal home, his struggles and those of his brothers' to gain an education, and then added, "O yes, home first, but college next in my life."

This rapid spetch of Mr. Goldwin's personal history seemed quite to surprise and capture Jonas. For a moment he was silent, and then he asked, "But what's the use of studying so much Latin and Greek? Nobody talks those languages now, does he?"

"No Jonas, they are not called spoken languages. And yet in one sense they are and always will be spoken. They enter essentially into the language of almost every civilized people. They are the main fertilizers of our English speech. English, French, German—strike down in any of these languages and you soon come to Latin and Greek roots. To know a boy well you must know his parents, and to know your mother tongue well, know Latin and Greek ."

"But," persisted Jonas, "don't college boys forget their Latin as soon as they can after leaving college?"

Mr. Goldwin smiled; "Yes, in one sense, many of them do. But so they do their Algebra and Trigonometry. In a few years you'll have forgotten those fish, and yet some of them will probably be wrought into your muscle and brain. Besides, there is great choice in diet and I think mind grows fastest and lustiest on a diet of Latin and Greek and Mathematics, with, of course, a plenty of Science and Philosophy."

"But then, ar'n't there English translations? Why not read them and be done with it?"

"For several reasons," replied Mr. Goldwin. "In the first place no translation does full justice to the original text. Something of the thought and much of the beauty escapes in the transfer. But, still more, the strengthening and sharpening of our minds is the important object. Nothing disciplines and trains the thinking powers like digging out some of the best thoughts of the ages and learning to express them in our own language. Splendid practice it is in discerning and expressing nice and delicate shades of thought."

"Yes," said the boy, "but doesn't anything that we have to dig for sharpen us?"

"It certainly does; you're right there, Jonas. Nevertheless there is great choice of whetstones. It would take you a long time to sharpen your scythe on a brickbat. So for the mind, take the college whetstones."

"It costs a fortune to go away to school. Why couldn't I study college books at home? Couldn't you teach me, Mr. Goldwin?" said the indomitable Jonas.

"Hardly," was the reply. I might help you some, and certainly will if you wish it. Still, I could not be a college to you. College is a little world that you can learn to move about in and carry your part in. It compels you to measure yourself not only by equals, but by your superiors. It throws you into the stream.

"Supposing I can't swim."

"O, but you can. Almost anyone can when its swim or sink. Besides, the college waters are carefully graded in depth to the growing capacity of the would be swimmer, and are well supplied with life protectors."

"Hawkins says college boys get the bighead," said Jonas, with an equivocal look, for he knew Hawkins was weak authority.

"Well, as to that," said Mr. Goldwin, "some go through college and some the college goes through them—a big difference. While self-conceit, or the bighead, as you say, comes from ignorance; proper self-confidence comes from knowledge. Nothing like rubbing mind against mind, classmate with classmate, pupil with teacher; wears off the moss of prejudice, starts the whole machinery. One meets in college some rare, rich soul, some professor or president, who has been there before him, and knows all about it; knows how to open just the right door for him—lives, and knows how to make him live. Hang your coat on that spicewood bush, and when you go home your garment carries the odor with it. So, much more one carries with him something of his wonderful teacher's character and manhood."

"But you wouldn't send every boy to college, would you?"

"No, indeed. Depends on the boy; prior to everything the raw material must be good. Yet I would like to send every boy to college who hungers to know something and be something. But a school of fish is what we want just now," said Goldwin, rising and drawing in his line.

He was surprised and delighted to see Jonas throwing off his shell and throwing out his feelers, although at the same time he instinctively felt that he must be a little wary and not betray too much surprise or pleasure, lest the boy should be frightened and hastily retreat under his crust. As he baited his fish hook for a final temptation, he said, "Jonas I would like to see you on the way to college."

"O, Mr. Goldwin, that's only one of my

dreams. It'll do just to talk about, but please don't mention it to anybody. Please don't Mr. Goldwin; it would seem so ridiculous."

"Certainly, Jonas, you can trust me for that. But then who knows? Perhaps we can make a way somehow. College may be for you yet. At any rate, it'll do to think about. But the dark is catching us. Hadn't we better haul in and start for home?"

Jonas went home thoughtful, and there was a stir within him. As for Mr. Goldwin, he felt that he had not only been near to "Nature's heart," but near to the heart of a good boy, and that he had thrown out a line which it were well to watch.

CHAPTER XIV.

"Mr. Barnett, will you please put aside the curtains, and let me look at the morning?"

The night had brought little refreshment to Pierpont, and he was glad to espy the day. His apartment commanded a wide view; tall hickories and maples and walnuts in the foreground casting their long shadows; in the distance the winding road, and, still beyond the glint of the river; and poured around all the chatter and song of a thousand merry throated birds; sight and sound and atmosphere of rest and beguilement.

Mr. Pierpont for sometime looked and listened. These venerable trees, he thought, with what peaceful and majestic grace they wave their green banners, while the sunlight streams in long bars beneath them, just as if this were not a world of accident and tragedy; insects revel in strident notes, and birds in jubilant song, as if morning never brought sorrow or pain; and yonder river, ceaseless river; its rythmic flow tells no tale of destruction and death. An atom smites us, a sliver pricks us, and we are gone; but the winds whisper it not; the sun still shines: Nature keeps step in her unrecking march in irony of our frailty.

A knock at the door and Sibyl appeared, bearing a tray smoking with appetizing substantials and delicacies.

"Ah, Sibyl, you're a jewel! I'm treated like a king, here," said Pierpont as he extended his hand to her.

"Well, if you are a king, then I am to be cup bearer to the king," said Sibyl.

"O, a lily for breakfast! Pray tell, whose thought is this?" inquired Pierpont as he took the flower from the tray.

"O, Emily's of course!" said Sibyl.

"Well, now, that is just perfect. Please thank her for me, and tell her I didn't know that even a lily could look so pure and smell so sweet."

"Hope the coffee 'll suit you?" said Sibyl.

"Entirely so. You people here seem determined to make me fall in love with my fate."

"Seems to me," said Barnett, "I'd fall in love. with something better than that. Wouldn't you Sibyl?"

"Indeed, I would. Good bye," and off she danced to the dining room.

"Now Barnett," said Pierpont, "do drink that cup of coffee for me. I don't feel as though I could taste a morsel, but I couldn't tell that blossom, Sibyl, so."

"O, but you must eat something. Try it," said Barnett; and so urgent was he that the patient did make a few sorry attempts; but soon gave over, and taking the lily and turning it over and over, gazed at it with that absent look which saw Emily more than it saw the lily. He loved Emily, and why had he not told her so? True, he had little to offer her as yet, except himself. But if, thought he, Emily Sherburne is the true woman that I take her to be, and loves me, there's an end of debate. At any rate I'll plead my case with my earliest release from this bondage.

Meanwhile at the Tupper breakfast table the young people were giving their several versions of the unfortunate occurrence, with spcial notes and comments. With one voice they extolled Mr. Goldwin; so quiet, and yet so prompt to see what to do, and especially what not to do.

"Such a delicious hour; and to have it end so shockingly," said Emily, as she languidly made pretense of breakfasting, for appetite, she had none.

"Do you know," said Isabel, "my first thought was that you, Emily, was hurt."

"I am not so sure that Emily is not hurt," said George, with an assumed air of solicitude. "Has anyone examined your heart, coz?"

"No, George; that was an unpardonable oversight. Hadn't you better go for Dr. Bancroft?"

Just then Sibyl entered. "Well Sib., dear, how is he?" said Gen. Tupper, as she gave him her morning kiss.

"O, he's chipper, she replied. "But I do

believe it's more than half put on. He looks awfully haggard. But, Emily, that lily went right to the spot."

"By Jove! I guess he has an affection of the heart," said George.

Mrs. Tupper did not fail to see that Emily wore a look of satisfaction, and attempted no evasion of the "soft impeachment."

A few mornings later and Sibyl, ever faithful in her self appointed office of cup bearer to the sick, bounded into the dining room nearly breathless, and exclaimed, "Who is Mabel? Who is Mabel? Would you believe it, as I stepped into Mr. Pierpont's room, he raised himself right up and wildly called, 'Mabel, where are you, Mabel? Come to me. Come quick, quick?' And then all at once he looked straight at me and said, "Ah! there you are Mabel. Now you'll never go away; stay with me, won't you; yes stay with me forever!' Good land! But I was stunned! But Mr. Barnett said in a low voice, 'Don't be frightened, he's had a high fever to-night and he's just waking, and hardly out of his dreams.' And, sure enough, in a moment he was all right again, and called me Sibyl."

With this dramatic rendition, Sibyl dropped into her chair, and for a moment in silence, there were various interpretations of Sibyl's report. Was he worse, was he delirious, or was it, as Mr. Barnett intimated, only a feverish dream? Dr. Bancroft will be in soon, thought Mrs. Tupper.

"But who is Mabel? That's what I'd like to know," said Sibyl.

"Probably his dulcinea," said George; "his sweetheart down in New York. I always thought he had one down there."

Emily's face reddened; then she grew pale with vexation because she had blushed.

When in her own room, the whole scene as described by Sibyl, together with George's interpretation, came over her like a nightmare. Mr. Pierpont's heart could never be hers. It had long been given to another. How foolish, how premature she had been. And yet, she could but feel that, whether designedly or undesignedly, he had given her some reason to hope. She could not be blamed for loving him. She could not help it. But that must be her secret. She must keep it. And yet how could she remain here and keep it? She must keep away; she must go home. If Mr. Pierpont really loved her and not another, a few hundred miles between them would not prevent his avowing it.

Besides, there seemed to be a conspiracy of events which she could not overlook. That very morning she had received a letter from her sister Ruth, asking her whether she was not about ready to come home; adding, "We know you are enjoying every moment at Uncle's, and dear lonely Papa never says come home; but oh! it would do him so much good to have you with us again. The housekeeper is getting so old and peevish and obstinate that she can't control the servants, and so my poor little headship is often called upon to settle their wrangles. Dear old Mammy, too, is such a child, and, if she sees me step out of the house, she runs after me to call me back, just as she used to when I was a four-year-old. Both of them will have to be put on the retired list, and some young blood be set flowing in the house of the Sherburne's. All this when you come home.

"Pomp is coachman now, and you ought to see how he inflates and swells. I am almst mortified with his obsequiousness. You'd smile out loud to see him strut and put on airs. But he'll get over it. This morning Dinah came out and raked him down somewhat after this fashion. "Se heah, Pom Randolph, yo' big fool, done yo' know dem hosses 'long to Massa and de Lawd; dey ain't your'n nohow, yo' big fool.' And then she chuckled.

"Pomp keeps Papa out driving half the time, which I encourage. Dear Papa will go to the cemetery too often, and always comes home with that despairing look which breaks my heart. If dear Mama had not been snatched from him so suddenly, and in the evening of his life when he needed her the most, he might have rallied and been himself again.

"Harry Burnham calls quite often of late, ostensibly to have an evening chat with me, but, mind you, he never leaves until he knows all that I know about when you are coming home. With this depressing fact staring me in the face, don't you think I'm a marvel of self-sacrifice to wish you to come home? But *sub rosa*, dear Em, I freely avow that there isn't a better than Harry Burnham in all Richmond. He is no longer tutor now, but has a professorship and isn't a bit puffed up over it. Papa thinks he smells a little heresy about him, but I call him the stiffest kind of a churchman. Papa, you know, isn't much for the new notions, and I fancy you'll come home limbered up just a little.

Now, Em, dear, if this old house on the hill draws you pretty strongly, we shall none of us say nay.

Your own loving,
RUTH."

Yes, Emily resolved that she would go home. She came to Riverton in search of better health and she had found it. Indeed, she was quite well. And she had found a good deal beside health. With her fondness for children and her disposition to launch out and try herself, she had taken the school in Riverton for a year, and been very successful and happy in it. She had found a blessing, too, in helping the young church and its young minister, and in forming the acquaintance of a noble, true-hearted young man, Daniel Pierpont. But this latter she must hide away in the inner sanctuary of her soul.

With swift resolution she wrote to her sister, "I am coming."

Emily was ever proud to say that she was born, nurtured, and educated in Richmond, Virginia. Blent with her earliest and fondest recollections was the boast, "I am a Virginian." How often her father had directed her eyes to the capitol, standing in its grandeur and majesty on the summit of Shockoe hill, as a most fitting symbol of the collossal position occupied by Virginia among her sister States. With a face glowing with patriotic fervor, he would point, perchance, to the bronze figure of Jefferson and rehearse to his children how that the same hand which drafted that immortal document, the Declaration of Independence, designed likewise that stately and venerated edifice of legislation. Born and reared almost under the very shadow of the imposing forms in marble or bronze of Washington, Patrick Henry, Jefferson, John Marshall, and others whom the friends of man delight to honor, these great names were to the Sherburnes, something more than names, more than shadows of a glorious past,—were a living presence, a mighty and beneficent inspiration.

Emily's father, Captain Paul Marion Sherburne, was a man of fortitude, and of uncomplaining spirit, but he had never recovered from the shock of losing his cultured and beautiful wife, who was as good as she was beautiful; one of those who, in this faulty world, keep "our faith in goodness strong."

During his active business life, Capt. Sherburne had been engaged in extensive shipping interests, for in his day, Richmond was one of the most opulent commercial emporiums of the South. He was widely known and as widely respected as a gentleman of the good old type. For many years the family mansion, with its attractive grounds, had been one of the landmarks on Church Hill, and was no great distance from the venerable St. John's church, where, for so many years, the Sherburnes had worshipped. Often, while seated in the family pew, Emily, as a little girl, would in thought wander away from service and sermon, and picture to herself the Virginia Convention of 1775 which convened within its walls—sat in those very seats; and would imagine herself listening to Patrick Henry as he then poured forth his fearless words, closing with, "Give me Liberty or give me Death;"—words which echoed not alone within those sacred arches, but from Boston to Charleston, and above the roar of the Atlantic to the throne of King George. Here, too, thirteen years later, the colonies, now no longer colonies, but sovereign States, another hardly less memorable Virginia Convention assembled which discussed and ratified the Federal Constitution.

The thought of returning home to Richmond brought to Emily Sherburne, with almost painful distinctness, the face of one dear inmate of that home, her invalid brother, now twenty-six years of age. If ever the celestial Gardener opened a bud of rare promise, it was at the birth of Jamie Sherburne. Never was child more welcome, never more tenderly, lovingly, wisely mothered. The babe grew and exhibited in prompt succession, all the wonders of child history. Infancy, little beginning of immortality! Kingdom of mystery, new to every parent! Sealed book, and no one has been found to break the seal and open the book. Jamie grew,—a jolly, pranksome, roguish boy; a little questioner; now and then he would put on his little thinking cap and for a moment would actually look sober and serious, and would bounce out some problem, some "how" or "whence," or flash out some "cute" child saying, the puzzle and pleasure of the household. Little star around which the galaxy of home revolved!

Was it a careless nurse that allowed him to fall from his carriage and strike his head upon the pavement? Was it some contusion of the only too susceptible brain? or some sudden chill and congestion? any or all of these, who knoweth? Jamie was suddenly very ill. The family physician shook his head, looked very apprehensive, and whispered something of brain fever. For days and days Jamie gave no sign of recognition of anything. At last he was seen to turn his head a very little and seem to follow with his eyes the spoon and cup from which nourishment was cautiously dealt to him. More days passed and then it was eagerly reported that he opened his lips and for once said "Papa."

Poor Jamie had to begin life over; had to learn, for the second time, slowly learn to walk and to talk. But the fever had left lesion of the brain and paralysis of the left side of the body. Jamie, now twenty-six years old, and yet a child! Growth of body and mind long ago arrested! There were intervals—days—of comparative respite and of brightness;—enough to show how much light had been eclipsed; but there was always suspended over the boy the dread certainty of relapse, and the dread uncertainty, the peril of every moment.

Gradually Jamie's world narrowed, till it finally was all included within the four walls of home. He was profoundly affectionate. Home and its little round were everything to him, and he clung to Papa and Mama as a vine does to the strong tree. He lived on the love and sympathy of the household, and he felt any seeming or supposed neglect like a wound. Conscientious he was, often morbidly so. As a rule, he was patient, and suffered in silence; but occasionally a word would escape, which told with what horror he went down into the deep waters. Those long, long, days of physical revulsion and of struggle as with demons! Kind Nature then in part, and for a time, drew a vail over the senses. Often the nerves were sorely taxed and strained, and were as if mercilessly laid bare; and then he would give way to impatience and ill impulse; how could it be otherwise? but only to follow it with bitter wailing lest he had done wrong, and had spoiled his record for the day. It was most pathetic to behold his struggles to be good and kind against such odds.

The horizon of thought and memory grew more narrow with the flow of years. The present made slight impression, soon effaced. More and more he thought and dreamed in the life and memories of earlier days, which had made their record on the sensorium when it was still responsive and retentive. But some faces and events he never forgot; for example, an Aunt tenderly loved, but now of long time deceased, and, later, his dear, dear mother suddenly taken to the skies, were never lost from his memory. Many a morning when he was fairly himself, with his cheery smile he would say, "I dreamed about Auntie," or "I saw mama last night." Songs, too, which he learned before he was ten years of age he never entirely forgot. He retained the sweet child voice, although it was not so strong as the impairing years came. He loved to go through his little *repertoire* of a score or more of songs and hymns which were his favorites, while Ruth or Emily accompanied him at the piano. When his mother came to face the last, how natural, and yet how piercing to the soul, to hear her exclaim, "Must I go and leave poor Jamie?" The last year of Jamie's life was darkness, and then— Light.

CHAPTER XV.

Quite four weeks from the day of the luckless casualty, Daniel Pierpont hobbled into the Tupper sitting room. This made it a joyous day for all the household. Nevertheless, a shadow overhung them all, since Emily, the universal favorite, was to leave by the morrow morning stage for her Southern home; and a shadow, indeed, it was to Pierpont and to Emily; the deeper, too, because it must be concealed. Emily, although a little pale, was never more beautiful than that evening, but with all her affability and kindliness, there was a reserve and forced composure and resoluteness which strong natures can summon while they suffer.

Mr. Goldwin and Mr. and Mrs. Barnett had dropped in to offer congratulations and good byes, and Miss Sherburne's departure was so much a regret to them all, that it was a relief to have the conversation turn to a subject as far away as last Sunday's sermon on Temperance.

"You were particularly close and searching in your sermon, Mr. Goldwin, but not one whit too much so," said Mrs. Tupper.

"I found my sermon," he replied, "in the wretched home of John Barnes. John is naturally a bright man, and a kinder heart than his doesn't beat. But now drink has made a beast of him, and he is slowly murdering his poor wife he once so fondly loved, and his children will soon be worse than orphans. When I entered the room John lay upon the floor in one corner, just beginning to sleep after a three days' debauch. Mrs. Barnes lay upon her bed, haggard, exhausted, and such a picture of despair; and there was the little motherly Laura trying to comfort the frightened and sobbing children; telling them Papa would'nt beat them so, if it wasn't for the naughty whiskey. Then they begged of me, "Please, Mr. Goldwin, take all the whisky out of Riverton before Papa wakes up."

The silence of deep emotion pervaded the group as Mr. Goldwin continued, "I felt so helpless to comfort that stricken woman. Death was facing her, and the delirium of drink her husband. 'Poor dear John,' she sighed, 'may God forgive him. Once there wasn't a happier home than ours in Riverton. But drink robbed us of everything. When I am gone, Mr. Goldwin, please do all you can for my dear, dear children. I know you will, and O, save them from the fate of their parents.' Then she sunk back completely exhausted, and for a moment, I almost thought she was gone.

And' what makes it more shocking, in effect, that scene is duplicated in more than one home which I have visited in Riverton.

The law sanctioned by the people of Riverton, protects the drink shops, but where is the law which protects Mrs. Barnes and her children?"

This recital from Mr. Goldwin brought tears to the eyes of Emily and Isabel, who were good Samaritans in this and so many other homes of want and sorrow. Even George, who vapored much about "personal liberty," was silent and thoughtful.

By this time Colonel and Mrs. Grande had dropped in, and, with how great sincerity it is not necessary to say, joined in the discussion of ways and means of reform.

"Of course my hotel must have a bar," said the Colonel depreciatingly, "but how can we get rid of O'Flannigan's corner and Schnapps beer hole, and Elias Whitcomb's place, too; for they say he sells a deal besides groceries—somthing to wash them down.

Here Mr. Pierpont, with a warmth and emphasis which he could poorly suppress, replied to Col. Grande's weak protest, "We can get rid of Schnapps' and O'Flannigan's and all others of that ilk, just as soon as you and other citizens want to get rid of them." This remark was reassuring to Mr. Goldwin, who reflected that in Mr. Pierpont, he had a good soldier of temperance.

As Mr. Goldwin rose to go he pressed Emily's hand very warmly, saying, "I can't tell you how much you have helped me in many ways. I shall never forget how you came to my rescue in those first days when I tried to play both preacher and chorister."

General Tupper followed him to the door to say what had been impressed on him of late: you are looking a little worn, Mr Goldwin. Ar'n't you working too hard?"

"Perhaps I am, General, and I have been thinking of late that I would soon give you all a litle rest for a few weeks, and pay a visit to old Vermont and my good mother once more." A twenty dollar gold piece just then adroitly found its way into the pastor's hand; which meant "Go, and my blessing with you." As Mr. Goldwin walked to his room, he smiled as he thought, "that twenty dollar piece will be very lonely in my pocket-book, but it does help to decide some things."

As Gen. Tupper resumed his seat, George was saying with great animation, "It just did me good last Sunday, when Mr. Goldwin, without a scrap of paper before him, poured out the hot shot right and left. No chance to get in my nap! Why can't he preach that way all the time?"

"Your question opens a pretty large subject, my boy," said the General.

"With or without paper," said Pierpont, "what surprises me is that a man for fiftytwo Sundays in a year, can give us two such fresh and brainy sermons a week. Why we attorneys think we are doing famously if we make six or eight well wrought arguments a year."

"You lawyers never write your speeches, do you?" asked Sibyl.

"No," said Pierpont, "although in the higher courts arguments are often submitted in writing. It does us good to face our thoughts in writing. Many a plea never could stand the test of being transfered to manuscript."

"After all, with the lawyer and preacher, isn't it a question of aptitudes," said General Tupper. "Manuscript, brief, skeleton or no skeleton, a speaker must capture and carry his audience; and that's the long and short of it."

"Yes, for instance," said Emily, "it sets one all in a fidget to hear our Dr. Nicholson, of Richmond, try to speak without his manuscript, but he talks grandly on paper."

"When," said Pierpont, "a man sits down to clothe his thoughts in pen-and-ink propriety, he soons finds out whether he has any thoughts to clothe;" and then with a droll look he added, "when I sat down to write my first plea, I began by sharpening my new pencil, and by the time pencil and I had a point, I had no pencil."

"Tried to make too fine a point, perhaps," said the General.

Meanwhile Col. Grande, after laboring in vain to make his scant and frowsy hair lie still and submisive over the bald top of his head, struck a new attitude and rested his hands on his knees and studied the carpet; and George winked to Pierpont, for they knew that the Colonel was grooming up the "Sage of Ashland" once more, and with even half a chance would trot him out.

"Well, Colonel," said George, "tell us what's on your mind."

"O," said he, "I was only recalling the time when I heard Henry Clay. But then there's but one Henry Clay."

"But don't you think," said Emily, "that the lawyer or the politician has this advantage, that he is in a debate? Its an intelectual tournament and everybody is eager to see the contest."

"To see who beats," said Barnett.

"Yes, Miss Sherburne, I think that is true," said Pierpont. "At the bar or at the hustings, the fire is already kindled, indeed, generally is at white heat; while in the pulpit the minister must strike the flint until he has kindled a fire. And yet, with barrister or clergyman, or political speaker, I fancy it is the same universal principle of right, which, after all, is the orator's best grip."

"One thing which pleases me," said Mrs. Tupper, "our minister is a good reader. His reading of the Bible is a new interpretation of it to me."

"And those good old hymns, too," added Isabel; "how it does set me on pins to hear ministers sing-song them, or else rattle them off like an auctioneer."

"Yes, reading in such a way as to give the exact meaning; that is just it," said Emily; "and don't you think half the commentaries and half the pulpit comments would be superfluous, if the minister simply read the Bible with a true spiritual insight? It seems to me so often as though the connection was broken, and the reader was not in touch with what he reads."

"Ah, we all understand that feeling," said the General, "and there is just one thing which is worse, and that is when the Bible reader turns actor, or tries to exhibit his elocution. That, I do think, is sacreligious."

"I never shall forget,' said Pierpont, hearing Fanny Kimball read, 'The Tempest.' It was like a revelation—the mind of Shakespeare himself. She read so perfectly that I hardly knew she was reading."

"What I like about Mr. Goldwin," said Mr. Barnett, "he has such good sense, gets right down to business, and stops the mill the very moment the corn is ground. Why, there was Father Tomes, up in the Vermont hills; he always gave us so much thin soup that we never got at the substantials."

"All soup and toothpicks, wasn't he?" suggested George.

"After all, Mr. Goldwin lacks one thing," said Col. Grande, and shook his head very wisely, as he arose to leave. "He'll never be complete until he has a wife."

"O that depends;" said the Tuppers.

"Yes, that depends," said the Colonel and Mrs. Grande.

CHAPTER XVI.

It was the "still hour" of early morning. No sounds throughout the slumbering house. Mr. Goldwin had quietly arisen, and was seated at the window. His thoughts, meanwhile, were "taking the wings of the morning." His eye rested on what was, to him, a new scene, a tranquil landscape, mid way between Riverton and the hills of Vermont. Comfortable villas, gardens, orchards, pasture lands, and fields of maize, and the yellow clay marking the road which wound about, sometimes lost to view, and then reappearing on the brow of some hill; a church spire flashing the first sunbeams, and a church yard, gray with its rows of little white headstones; and off to the right, the roof just visible above the trees, Holton Academy—these were some of the features of the landscape on which Goldwin, sitting with his arms resting on the window sill, was intently gazing. Thus far on his way to Vermont, he was here at the hospitable home of Father Halliday, who, as pastor, had, as the Deacon so often told the Lord in prayer, "gone in and out before this people for more than a generation."

Before leaving Riverton, Mr. Goldwin had received a little package and a newspaper from Boston. The package contained letters from Mr. Goldwin to Miss Marian Braddock and bearing date of several years previous, and accompanying the package was a clipping from a late issue of a Boston journal which told these grave words:

"Died in this city, June 27th, Miss Marian Braddock, late preceptress of Latin in the Beacon Street Classical School. The deceased had filled this responsible position with great acceptability for three years, and had easily won the high admiration and esteem of all who knew her. Thus a mysterious Providence has suddenly closed to earth a life which gave brilliant promise of years of usefulness and distinction as a scholar and instructor. The body will be conveyed to her early home, Ryeburgh, Vermont, where it will be consigned to its long rest. We beg the privilege of mingling our tears with those of the aged and revered parents, sole survivors in that hillside home."

A note, written evidently with a feeble and trembling hand, but Marian's own, accompanied the package of letters:

"Dear John:

The friends who are about me tell me that I am not seriously ill; but something in my own heart tells me that I shall never rise from this bed. These letters you wrote to me in what seems to me now the long ago, were then, and always have been, a sacred possession. I can not destroy them; I cannot think of their falling under any eyes but yours. Dear John, I was not worthy of you. I knew it then and tenfold more do I know it now. God bless you, John, and good bye.

MARIAN."

Seismal convulsions have oftened opened springs that had long been closed. Those letters and that last of earth to Marian Braddock revived an old fountain in Goldwin's heart. He pondered the ever changeful, ever new mystery of life-histories. How different, thought he, it might have been. Their destinies, how near they ran; two ships touching and interchanging and then diverging for all the future. 'Man deviseth, but Another directeth," said Goldwin, "and let me be lapped in the wisdom and love of that Disposer."

With a heart serene as this August morning, Mr. Goldwin was looking upon the sunburnished landscape; looking and yet not looking. In that pensive hour he was traversing one sacred field of memory, carefully enclosed and guarded, where foot of mortal, save his own and one other, never pressed. In it now stood a stone of memorial, and on it grew an amaranthine wreath to the remembrance of Marian Braddock. Time had borne him on, guided and sheltered in the Eternal Wisdom, but that landmark remained. Life had grown richer, fuller; and with chastened, but deeper emotions, now, he looked upon the landscape of existence.

It had a profounder interpretation than when he first passed that way mark.

Father Halliday and wife thoroughly believed that it was not good for man or woman to be alone. Now a niece of the revered pastor was teaching in the Holton Academy; had been teaching for several years; quite years enough, as he and his second agreed. "Time Jane Elizabeth had been paired off. Here's this Mr. Goldwin—a rare man, unexceptionable, who knows but there is a Providence in his coming at this time. Who knows but this may be his Padanaram."

"Or mount of sacrifice," archly suggested his wife.

"No, no, my dear; here the well-side where he shall meet his Rachel. Now the next thing is to bring these two people together. Wife, why not send around to Jane Elizabeth inviting her to tea this evening."

"Very well, husband; we'll do that, and while we are about it, why not ask Miss Howard and the Principal, Mr. Everett? I would rather get a supper for four visitors than for two."

"Very good, my dear; do so. Margaret Howard will do finely as a foil to set off Jane Elizabeth—serves well as an accompaniment."

Six o'clock. The sun, having borne himself openly for a day, was retiring behind curtains of dappled glory, and the carryall of the Holton Academy held up at the parsonage. Mr. Everett alighted; a sleek, precise, methodical gentleman of about thirty-five summers; then came Miss Howard, some ten years his junior, whom Mr. Everett handed down with marked deference and gallantry, as though he quite enjoyed the privilege.

Miss Applebee, for once the last to alight, was on terra firma before Mr. Everett could so much as give her a hand, albeit, that worthy gentleman turned himself about as quickly as a man could, circumvallated as he was in a great stock and high collar. Miss Applebee presented a tall and rather broad form, erect and a little more, in a bright terra cotta colored gown, not unlike the hue of her hair which rolled in thick folds around an aspiring knot on the top of her head, and lay in serpentine waves over her smooth and retreating forehead, which rested on high abutting eyebrows, under which lurked large gray eyes; sometimes you would have said they were dark eyes, and always piercing as bayonets. In or out of the school room, it was Miss Applebee's nature and preference to take the lead. She was the school mistress, pronounced and dogmatic everywhere. A habit she had of punctuating her remarks with a light half developed laugh, which, at first not unpleasant, was thrown in so promiscuously as soon to become humdrum and rasping. Her pupils, indeed, had come to look upon this conciliatory titter, or "refined giggle" as they half ironically styled it, as the precursor of some axe she wished them to grind for her. She often seemed conspicuously kind; although, not unlike some others, her kindness generally proved to be well aimed at some ulterior end.

A few personalities and formalities, and as the ice began to crack, the little company drew around the tea table, and there was a general thaw, and every atom of congealment floated away. Blessings on tea! Great social benefactor. What intrenchment of silence or reserve can resist its benign warmth. Blessed potation, which Miss Applebee said, "cheered, but did not inebriate," and sipped her second cup. The conversation ambled along, touching lightly and, of course, eulogistically, on Mrs. Halliday's light biscuit, cold tongue, jellies, sponge cake and cream custard; touching also lightly, if not eulogistically on politics and the state of the nation, wherein Prof. Everett stood alone in the role of champion of Andrew Jackson; then they alighted on such themes as temperance, slavery, and education,—ways and means thereof.

Here were counter currents, mild little eddies. For as soon appeared, Miss Applebee was sworn enemy to co-education beyond the academy. Promiscous schools for more advanced pupils, she declared to be little short of heathenish. To this Mr. Goldwin ventured a demurrer, and drew upon himself those bayonet gleams.

"We are," said he, "all accustomed to think that home the more fortunate where there are both brothers and sisters." A proposition to which Prof. Everett bowed a ready acquiescence; that is so far as his broad stock and high collar would allow, for the latter, like two white knives held his ears in constant menace of abridgment. Miss Howard, too, whose home had in it many brothers and sisters, quite cordially confirmed Mr. Goldwin's pleasant illustration.

"And I think," Mr. Goldwin proceeded to say, "that this compulsory sundering of young ladies and gentlemen in the great work of education is, to say the least, somewhat unnatural."

"O, Mr. Goldwin," said Miss Applebee, "you can have no idea how such a school and college system would degenerate. The freedom would be misused. Why right here in Holton Academy, I have had my opinion confirmed. My own sister, Annie, had not been in the school a whole term before there was a young man at her heels, and he kept at her heels till both he and she had finished the course, and then of course they had to get married."

This was too much for the equanimity of Father Halliday. "Now Jane Elizabeth," said he, bringing his fist down on the table, "there never was a better behaved girl in Holton Academy than Annie Applebee, and the young man you are berating stood first in his class in morals and scholarship, and if ever there was a match made in Heaven, that was."

"Thank you, Father Halliday," said Mr. Goldwin, "you are reaching the very point I wanted to emphasize. A young man and a young woman trained in the same school, and having similar tastes and acquirements, have rare opportunity to know each other thoroughly, and when they come to marry, it is no venture into an unknown sea."

Miss Applebee glowered and Miss Howard's eyes twinkled.

"Nevertheless," said the immovable Miss Applebee, "I maintain my position that the freedom would be misused."

"In some cases, doubtless, it would be," said Mr. Goldwin. Everything good is abused. Nevertheless, give us liberty; freedom is in many cases the best cure for its abuse. Artificial and unnatural restrictions beget abnormal results; very often instigate the very conduct that they are designed to preclude. However, this word co-education is only just coming into our vocabulary, but it contains a truth which is bound to make its way. Our seminaries and colleges which are limited to one sex are doing a grand work, and there will long be room for them."

"What I would like to plead for," said Miss Howard, "is that the door should be opened to woman into our highest institutions of learning—our best colleges and universities.

To be sure, at first not many women would enter these instintutions, but the opportunity would itself be a grand incentive. This subject is one on which Miss Applebee and I have had many a sharp discussion."

"Your face is toward the morning, Miss Howard," said Mr. Goldwin; "I hope you will keep right on pleading for the privileges which, in fairness, belong alike to both men and women.

"What a demoralizing effect it does have on some men to go West," said Miss Applebee. "I am thinking what a paradise of fools and wild eyed cranks you would have."

"O," said Mr. Goldwin, "fanatics and hobbyists jump on to every new reform. Barnacles love good timber. Where's the good cause which does not suffer from selfish and sinister retainers?"

"Flies gather where the sweets are thickest," said the good housewife, Mrs. Halliday.

"Now don't let me be misunderstood," said Mr. Goldwin. "I know that I occupy advanced ground, but all I would say is, give woman her chance and her place which is beside man; each free and neither complete without the other."

"That's it; that's it," said Father Halliday and the Professor, although neither of them appeared to realize the full import of that to which they so readily assented.

The lustre of tea table vivacity hardly seemed to belong to Prof. Everett. In speech and manners, he labored to be preeminently proper. He was a routinest. Certain text books he could repeat, verbatim, and when the conversation led to it, he could give you axioms and round periods from Adam Smith or Ricardo or Locke or Brown, and so appear very sage and philosophic. But as for evolving anything from his own mind, any reflections which had a personal flavor, like apples which have extracted a peculiarly rich flavor from the rich soil—as well expect to gather oranges from fence posts, or to spear whales in Sahara. His pupils thought him a man of prodigous learning, and the trustees of the school pronounced him to be a very superior instructor. And judged by a common standard, so he was. Take him anywhere outside of his daily beat, and he was a vaccuum. His one talent he kept wrapped in a napkin of routine. Miss Applebee's glib command of humdrum exactly suited him, and her *repertoire* of familiar quotations charmed him. Miss Howard's mental freshness and ideality were lost on him. Native talent he would carefully prune away as only a superfluity.

Why is it that persons favored with educational advantages, and, it may be, by their calling supposed to move amid thoughts and truths and knowledge, often talk together for a half hour and reach nothing beyond mere talk and triteness? What a dull time their recording angel must have. Is it that they are so very chary of their better thoughts, or is it that they have no thoughts?

In conversation, Miss Applebee sprinkled quotations, like flowers strewn here and there amid grasses and weeds; some of them long withered, dessicated; flowers plucked from foreign gardens; not those which had planted themselves, nor those which she had planted and grown until they had become a part of her own lawn and garden plot. Her couplets, wise saws, borrowed phrases and etceteras, were sufficient to scintilate one or two occasions without being dulled by reintroduction, but to the close observer, they were too much like ornaments puttied on to a wooden figure head. Thoughts, felicitous conceptions and reflections, ones own and others, which interwined and interrooted and grew because they must grow and loved to grow; these neither she nor the Professor, nor the veteran pastor of Holton possessed; or if they did possess them, they had laid them away so carefully that they were unable to find them. Some persons are a garner house of facts and data; touch them where you will, you learn something. And now and then there is one who has pierced beyond this outter shell of fact; he has that imagination, that vision of the ideal, the real, which thinks and sees, revels in its own discoveries and creations, and imparts to all thoughts its own individual stamp. To converse with such a mind is to banquet with the gods.

As the evening wore on, Mrs. Halliday and Miss Applebee put their heads together over some matters pertaining to the church sewing society, and Father Halliday and Prof. Everett were exchanging platitudes and supposing they were practicing the high art of conversation.

Mr. Goldwin, in the meantime, chatted with Miss Howard. He was amused and gratified to find so much enthusiasm and high ideal under that quiet exterior. Instead of the trifles and small ambitions which fill the life of so many women, she was absorbed in her one work of teaching, which to her was no mere routine or machine work, nor any mere literary bespattering, but was no less than mind and character growing; leading the young pupil into a life-long enrichment and enriching. Her brown eyes were wonderfully expressive, her whole face beamed, as she spoke of those studies which hardly more than are opened to their first page in the academy, little more, indeed, in this brief academy existence—human life; spoke, too, of her classes, of minds just catching a hint of the dawn, and of selectest personal histories now in the making. And how she listened enwrapt, her whole soul in her eyes, as she led Mr. Goldwin into a narrative of his pioneer toils in the West, of the forces contending for the mastery in those rushing communities, of his difficulties and obstacles, his pleasant discoveries, and his large cheer and hope. He thought, as he conversed with Miss Howard, "Here is the lofty imagination and spiritual vision for greatest things; the very stuff for the heroic."

After their guests were gone, Mr. and Mrs. Halliday sat hand in hand by the open window, looking out into the moon light, just as they had done fifty years before when life was young. As they reviewed the evening, on the whole they were pleased. Mr. Goldwin, as both agreed, had borne his part most credtiably. "Fortunately," said Father Halliday, "Miss Howard was unusually reserved, so that Jane Elizabeth had the field, and I think Mr. Goldwin must see that she is a woman who has opinions and knows how to express them." Mrs. Halliday assented mildly, having her own view of JaneElizabeth's opinions. "As they were leaving," said Mrs. Halliday, "I noticed that she invited Mr. Goldwin to take tea with her at the academy to-morrow night."

"Did she? That' a good stroke. You see, wife, we have set the ball rolling in the right direction. Providence will take care of it now."

"Yes, husband, I don't see that Providence needs any more of our help."

For two Sabbaths Mr. Goldwin supplied the pulpit in Holton. Father Halliday very much enjoyed his assistance. Mr. Goldwin's direct way of presenting his thoughts, his Western freedom and informality, bespoke attention, and started mind and heart. It was a change from the usual Sunday fare at Holton. There was no disguising the fact that, with advancing years, Father Halliday had grown tame and juiceless. His truisms together with his dogmas, hewn and squared in a former generation, although of some avail once, were rather unsatisfactory and wearisome to the wide awake and questioning youth. Henry Grimes, just home from an Eastern college, called Father Halliday's sermons old straw threshed over for half a century. Mr. Goldwin's studies in the Bible, and in every day life, gave him sermons at first hand, and they had the charm of the real. Even old Deacon Jones, who for years, had been one of the sound sleepers of the church, listend with mouth wide open. Merchant Clark said, "he gives us something to think about," and young Mr. Stover said, "He puts things so that we can see them." Philip Griswold, son of the rich man of the town, loved "short graces and long dinners," and lounged indolently into church and bestowed his patronizing smile. Even he condescended to say that "Mr. Goldwin was wise enough not to attempt to exhaust his subject, and so never exhausted his hearers." Father Halliday had given his strength and more than half his days to doing good in Holton. Some always remembered this with gratitude; some forgot it and ill judged him.

The young ministerial guest, in company

with the parson and his worthy lady, was invited out, dined and tead among the dames and damsels of Holton. Often Miss Applebee and Miss Howard were also guests on these occasions. Mr. Goldwin soon knew all the roads of the vicinage, and they all seemed to lead to the Holton Academy. The pupils thought him extremely devoted to their school library, and some wondered whether that were really the center of his devotion. Miss Applebee expatiated in her sweetest half-grown laugh on his remarkable interest in the school.

It chanced that on the last evening which Mr. Goldwin was to spend in Holton, he and the teachers of the academy were invited to an evening's visit with Deacon and Mrs. Jones and their fair daughters. Pastor Halliday then suggested that as the academy "bang about" was not the most comfortable, nor over roomy, Mr. Goldwin would do well to take the parsonage horse and buggy, with one of the young lady teachers as a companion.

"Thank you, Father Halliday," said Mr. Goldwin, "your offer is very kind and most opportune. Nothing would suit me better."

Father Halliday reflected that nothing suited him better, for hadn't he heard Jane Elizabeth less than a week ago declare that matrimony was a deplorable state of bondage, and that she was sure she should never put her foot into it? This remark was reassuring to Father Halliday for he had noticed that maidens, young and old, who talked thus derisively of marriage, were the first to surrender to the tender passion, and furthermore, he had noticed that Mr. Goldwin had spent several long evenings, of late, at the academy.

Now Deacon Jones hospitable home was by direct road two miles, and by a more circuitous route four miles, from the village; and Mr. Goldwin, on this occasion, concluded that the longest road would be the shortest, much to the disgust of the parson's horse, he being sure that he knew the shortest road to the good Deacon's oat bin.

The evening wore on, and the other guests were arrived, and the question went around, "What has become of Mr. Goldwin and his lady?" Just then the couple were announced. "So glad to see you, you are so late that we began to fear something serious had happened to you;" said several voices. Mr. Goldwin felt pretty sure that something had happened to them; but for all the charges of being tardy, the parson's horse came in as the scape goat, for wasn't he old and opinionated and a slow-goer? Miss Applebee smiled most mysteriously and said "she had long thought the people ought to present Father Halliday with a swifter horse, and now she was sure of it." Deacon Jones thought that their faithful veteran minister found no difficulty in coming around promptly, and that there must be a difference in drivers." Prof. Everett thought that Mr. Goldwin would do better if he let the lady drive. Mr. Goldwin quite enjoyed the merriment, even though it was at his expense, and helped on the jesting famously. His repartee was remarked as unusually felicitous.

As the young minister and his lady companion rode homeward, the clouds were scurrying over the face of the sky, and the stars gleamed fitfully. But it is very doubtful whether the occupants of the clerical vehicle could, if questioned, have given on that evening any very coherent description of the earth or the sky. Perhaps they fancied they were neither of earth or sky, but floating deliciously somewhere between. One thing they knew, henceforth they were pledged to each other for life.

CHAPTER XVIII.

A few weeks have passed, and with them is passing the glory of summer. Nature is painting in gorgeous suncolors, and Love is casting colors still more beautiful and more unfading over two lives that henceforth are one.

Mr. Goldwin had spent a month in Vermont visiting his beloved mother, and renewing the memories and delights of his youth. Thomas he missed, who was now somewhere in the then far West, and Arthur was just graduated from college. John, the Riverton minister, gave his Sabbaths to supplying a pulpit in Rowland. "Why can we not secure this young man with us permanently?" said his hearers. But in vain did they suggest this. Mr. Goldwin's heart was in the far West, and lingered at Riverton. Again he said what he had so often said before, "No, I must work where, if I do not go, the work will be left undone.

That which sometime comes to us all, and which rounds and perfects the orb of life, had come to two more mortals. Letters from Vermont, letters in a strange and masculine hand had come for the last month by swift and regular post, to Miss Margaret Howard.

How much she learned from those letters! They led her into a deeper and more vital acquaintance with her affianced than even his personal presence and conversation had done. Was she sometimes lost to everything around her; her eyes beholding something far, far away; her heart travelling on swift wings of fancy, her imagination building beautiful worlds in her future? Did some of her pupils and fellow teachers discern this? She was drinking of the overflowing goblet of wedded troth. A new light shone in her face, and a larger meaning and loftier eloquence were in her daily teachings. Love enriches all true souls. In all practical trivalties the pupils referred to Miss Applebee; but when they had any serious difficulty, any life trouble, they sought out Miss Howard. Her sympathy, insight, and, sincere fellow interest gave her just the ministry for each tried heart. How they mourned her departure from the school; but Prof. Everett, with his accustomed equanimity and stiffness bowed his acquiescence, and said that matrimonial engagements superseded all others, and said that they might as well bend gracefully before the inevitable, and especially, now that a dear friend of Miss Howard had been secured to step at once into her place.

It was not without a struggle that Miss Howard gave up her position in the school. It afforded the work she had deliberately chosen because of its extra opportunities for doing good, and at first she revolted from any suggestion of abandoning her espoused life work. This disposition, however, only drew the young minister the more strongly toward her.

Miss Howard was a neat, agile body, above medium stature, hair soft and brown, eyes that everybody loved to look into, drooping eyelashes under which harbored sympathy, benevolence, intellectual alertness, fun and fire; cheeks of that fine flesh tint which is the admiration and despair of artists, thin and well molded lips, firm mouth and a round, plump chin which was enlivened with a coquetish hint of a dimple. "She isn't a beauty, I suppose, mother," said John Goldwin, "to anybody but me. Those who meet her are drawn to her and she holds them. Her energy is almost unbounded and I only fear it will carry her beyond her strength."

One day soon after Mr. Goldwin had left Holton for the East, Father Halliday came in from a meeting of the trustees of the academy with an unusually quick step, and an excited manner.

"What's the matter, dear?" said his wife. "What's happened? Any news?"

"Yes, news enough for one day. Miss Howard's sent in her resignation, trustees have accepted it, and she's going home; more than that, rumor says she's engaged to Mr. Goldwin and they are soon to be married."

"Indeed! Really!" said Mrs. Halliday, "now that is news to you, isn't it?"

"Sarah, do you mean to say that it isn't news to you?"

"No, dear, not exactly, but I can't say that its unexpected; and who could better it? What is it about the best laid schemes of mice and men?"

"Wife," said laughing Father Halliday, "that isn't in the Bible, but its true as preaching. Providence rather outwitted us this time."

"Yes, husband, Providence, or Mr. Goldwin or both."

"After all," said Father Halliday, "Mr. Goldwin is the one to be suited, and Miss Howard is a gem—no disputing that."

At the home of Miss Howard, Father Halliday pronounced the solemn words which sealed the union. The brothers and sisters and Miss Applebee and Mrs. Halliday and one or two old family friends were interested witnesses. But easily first among them all was Mother Howard, beautiful in that lovliness which only experience and divine faith can give. She thought of the dear husband now for many years among the shining ones, and wondered whether he was looking upon this scene. Forgive her if in this hour she was so lonely. She had given her approval and blessing to all Margaret had done; and yet, who dare remonstrate, if to give up what seemed her selectest daughter to go into the far West, so remote, and, as it was then, so difficult of access, seemed a sacrifice almost too costly. How the mother heart foresaw the frosts and tempests, and longed to shield the lovely flower.

Mrs. Halliday said, *sotto voce*, to the contented bridegroom, "I can't help saying that I admire your choice;" for which word he gave her a grateful and significant glance. At this a beautiful flush stole over the cheeks of the bride, which told that her quick ear had caught the word. As she lifted those tenderly bewitching eyelashes, Mrs. Halliday, as well as Mr. Goldwin, thought she never saw any more beautiful.

"That remark was not for your ears," said Mrs. Halliday.

"Ah, no secrets now that I do not share," archly replied the bride.

Miss Applebee bustled about dispensing the little cubes of sugar for the coffee, and little comfortable giggles in the conversation. Some preferred less condiment in the coffee, and many less confectionery in the conversation.

Brother Jo skipped about, tossing jokes at everyone;sad enough down in his heart,but determined no one should know it; skipped up behind the devoted pair as they were conferring and whispered, "New broom! New broom!"

"Always new, Jo," retorted Margaret, in her richest alto voice. How a little word will echo and reecho in after years.

The bridal tour to Riverton—a journey of nearly three weeks—let it pass with brief notice. Irksome and harassing as it certainly was, it abounded in the new found joy of great souls communing with and discovering each other. Let it pass,—a society where we will not intrude.

For many reasons that journey, once made, could never be forgotten. There was the trip by lake, by stage, by oxcart; and then several days of paddling down the Pocanock river in a dugout, or pirogue, the French name given to the craft among ears polite. The bride seated herself at one end, and the bridegroom, with his paddle, occupied the other end, while the worldly belongings were in the center. Within certain narrow limitations, the canoe could be trusted to maintain uprightness, but was swift to resent any flirtations with the water, or with the foliage and flowers which crept enticingly down the banks or along the islands. The autumnal gold was displacing the green of the forest which everhung the stream, and the sumac and sassafras gleamed here and there like torches. Add to this the river perfectly reflecting its sometimes pebbly, sometimes solid rock bottom, and now running smoothly and scarcely appearing to flow at all, now boiled and fretted against the rocks, now tumbling in rythmic roar over some fish dam, and you have that which seemed to Margaret the very soul of romance. Nor in her eyes did it detract from the romance, when she lay down in the pirogue, while her best man, standing in the water, lifted the canoe with its precious cargo over a dam. And then sometimes from the bottom of the canoe she would merrily call out, "Is the broom new, now John?" To which he would retort, "Aye, aye, Margaret, always new."

And now the end of the journey was almost in view. It was noon, and the evening shades would doubtless close around them in Riverton. The paddle was laid to rest for an hour, and spreading their blanket on the untrodden grass, they took their simple lunch. To Margaret, bounding on the crest of the billows of hope, all this was the poetry of life. To Mr. Goldwin, now that they were about stepping into the realities so familiar, there came a more serious and somber cast of thought.

Margaret, hiding under the bending boughs from the noontide sun, and watching the little gossamer dressed seeds floating in the air, found the tears moistening her eyes, as she recalled how she was floating away from all the dear faces she had always loved, but tears they were of loving trust, as she thought what perfect provision the Father had made to convey that little seed; what downy sails to bear the tiny seed ship, what filmy threads to cable it in its port; how wind, ill wind as we call it, and sky and light and air and soil conspire at God's bidding to convoy or harbor and encourage it. "Surely,' was her thought, "I too am sailing in his great sea, and he guides my little boat."

"Tears, idle tears," we read that there are; tears, too, there are which are the outlet of the heart, grief laden; and also tears of joy and faith and hope, which tell of life, and love too great for heart to tell. Earth has no spectoroscope subtle enough to analyse a tear.

Mr. Goldwin, as he approached Riverton, underwent a conflict of feelings. Duty and Hope seemed met and challenged by Fear and Doubt. He experienced the emotions said to come sometimes, even to bravest soldiers, in the moment just before the battle. He was cabled to Riverton by the triple strands of Faith, Hope and Love, and never for an instant did he think of slipping the cable. Still he was like a boat made fast to shore by a slack hawser; fast; securely so; but sensitive to the slightest motion of wind or wave; floating in and out, and now to this and now to that side. At one moment his eager heart carried him boldly to the landing; at another, reflecting, he drew back for a larger and more cautious survey; only again, however, to respond to the drawing of that triple strand which moored him to God and man. Those words of the Hebrew poet came singing on the lute strings of memory; "He led them forth by the right way."

Margaret, "niched" in the little canoe, and gathering her wraps about her, sat silent, reposing on the still evening, which as an infinite Beneficence, was enfolding this little world, as a mother folds her babe to sleep on her cheek. The moon's crescent horn hung low in the sky. Orion's girdle was beginning to gleam as of old, and the sister Pleiades to sparkle. Margaret could think just where they glowed above her dear home, and how she had traced them while she stood on the old threshold. Her heart asked, "Is mother looking into those "eyes of God" and thinking of me to-night?"

As, that moment, their canoe glided around a point and brought them in sight of the chimneys of Riverton, they came suddenly upon Christian Stubbs and Deborah Dale, gaily paddling across their course. Stubbs stopped short and looked, pushed back the brim of his hat for a second look, and shouted, "It is, It is Mr. Goldwin," and his swarthy face gleamed like the sunrise. Deborah was no less pleased, though less demonstrative, and perhaps more intent on the other person in the minister's boat. These young representatives of Riverton were just coming in from an hour's ride on the river; and, indeed, Stubbs felt as though the sun had that instant appeared out of a six week's eclipse. He insisted on his privilege of taking charge of the baggage, while Mr. and Mrs. Goldwin should proceed at once into the village.

As John took Margaret's hand and climbed the river bank, he whispered drolly, "Thus hand in hand, Adam and Eve took their solitary way out of Eden."

"No, John," retorted Margaret, "into Eden! Hand in hand into Paradise regained!"

CHAPTER XVIII.

A frontier town, and indeed any growing town, is a net which catches all manner of fish. We have often watched the fishermen, with what complacency they gathered in the bass and pickerel, and with what disdain they "chucked" the suckers and "small fry" back into the water; and we have sometimes wished for power to make like assortment from the human nets. But doubtless, we should make sorry work of it. Divine Wisdom has determined that this separation shall be made neither here nor now, nor by us.

Riverton was steadily receiving accession to its population, and among these, notably was Edward Mortimer. He was a son of an English Dean; had been to Eton and Oxford; had shown good abilities; had enjoyed every opportunity and incentive which wealth and devoted parents could furnish; had revolted from their design to have him take church orders; had developed a disposition to travel and wander over the earth; and had finally prevailed upon his father to grant him an annual allowance, and leave him to his own preferences. The father, driven to despair of his designs for the church in his son Edward and disgusted with his reckless, self-indulgent habits, at length, to satisfy conscience and end his own responsibility, provided this annuity, sometimes having faint hope that travel and experience might bring wisdom to the errant son.

Young Mortimer had roamed over the British Isles and on the continent, and conducted himself in such a way as made frequent changes not only desirable but necessary. Finally he found it essential to his convenience secretly to take passage for New York. Here he led a precarious life as a young and dashing sport; sometimes taking the current at the flood, sometimes floundering amid shallows, but always hopeful, and fertile in resources, and never troubled by any scruples of conscience.

On one of these occasions when he seemed to be coming in on a full tide, he had steered his bark into the sea of matrimony; wedded a lady of character and position in New York city; set forth on the connubial deep with banners flying; made a quick voyage, soon ran ashore and abandoning his pledged lifemate to the ship and the mercy of the pitiless elements, suddenly appeared in the role of a land speculator at Riverton. Son of an English dean, possessed, as it would seem, of money, traveled, informed, of polite manners, engaging and attractive bearing, and a ready adaptability to whatever social atmosphere he might enter, he was soon well known and had the entre of the society of Riverton. No lean and hungry look was his. Round, sleek and oily, he carried an air of Johnny Bull frankness, under which he was always in reality scheming and plotting for his own selfish ends.

Colonel Grande had run his course as hotel keeper, and, involved in pecuniary toils, had been obliged to abandon the hotel; suddenly found it too confining for his health, and opened, as he termed it, a select boarding house. Here Edward Mortimer had taken rooms. Little time did he allow to escape before he had acquainted the house with his rare antecedents. This house consisted of several boarders, the school teacher who was Mrs. Grande's maiden sister, and the daughter of Colonel and Mrs. Grande, just returned from a very superficial but very pretentious boarding school career at Indianapolis. This young lady, Kate Grande, was taught by her parents to think that she was quite too rare a flower to be suffered to expend her sweetness in the common walks of Riverton life; a lesson she learned more readily than others which had been assigned her.

Mortimer by tacit, but mutual consent, was the oracle, code of reference, and central luminary of this circle. With many a Munchausen tale of his exploits did he regale his eager and select audience, while he regaled himself luxuriously with Mrs. Grande's excellent coffee. The Colonel, who was by nature, an idolator, made haste to set up this new image and bow before this new shrine; and Mrs. Grande was captured by the courtly manners and elegant discourse of this scion of English nobility. And this not without reason. For, although Mr. Mortimer had not profited as he should by his rare opportunities and good natural gifts, he had not been blind nor unobservant, and had perforce absorbed much knowledge of society, and of all which "adorns and embellishes civilized life."

While wearing the appearance of entire freedom and engaging frankness in speaking of himself, no one was really more circumspect and reticent than he concerning the vital facts of his history. Sordid sensualist that he was, he was nevertheless like those insects which promptly assume the color of any object on which they alight, and when he was in highly reputable circles, he easily bore his share in their affabilities and amenities, and in his own view he found no difficulty in styling himself "a good, generous fellow." To be sure, as he must admit, there were for him some heavy scores on the debit side; but by his own ingenious method of moral book-keeping, he was able to balance his acounts to his entire satisfaction. Sometimes, after being discovered in some heinous defalcation, sheriff conscience would succeed in arresting him, and then forthwith he was exceedingly penitent and said penitence, he never failed to reckon as a very large return in his credit column;—sufficient amply to liquidate whatever had accrued against him. A man of fortune, wide travel, and, as Mrs. Grande phrased it, "very highly connected," it is not strange that Edward Mortimer was regarded as a rare acquisition to the society of Riverton. Nor is it strange that Mrs. Grande immediately had thoughts of her daughter, Miss Kate, a gorgeous plant just out of the boarding school hot house. But this, our Caesar, was very choice upon what meats he fed. Miss Kate danced between this man, who she hoped, was to be her lover, and her looking glass. Poor little moth! Fluttering too near the flame.

Mr. Mortimer rather plumed himself upon being able to say that he was a faithful attendant upon "divine service," and he lost no time in forming the acquaintance of Mr. Goldwin, and in congratulating him upon his return to his parish, adding that, although he had never before had the pleasure of meeting him, he had heard in Riverton so many flattering references to him, that he almost felt as though he had known him. He remarked also that personally he was rejoiced in Mr. Goldwin's return to his pulpit, for, though he was by no means as good as he hoped to be, he made it a rule, he said, to attend church, and he had felt very much lost for the last month, with Mr. Goldwin's church closed; for, he added, although brought up after the strictest sect of the church of England, he was free to confess himself thoroughly enamored with the severe simplicity of the non-ritualistic faith and mode of worship.

Seated in church at Riverton, if we come to the exact facts, Mortimer deftly cast incendiary glances at the ladies, and fastened his mind far more upon Miss Drake, Miss Isabel, Sibyl, and Mrs. Dale's daughters, and the pastor's lovely bride, than he did upon Mr. Goldwin; although he seldom retired from the service without complimenting the pastor upon his excellent sermon. He affirmed that he had listened to the famous pulpit orators of England and America, but that none met his case as well as did Mr. Goldwin. The latter received such statements as friendly exaggerations, and yet there was more than one grain of truth in them, for Mr. Goldwin's preaching "found" his hearers. Nor is it necessary to suppose Mortimer wholly insincere, or merely diplomatic in complimenting his pastor, as he called Mr. Goldwin. He, selfish Englishman though he was, responded readily to his surroundings, and he verily sometimes envied the good their peace and quiet joy; sometimes winced under the stings of plain truth; sometimes, too, felt the touch of his blessed mother. Even the darkest fabric, when it fronts the sun, throws off some light; and no stream, however direct its general course, but that sometimes doubles on itself. Mr. Goldwin was not insensible to the attractive qualities of his new hearer, and not without earnest desire and hope of happily reversing the disposition of his life.

CHAPTER XIX.

To one brought up amid the inflexible forms and moss grown precedents of English nobility, the change to the new and unconventional society of Riverton was very discernible. It was like suddenly giving to one long confronted on every side with prohibition and anathema, the freedom of the universe. Nor to one of Mortimer's adventurous disposition was this informality and luxuriant personality at all disagreeable. For a time, at least, the novelty and *abandon* of these settlements quite occupied and satisfied him. He was a good natured saunterer, ready to follow any path, bound upon pleasure, and careless how or whither.

Strolling one evening in a "wood lot" close at hand, he came upon a half score of cows browsing liesurely toward their milking stalls. They paused and fixed an inquiring eye on the intruding stranger. He, too, paused to admire the sleek, well-to-do creatures, with their distended udders, and he said, "English cattle can't beat this." Hark! In the distance a clear falsetto, "Come Mooly. Come Mooly." The bell cow, Mooly, listened with a philosophic calm for a moment, and then her bell began to ding as she concluded to "move on." The little drove separated and Crumple Horn, White Face, and Pink Eye demurely followed Mooly. Dance, Jonas Drake's beautiful hiefer, that stood eyeing the infrequent visitor until all her associates had passed on, at the swing of the alien's cane, swung up her tail and her heels and cantered away. A few rods in advance was a fence and in it a set of bars which had been let down. Following a well worn path, the cows, led by Mooly, filed through this gap into the pasture lot, on the opposite side of which now broke upon the view the back yard, sheds, and barns of the Drake place.

Now it was plain who had called Mooly, for there in a short dress and an all-enveloping apron, and with milk pail on her arm, and milk stool in her hand, stood Rachel Drake. Jonas, minus coat and waistcoat, and barefooted, bareheaded Waxie, were coming to join her; the latter hopping and skipping and tra-la-la-ing at the top of her voice.

Mortimer had met Miss Drake once or twice, and now observed in her the same charm of form and graceful poise which his quick eye had noted the first time he saw her. He was eager to pursue his acquaintance, and now that good fortune had let down the bars, he was not the one to decline to enter. So he approached and with his politest bow, said,

"Good evening, Miss Drake."

"Good evening," rejoined Rachel, with a

faint flush playing over her cheek. So it is you, Mr. Mortimer, that we have to thank for the cows coming home so promptly."

"Now I vow," said he, "this is jolly; strolling by an unknown path, and following the cows, to come out so unexpected at your gate!"

Then he fell to discussing with Jonas the fine points in the stock, and the latter was surprised to find the English gentleman so excellent a judge of cattle.

"You'll excuse us a few moments, Mr. Mortimer," said Rachel. "Business is business, as father says."

"Certainly, certainly," he exclamed, gra- graciously bowing, "I am the one to be excused."

With that Rachel made Mooly "hist," and seated on her stool, forthwith the lacteal streams began to go pit pat, and play in snowy cascades and whirlpools in her bright tin pail. Waxie, meanwhile, swished her sassafras bush about the flanks and legs of the cows and kept the flies on the wing.

Now Crumple Horn looked meek as a saint, but woe to him who counted on her saintship. She was known to let fly with her hinder legs at most unexpected times and places, and had even been known to "push with her horns." On the other hand Pink Eye and White Face practiced faithfully the doctrine of non-resinstance. So Jonas always began with Crumple Horn, on the principle that it is wise to storm the stronghold first. He threw a rope over her horns and tied it to a post. Then while milking her he held his head firmly against her side in the place where the germ of the kick evolved, and crushed it in the germ. The same tact with which Jonas adroitly managed Crumple Horn, served him well in later years in managing men.

Just then the gate clicked. Mr. Drake was coming, and every cow looked up with the hope, this time illusive, of a lick of salt, or a bite of pumpkin or a nubbin of corn.

"So-o there," cried Rachel, as Mooly, absorbed in great expectations, was about to step. Creatures of one idea are apt to upset the dish.

But now Mooly is "stripped dry," and Rachel's pail is full and foaming over, and Mr. Mortimer, taking it, acompanies her to the milk house. Reader did you ever visit that milk house?—a very modest structure down amid the grasses and cowslips and buttercups, and just below the ever flowing spring; the clearest, coldest water. Years have sown their moss and licken thickly over many of the writer's fondest memories, but he still sees that spring, and sees and hears the little gurgling stream it formed, which trickled in a little artificial channel across the stone floor of the milk house. What words can fitly express the creature comfort with which many's the time he has surveyed those rolls of yellow butter, Mrs. Drake's phenomenal butter; those rows of bright milk pans, those jars of richest golden cream. Unadulterated extracts and essences of green fields, pearly dew and laughing sunshine, friends of our better days, whither have ye fled, and given place to the mocking, gibbering shades of butterine, oleomargarine and "doctored" milk?

No marvel that Mortimer looked on with wonder and talked of the idylic, while Rachel strained her pailful and talked of the practical. No marvel that Mortimer a few moments later, drew up with the family to the evening meal—butter, honey, milk and wheaten loaves of snowy white—with a zest which no guest at a king's table ever knew. No marvel that as Rachel appeared at the table in a modest blue gown which suited so well her fair complexion, and bore herself with such accustomed ease and propriety, he was more than ever impressed with her interesting and thoughtful face. No marvel that as the master of the house spun yarns of his early woodsman life, and of the "dark and bloody days" of Kentucky and Daniel Boone, this chance guest had a tale from his travels and adventures to match every one of them.

Jonas had brought to light from some neighbor's shelf a book of travels in the Old World, and he was ready now and then with his eager questions, and all listened intently, both entertained and instructed by these descriptions from an eye witness.

As Mortimer walked back to his room that night, he felt the spell of that simple, pure and affectionate home. He could but do homage to it; could but recall what might have been with himself; and became restive under self-reproach. What right had he to set foot on such hallowed ground? He! a ruthless despoiler of home! But he brushed aside these thoughts and said to himself, "That Miss Drake—what native grace and dignity—what unaffected beauty! By Jove, her attractions would do honor to the court of St. James!"

A few evenings later, and as Stubbs was passing O'Flannigan's country store, where whiskey was the prominent export and import, his attention was arrested by loud, hilarious voices. It was late, and the doors and shutters were closed, but the voices within seemed familiar. "Hark," said he, "is it them?" He could distinguish the clink of glasses, and boisterous guffaws, mingled with oaths, as one or another of them threw down a lucky card, or drew a blank. "A drinking, gambling crew," thought Stubbs. Just then came words of coarse banter. "Can it be?" he exclaimed. "Yes, that's Grande and Hawkins and O'Flannigan and Mortimer! Ho! ho! so that's the kind of man this genteel blue blood, Mortimer is! Riverton little suspects him of such things." Hark!

Mortimer breaks out in song the frequent refrain of which as Stubbs catches it is,

"Then drink boys, drink,
And we won't go home till morning."

Now it came to pass in these days that the autumn house cleaning and renovating in anticipation of the long winter was in process at the Dale home. One period in this process was the washing of the blankets, quilts and coverlets, and the sunrise found Deborah and Stubbs, or as they called each other, Deb. and Chris.," who was generally at hand when he could lend a hand to "his Deb.," carrying swung between them on a pole, a large iron kettle down to the river bank just back of the Dale house. It was one of those superb mornings which make it a joy to exist. Deb. was in a short coarse frock which seemed to struggle to grasp the redundant form, and which left her bare feet and ankles disencumbered. She was a magnificent illustration of a certain kind of beauty,—that of youth, health, physical perfection and superabounding vitality. Her mother was captain, but Deb. was second in command of the Dale forces, and an able second, too. If you had seen her, her firm, assured tread, the independent toss of her head, the ease and eagerness with which she marched off with her end of the pole on which hung the kettle, you as well as Chris, would have accredited her, now at least, with meriting to be called "the better half." Assuming a very innocent and far off look, Deb suddenly raised the pole and sent the kettle tilting and sliding over to Chris,—a joke which he could return in the same kind.

With many a banter and jest, they built a roaring fire under the suspended kettle, and filled the latter with water, Deb. roguishly spattering her lover; which, however, did not dampen the flame of his love. They sat down on a log for a few blissful moments, and watched the fire as it climbed the sides of the kettle. Then Chris., springing to his feet, exclaimed, "Farewell Deb., I must be off," and ran up the bank, bound for Gen. Tupper's, where he said he had a little jog of work; when suddenly he caught sight of Mortimer lolling under a tree near by. "Well, well," thought Stubbs, with a shrug of the shoulders, "what brings our London exquisite around so early?" At the same time his face darkened and his hands closed, and can you wonder that he had a feeling akin to that of Ithuriel when he discovered Satan squat like a toad at the ear of Eve? What new passion was this which leaped within Stubbs like a lion from his lair, and so at variance with that which lighted up his face but a moment before. He shook himself and tried to laugh, but he did wish he had not that engagement at Gen, Tupper's, and the instinctive ill judgment which he had formed of Mortimer the first time he saw him, it must be admitted, had not been removed by subsequent knowledge of him. So in no very amiable frame of mind he hurried to his morning task.

Meanwhile, Mortimer from his covert was admiring those plump, round arms as they punched the blankets down into the hot water with clothes stick, and was completely captured by those stout pink and white ankles. He was gloating over the attractions of this water nymph and yearning to come into close fellowship with her.

Then Deb., who, quite unconscious of observers, had been singing some household song, called to her sister to run to the house for more soap, charging her to hurry back, so as to help lift the kettle off.

But her sister was not one of those who often hurry, and the water was boiling over and hissing and sizzing in the fire and scattering ashes and smoke. Mortimer at once perceived and seized his opportunity. Sauntering along as though his approach was the merest accident, he offered his assistance, at the same time laying hold of the pole on which the iron boiler was sunspended. The pole was much warmer than was agreeable to the hands of this sprig of the nobility, but gallant knight never clung to his good sword more faithfully, and with the help of Deb's muscular lifting, the sputtering iron kettle was safely landed on terra firma.

Now it would not be just to Deborah Dale to say that she had no vanity, or to say that she did not feel flattered and just a little elated to find herself the object of deference and politest attention from this gentleman par excellence, in perfect attire, rings set with gems on his fingers, and a gold chain flashing from his velvet waistcoat; and, although she was coy, and replied to him for the most part in monosyllables, it was manifest enough that she was pleased to have him talk to her.

Here Stubbs returned, and as he beheld Mortimer seated on the log, quite at his ease, and evidently entertaining Deb., her face, lu spite of herself, suffused with gratification, they both saw fire in Stubb's eyes, and blackness on his brow,—lightning stored beneath a midnight cloud. Nor did the coquettish vein which seems to belong to the circulatory system of woman, fail to come to the surface, and Deborah was in the mood to sport with that cloud, rather than to beam it away.

Soon Mortimer, bowing graciously to the blushing nymph, and avowing his sincere hope that he might be allowed to pursue an acquaintance begun under such novel and charming circumstances, took his departure, bestowing no notice upon Stubbs.

How sensitive is love. Thermometer of the soul, and prompt indicator of every slightest variation of its temperature. The mercury had suddenly encountered a chilling wave. It was only temporary, and, like the rose scent of Mortimer's handsome black hair, would soon pass by.

"Deb." said Stubbs, "if I ever see that fellow near you again, I will kick him."

"What! jealous are you, Chris?" said Deb. most tormentingly, at the same time patting his cheek with her wet, slippery hand.

"I say it again, Deb., if I ever see that black leg near you again, I'll kick him."

Several days passed before Deb. and Chris. met again. Deb had cleared the tea things away, and seated outside the porch, was paring apples. Her mind had traveled more than once over her sudden and romantic interview with Mortimer, and she had come out of the spell which his presence had thrown about her. She had her weaknesses; like Mother Eve, was susceptible to flattery. Nevertheless, she had a prevailing modicum of good sense, and while she could see no justification of Stubb's obvious aversion to Mortimer, she admitted to herself that she had taken a little unjustifiable pleasure in feeding Stubb's fear of a successful rival. She said, "The idea that this blue-blood Londoner really cares anything for me!" The more she thought of it, the more preposterous it seemed; and as the gate turned on its hinges and she saw the manly form of her honest lover, she gave him such a frank, love-lighted face, as at once told him her heart, and left no space for shadows or cloud.

"Sit down, Chris, I was wishing I could see you. Don't you think I am a little naughty?"

Stubbs laughed, and said, "I expect you thought I was kind of touchy like."

"No—yes—well perhaps both of us were foolish. At any rate I guess I was," said Deb. But now, Chris, pray tell, why are you so dead against Mr. Mortimer; for it is plain to be seen that you don't like him."

"Well," replied Stubbs, "I don't know as I can tell exactly. The very first time I set eyes on this man, I suspicioned him; same as the first time I saw Mr. Goldwin, I said, "There's a good man." Chris relied much on his intuitive judgment of men.

"And is that all?" asked Deb. "You don't like him, because you don't like him?"

Then Stubbs told her that he had the best of reasons for not liking the man, and that some day he would tell her all about it. "And then knowing the fellow as I do," said he, "when I started on that morning for Gen. Tupper's, and saw him sitting behind the bushes under the beech tree, and watching you, I could think only of a rattle snake."

"Watching me! Why, as much as two hours after you left, he came along, whistling and swinging his cane, and said that he had that minute left his writing desk for a little recreation, and accidentally, or as he should say, providentially came upon me, just when, as he said, he could have the extreme pleasure of assisting me; said he had seen me at church so often that he could not look upon me quite as a stranger; always attended church himself, and had a great partiality for church-goers; had often admired me and hoped he might become acquainted with me, but had never dreamed of such a novel and truly romantic introduction as this morning had afforded him; some of the happiest friendships of his life had grown, he said, out of just such unexpected meetings; the straightforward, unceremonious, informal ways of the West, he added, charmed him, just suited him. All this stuff and a great deal more, and in such big words that I didn't half understand what he meant anyhow, seemed just to tumble out of him like water out of a jug."

"He's a puppy! that's what he is," said Chris. "Deb, some of these big red apples you're paring are wormy at the core; still, them that's used to it can mostly tell a good apple at seeing it."

CHAPTER XX.

As the autumn blasts were wantonly disrobing the wood, and prophesying of winter, Mr. Goldwin hastened to lead his wife into their new home. Nothing bleak or wintry there! It was a house on "the hill," alone, half cocealed in the freshly invaded forest.

With what glee Margaret traversed those four little rooms. How she enjoyed the odor of fresh wood work, and curling a shaving, she said, "Home, John, our home!" Wedged between great stumps and piles of underbrush, with hugh trees swaying, menacing boughs above it; with no fences, and distant a good quarter of a mile from Kelly's spring, the nearest supply of water—it was a home sufficiently rural, and lavish in opportunity for communing with nature in her changeful moods. Its roof was lowly, but its rooms were peopled with high thoughts, and its skies dipped into a glorious future. Its walls were plain, unadorned, but no day so dark that the sunbeams did not dance on them.

Mr. Goldwin had been advised to purchase a plot consisting of several town lots. Such could be bought then for a very moderate sum, and could not fail to yield large returns as an investment. But he was ever firmly resolved that, amid so much speculating and land-grabbing, it should be self-evident as the sunshine that he had come to Riverton wholly absorbed in higher intent.

For weeks it had been for the minister and his bride a continual round of visiting and tea drinking at the hospitable homes of Riverton, and this semi-dissipation prepared them the more keenly to enjoy the retirement of their own home. Home! That colors the rudest structure in hues immortal.

Mr. Goldwin, since bringing Mrs. Goldwin to Riverton, had taken, if possible, even higher place than before in the hearts of the people. Mothers and maidens were unanimous in admiration of his selection. Dear matronly Mrs. Tupper said to the General that "she felt drawn to Mrs. Goldwin almost as to her own daughter," and Mrs. Barnett declared that "to look in her face was enough to make anyone good." Her warm sympathies and her personal interest in humanity brought her close to all in their every day wants, and at the same time, there was ever that about her which suggested the higher. At the sick bed she was most welcome, and seemed on those occasions inspired to the fittest word and deed. Happy lives are those which make heaven seem real and not far away.

Mr. Goldwin noticed that while his wife spoke of Mr. Pierpont, admiring his intelligence, modesty and manliness; or of Dr. Bancroft, laughing at his brusque and humorous ways, and gratified with his clear cut opinions; she almost never mentioned Mr. Mortimer. This reticence concerning him was the more to be observed, since only a few days before, at Mrs. Martyn's, Mortimer had sat by Margaret at dinner, and had bestowed his attentions quite studiously upon her. The truth was that she, with a woman's quick intuitions, had taken an inventory of the man, and had set him down as having large liabilities and almost no assets. When the guests of Mrs. Martyn were about dispersing, Mrs. Grande detained Mr. and Mrs. Goldwin at the door to enlarge in very copious measure upon the wonderful Mr. Mortimer, and begged them to call often, very often, while he was at her house. But to this Mrs. Goldwin offered but scant response, which was not the kind of response Mrs. Grande had expected. The fact was that Mrs. Goldwin thought Mr. Mortimer with all his easy manners and air of elegance, was scheming and insincere. He had been careful to speak flatteringly to her of her husband, but he had also ventured cynicism or haughty sneer concerning the people of Riverton, and then he immediately discovered from Mrs. Goldwin's reserve that his tactics were at fault.

"Quite at home in ancient classics; profuse in Latin fragments," said Mr. Goldwin by way of eliciting an opinion from Margaret.

"Rightly you call them fragments," she replied, "for it seems to me that he quotes from the dead languages, not like a thorough scholar who almost thinks in them, but like one who has passed through the banquet hall of the Greeks and Latins and brought away a few scraps."

Mr. Goldwin smiled but made no reply and fell to reflecting on the acuteness of his wife's intuitions of character.

Meanwhile the parish of Mr. Goldwin was growing both in area and in density of population. He became every year more widely known, and was often called to solemnize a marriage, or to conduct the last sad rites of the dead, at points many miles distant, and difficult of access. Riverton was enlarging and his congregations were increasing. Almost every Sabbath brought new faces before him. The school room which the builders had supposed to be of ample dimensions for several more years, was insufficient to accommodate the audiences. The pastor returning from his eastern trip, seemed, if possible, to return to his pulpit with a joy and zest surpassing his former ministry, and the large Sunday school and the Bible class with the pastor's wife for teacher, were enlisting the children, and the young people. Parents, heretofore little accustomed to it, were now beginning to drop in on the Sabbath services, verifying the old word, " A little child shall lead them."

Moreover, as the days passed, it became

more and more evident that something new had come to Riverton. It was in the pulpit and in the audience, and in the Sunday school, and in many of the homes. No new gospel; no new messenger; no new agency or invention; but a new solemnity and attentiveness. Something was there; was in the very air; not noise, not simply excitement, not sensation. What more rational explanation than that the Spirit of God was there? "The Spirit of God moved upon the face of the waters." Till something better is given, we do well to accept this explanation.

Recently Mr. Goldwin had preceded the Sabbath evening service with a short meeting for prayer and religious conversation. The attendance on this informal meeting had increased until now it embraced nearly the whole of the customary Sabbath congregation. They who came to the meeting seemed to have one subject on their hearts and tongues. Voices were heard of men and women and youth; simple, plain, sometimes tearful, sometimes very broken words; nothing new in them, and yet there did seem in them a new meaning, and there was in them a new thrill. Chords long silent were touched and quivered.

It is Sunday evening. They are going to the school house. Let us go there. It is early twilight; scarcely time for the preliminary meeting. But hark! They have begun to sing. Seats are filling rapidly. My eyes!

There's Hawkins in the corner by the door. And in the next seat are Tim the blacksmith and Perkins. Yonder on the right, over against the wall is a sitting which commands the whole view. Since we are here to observe, we will walk up and take it.

The dear old hymns they are singing—how they bring up old scenes, and how they soften our hearts. Isabel and Sibyl and Mrs. Goldwin, in clear sweet voice guide the melody. That rich baritone a few seats back of them is from Mortimer. But it seems as though all were singing; even Chris and Jonas are attempting it, and likewise almost toothless Mrs. Smile with her quavering tones.

Now a few verses of Scripture, a few words from the pastor which lie close to his heart, and his prayer, short and simple and straight to God. Then someone is singing—a pure little rill, soon joined by others, till there's a general wave of song.

With the first opportunity, Mrs. Smile is on her feet with a word. Poor soul! She's a pessimist and doesn't know it. We wish she could learn a new strain and not so often whine and berate the church. Light weight; but she means well; and her one talent she never buries. On the whole, Mr. Goldwin may well congratulate himself that he is so exempt from hobbyists and prayer meeting killers.

Mr. Barnett rises. Everyone listens to him. He has the Sunday school on his heart.

A few words, and then he kneels in a tender plea to the Saviour for the young.

Mr. Pierpont is on the other side of the room, nearly opposite to us. We think we see an unwonted gleam in his large blue eye. There! his tall form is rising. He is struggling with deep emotions, which the audience percieve and share; but he controls his voice and says: "This morning Mr. Goldwin selected the words, 'Whatsoever he saith unto you do it.' The sermon followed but I could get no farther than those words. They smote me. I have been entrenching myself in mysteries and perplexities. I have stumbled at regeneration, or what is called the new birth. I have been lingering, wondering whether sometime the Almighty would seize me, as one siezes a garment, and by a single motion turn me inside out. When that is done, then, thought I, I shall be converted.

To me thus halting, questioning, perplexed, and excusing myself with my perplexities, Mr. Goldwin came this morning with those words, "Whatsoever he saith unto you do it.' God sent him to me with that message. I could not forget it. I could not pass beyond it. It pursued me to my room. I felt that the Lord was speaking to me. I was in agony. I cried out, 'Lord, I will, I will, whatsoever thou sayest I will do.' Then there came to me such a view of the love of Christ; oh, such as I never had, never even begun to have, before; such a view of his long, long patience with me, and of my blindness and of my wrong to him. I said, 'Why didn't I see this before? How strange that I didn't! Will he forgive—can he forgive me? Nevertheless, I said, I will do what he saith. I will strive to obey him. I prayed. I read my Bible. My agony left me. I felt as though I loved everybody. I had a strange but inexpressible peace."

"So, in obedience to this morning's text, I have ventured these words tonight. Oh, I need help. I am very weak. Won't you help me?" Then Mr. Pierpont alludes to his dear mother who for so many years has prayed for him; but his voice chokes and he sits down.

For a moment there is complete silence. It is the hush before a wind from heaven.

Then Mrs. Drake whose heart is always open heavenward and who appears always to have it given her just what to do, says, "Let us pray," and it seems as though every one does pray.

Hardly has the prayer closed, when a young girl arises and sobs out, "I want to be a Christian. Pray for me." Do you know that she is the daughter of O'Flannigan the whisky seller, and is from Mrs. Goldwin's class in Sunday school?

Hark! as if in direct reply to the girl's request, Mrs. Goldwin strikes up,

"Jesus, thou art the sinner's friend,
  As such I look to thee,
Now in the fullness of thy love,
  I pray remember me."

It is the plaintive trustful strains of the tune Naomi, and only three voices, Isabel, Sybil and Mrs. Goldwin. The words come to our souls like a fountain in the burning desert. In the second verse something gathers in Sibyl's throat, and she buries her face in her handkerchief. Her brother George— how he bites his lips and looks at the window and struggles against the tears in his eyes.

Mr. Goldwin did not preach that night.

This informal meeting ran on of its own will.. No, that does not adequately state the fact. A will higher than man led that meeting. The next night found the people again in the school house, and so every night except Saturday through the week. There was no noise, no animal excitement, only plain tender appeals to reason and conscience. It seems as though but one subject was on the mind of Riverton, and as though but one book, the Bible, was read. Everyone seemed to expect to converse on the one subject. The pastor went everywhere, inviting, urging, dropping a kind word here, a timely suggestion or encouragement there;

with all ingenuity and tact of love pressing each to immediate obedience to their divine Elder Brother. This personal pleading, together with conducting the meetings every night, as Mrs. Goldwin said, scarcely allowed him time to eat or sleep; then in her sweet soft voice she added, 'The Lord feedeth him.' His life was one all consuming passion for those around him, and he and his dear people were knit together like David and Jonathan. Prayer was offered in many homes where it had never been heard before. Jonas, Sibyl, Deborah Dale and a number of others who stood just outside came within the open door. Their happy faces and new joy naturally affected others deeply. Mortimer was restless and especially moved by whatever Sibyl said or did. He sometimes appeared to be seriously impressed, but kept himself fortified with doubts and skeptical difficulties. He was fond of walking home with Mr. Goldwin after church, and asking the how and the wherefore of those secret things which belong to God. Mr. Goldwin gave to him precious time and strength until Mrs. Goldwin's patience was entirely exhausted, and setting down her little decided foot, told Mr. Mortimer that if he heeded his plain undeniable duty half as diligently as he did his doubts and skepticism, he would be a model of goodness.

Mr. and Mrs. Perkins also debated very seriously with "I ought." How affectionately Mr. Goldwin prayed with them and besought them not to procrastinate. But they were bent on amassing a fortune and were doing it. Lucky man, as the world called him; he never even tossed up a penny with an Indian but that he won. He became one of the large land owners of Indiana, but to the great grief of Mr. Goldwin, neither he nor Mrs. Perkins could be prevailed upon to seek what is better than gold. To their dying day, they never again came so near to the Kingdom of Life.

At O'Flannigan's home Mr. Goldwin was received very coldly; hardly receivd at all. The mother and the daughter said nothing, and the latter wept freely, while the father abused and vilified everything, and said there should be no pious talk or praying in his house. The truth was, the people were going to the meetings and the whisky store was lonely. O'Flannigan cordially hated Mr. Goldwin for his well known temperance preaching and persuading. The daughter came no more to the meetings. O'Flannigan declared that if she went he would horsewhip her.

Merchant Martyn also felt the power which was manifested in those meetings, and his dear little wife longed to have him yield to it. He said religion was good enough for women and children, but, as for him, he had no time for it. He had pretty much his own way, until at last when he was sixty years old, he lost his health and lost his property. It took this to bring him to himself. So, a few years before he died he really began to live.

Phil. Arnold, a loose careless fellow, who applied his wits chiefly to dodging his creditors and the law, was no sooner under the control of these better influences, than he went around paying his debts. Even Hawkins confessed that there was something in that kind of religion, and Tim the blacksmith said he hoped the meeting would never stop.

Col. Grande, always a reflection of the prevailing mood of Riverton, now attended the meetings constantly. He occasionally had a word to say, and finally on a Sunday evening —the house crowded and many standing in and about the doorway, he brought out his red handkerchief with more than usual flourish, and then narrated what he called his experience. The night previous, as it would seem, he had not only seen stars but dreamed dreams, in which clouds and rainbows and birds and flowers and rivers and darkness and demons, and angels and choirs were strewn together in grotesque confusion, and there came a voice to his naturally bewildered soul, whispering "peace, peace," and now he was happy, and firmly resolved that for the future his should be a religious life. This experience given by Col. Grande was all news to Mrs. Grande, as well as to the rest of the audience. She did hope it was true.

There was need enough of better living. She ought to be a better woman, and then she could strengthen her husband. Such were her thoughts and resolves.

Poor Col. Grande! In a few months every vestige of his religion had fled, and, like his stars and dreams, left no trace behind. Perhaps, after all, he was not so insincere as he was shallow.

And there was Albert Slade, an odd genius everybody said, a wood chopper, bachelor, lived by himself in a lone cabin. He was a misanthrope, or in common parlance, was soured on everybody. Sunday was to him like other days, except that he chopped a little longer, or discharged his hunting piece oftener, and swore harder, on that than on other days.

One day last spring Mr. Goldwin rambled out to Slade's premises and chatted with him about everything under the sun except religion,—a thing which rather pleased and yet puzzled Slade, if not by a few shades disappointed him, for he was loaded, cocked and primed for the parson on religion. Something moved this recluse to drop into the meetings. He swore about them; said he wouldn't go again; declared them to be half fanaticism and half hypocrisy; but when night came, he found himself at the meetings. He slipped in and out alone, and no one conversed with him. Mr. Barnett, apparently by accident, although in truth of very serious intent, came upon him chopping wood one day and talked with him,—wisely refrained from controversy or argument, but kneeled down and prayed with him. Not everyone could have done this with Slade and not been insulted.

He had been, when a boy, under that kind of instruction which, in effect, robbed man of spiritual responsibility, and left him bound hand and foot in the forordination and decrees of God. His whole nature revolted from such teaching, and yet he had been trained and wound up in it, and was full of hostility to a God and a Bible which he supposed must inculcate it; and here, hundreds of miles from his kindred, in the woods with his axe, gun, and little cabin, he had flattered himself that he had gotten clear of all bother about religion; and now to his great vexation, religion had once more hunted him out. Sometimes he said, "I'll take my axe and gun and dog and strike out for the Mississippi or the Rocky Mountains." Sometimes he said, "What am I running away from? Might as well have it out where I am." Thus he debated and wrestled with himself, till at last he could scarcely eat or sleep. Sometimes in the overflowing congregation he could hardly refrain from springing to his feet and crying Lost! Lost! Lost!

One night Mr. Goldwin read to the audience from the Psalm 137. When he came to the seventh verse, he paused, fixed his eyes upon the people, or, as Slade thought, upon him, and, his voice tremulous with emotion, quoted, "Whither shall I go from thy Spirit?" Instantly Slade leaped to his feet and cried, "That's my question. I've been trying to run away from the Spirit of God. I give it up. I can't do it. Oh, pray for me. I'm lost;" and sunk down exhausted and trembling with agony.

The next morning, as Tim was blowing his forge, Hawkins dropped in and at once began "Well, Tim, I've heard a piece of news this morning that beats me. Wife says the revival meetings have caught 'Bert Slade.'"

"What! You don't mean it? You're joking," exclaimed Tim as he suddenly stopped plying his bellows.

"No fooling. Guess its all so," said Hawkins.

"Well, well, I vow! Who'd a believed it? Why, they'll get you and me next!" replied Tim.

"When they get me," replied Hawkins, "there'll be a mighty scuffling around, for then the devil 'll be dead."

"John Barnes, they say, has been sober a week," said Socrates Dale to his wife, as they sat down to breakfast. "Begins to look more like a man."

"Thank the Lord for that," exclaimed Mrs. Dale fervently. She, in common with other women of the church, had taken a deep interest in the Barnes family, and extended kind motherly wings over the poor motherless children. Death had brought blessed relief to Mrs. Barnes, and the wee babe, which slept in the mother's arms in the same grave. The kind women had supposed it would be necessary to separate the children and provide homes for them wherever they could. But little womanly Laura begged so hard to be allowed to keep her little brother and sisters around her, and cried so at the mention of separating them, that Mrs. Goldwin, Mrs. Dale, Isabel, Rachel and the rest held a council and decided to gratify Laura, and preserve the home, for a time at least; and meanwhile they agreed to exercise a good Samaritan protctorate over it. Laura and the little ones still clung to their Papa, in spite of his drunkenness; and there was a forlorn hope that their appealing faces might awaken the man in him.

Dr. Bancroft had kept Barnes about his office for several days, under pretense of his doing little jobs and errands for him. And so now, notwithstanding O'Flannigan & Co., he had really been sober a week. At first he shrank from all meetings, ashamed, both of himself and his shabby clothes; but by some female strategy, ere long he appeared in better clothes, and Mr. Barnett brought him into the meetings, and through the crowded aisle, up to a front seat.

One Sunday morning, among those who enlisted under the banner of the Saviour was

John Barnes and Little Laura, and more than one pair of eyes wept for joy over this signal victory. For if there was anybody who had been considered by all Riverton to be beyond rescue, it was John Barnes.

In truth, it must be admitted that once, a month or more later, John fell. One morning he found a bottle of rum out by the wood pile. Who put it there no one knew. Yes, everyone thought that O'Flannigan, and, perhaps, his comrades knew. Mr. Goldwin and others immediately sought John out and hardly left him for several days. But this was the last lapse. John bitterly repented and never drank again.

Dr. Bancroft had attended every meeting, so far as his professional calls allowed but only as a silent spectator; and what seemed so contrary to his habit, conversed as little as possible about what was then the theme of Riverton. He had been in his youthful days enfolded within the church, and he had never forgotten nor forsaken his early committal. Yet he had passed through trying scenes, and had been involved to some extent in moral bewilderment and innertness. However, though he was silent, he was musing and the fire was burning.

One night Mrs. Goldwin and others had sung very tenderly:

> "But floods of tears can ne'er repay
>   The debt of love I owe;
> Here, Lord, I give myself away,
>   'Tis all that I can do."

Hardly had the sound of these words died away, when the expansive form of Dr. Bancroft was seen rising. There was silence which continued and grew until it was almost audible and painful, as the Doctor deliberately, slowly, passed his eyes over the hushed and expectant audience, struggled for what seemed many moments with a torrent of emotion, and trembling under it like an oak in the tempest, at length sat down without uttering a word. The thoughtful stillness which followed this mute address was as the voice of the Lord. After that, the Doctor for the rest of his days found ready and earnest voice, and to the delight of his auditors, for he was prone to have something to say, and he had a character behind his words which emphasized them.

Mrs. Goldwin counted it her crowning joy that it was given to her to see all her Bible class entered on the Christian way; and many pupils of the Sunday School made at this time the blessed turning point of their lives.

Mr. Goldwin's work was four square; reconstructed those of every age, rank and condition. Work brought the pastor work; success augmented responsibility and solicitude, but also endowed him with new and higher strength and joy. Everyone, even the haters of Christianity, in their inmost soul confessed that this religious movement, so memorable in the history of Riverton, was inspired and led by a power above man. As Mrs. Goldwin and Mrs. Drake affirmed, "It is the Lord's doing, and it is marvellous in our eyes."

This spiritual awakening illuminated the fact that Christianity is practical; that it is the Spirit and teachings of Christ vitalizng the whole man and the whole living, every social relation and obligation, even as the blood vitalizes every particle of the body. This moral eye-opener evinced that when religion is Biblical it is all-inclusive, covers the field of human action; carries onward temperance, honesty, purity, industry, universal right doing, as the sun carries not only light, but verdure and harvest.

CHAPTER XXI.

Two years have elapsed between this and the last chapter. On a partly opened, ungraded street, which respectfully turns out for giant trees and stumps, but which ambitious, expectant Riverton calls Broadway, stands a neat frame church. You of the lofty nave and long aisles, gothic windows radiant with the saints and sacred symbols, blushing upholstery, paneled and frescoed ceilings, and rising over all the stately and awesome dome, can scarcely know the joy with which those modest walls went up in this potentially and prospectively important city of Indiana. Riverton was glad and rejoiced in her first house of worship. Some had contributed timbers, others siding, others flooring, others shingles. Some had given many a day of work on the building.

To be sure, every net draws all sorts of fish, and church nets are no exception to this rule. There was Mrs. Rosson. She and her husband were nicely settled, prosperous and well-to-do, on a large farm. After the floor was laid, but before the seats were placed, the ladies provided a dinner in the church, and rallied the people to dine, and to bring their free will offerings. Now, previously, Mrs.

Rosson conspicuously urged that the dinner should be upon a large and sumptuous scale. "Let's have a magnificent dinner, chicken pie, turkey, salads, mince pies and everything good," she urged; and Mrs. Martyn, chairman of the committee on refreshments, highly delighted and encouraged by Mrs. Rosson's exhortations to liberality, drew out memorandum book and pencil and exclaimed, "Good for you, Mrs. Rosson; just the one I want to head my list; tell me what you will contribute, and I will jot it right down."

"Oh, well," said Mrs. Rosson, at once dropping down to a low drawling tone, "well—well—I guess—I guess—I can bring a little milk—and—and" then she paused, and twisted her bonnet strings and paused. After waiting a painful instant, Mrs. Martin renewed her inquiry, but made no advance.

"Mrs. Rosson, I am waiting to write down your contribution, turkey, chicken pie, etc." Mrs. Rosson turned this way and that, studied and paused, started, stammered and stopped, but did not get beyond "A little milk—and—" Finally, after waiting what seemed ages, and while ill suppressed smiles were on every countenance, Mrs. Martyn, putting pencil to paper, said, "Very well, Mrs. Rosson, I will write it down then."

Mrs. Rosson—"A little milk—and—" Can you wonder that among the workers of the church, one lady came to be known as Mrs. "A little milk—and—"?

Mrs. Steele was a woman of quite different type from Mrs. Rosson; a brisk, *petite*, enthusiastic body; liberal, very liberal—so long as she was allowed her own way. She had a very sharp "I will" and "I won't," and was needles and daggers to everybody who did not smile serenely and submissively on her domineering. The lash, too, which she applied indiscriminately and repeatedly to those who differed from her, was the threat, "Well, if you don't do thus and so, I'll leave the church." But at last that lash wore out and the whip stalk broke.

Now, it happened at this very time, when the ladies of the congregation were arranging for the aforesaid dinner, that some of them were cushioning Mr. Goldwin's pulpit tastefully, and Mrs. Steele was, as usual, in and around, and, strange to say, they drew the line with Mrs. Steele, on a thing as small as a pulpit tassel.

"A tassel dangling from the pulpit! No, never. It's altogether too worldly. I'd as soon think of having a tassel on my coffin. If the pulpit's going to be tasseled out, I won't come to church. I won't have my mind diverted in the house of God by tassels," exclaimed the explosive Mrs. Steele.

Not that the good women of the church hung so very much on that tassel, but they felt that Mrs. Steele had made her accustomed threat quite long enough. And so, Mrs. Steele found she had made it just once too often. The tassel hung from the cushion, and Mrs. Steele was quietly, though regretfully taken at her word, and permitted to withdraw from the church. But the church dinner came off very successfully notwithstanding; and Mrs. Steele lived to mourn her stubborn and ill-tempered action, and to bite her lips with humiliation, as she saw how prosperously affairs moved on in the Riverton church without her money or her measures. However, Mrs. Rosson and Mrs. Steele were quite the exception, so please do not guage the church or the people of Riverton by them.

The church edifice having, as we have said, been completed, Rev. Dr. Ball, of Cranston, preached the dedication sermon. He gloried in being called the great champion of orthodoxy, and seemed to think it his duty to stiffen "the young brother's" theology. Dr. Ball was of the school that thought there was great danger of assuming to take God's work out of His hands, and that anything which was really a doctrine of freedom of the human will, was a doctrine of devils. He had much to say about "our book," and at first the congregation at Riverton supposed that he referred to the Bible; but Dr. Ball soon made it very clear, that with him, "our book," was the Westminster Confession of Faith. He inquired of the officers of the church whether Mr. Goldwin had been faithful in drilling his new members in "the book." I don't know as to that," said Bro. Barnett, "but I believe he is still drilling them in the Bible, and I hardly see how he could do better with beginners than that." Dr. Ball also asked, "Does Bro. Goldwin warn his people against New England heterodoxy, and above all, against Oberlinism, and the "New Measures?" "Doctor Ball," said Bro. Drake, "perhaps I'm not well up in new measures, and that sort o' thing, but I believe our pastor in his preaching brings forth things new and old." Doctor Bancroft overhearing the Minister's question concerning New England heterodoxy and "New Measures," felt his loyalty to dear old Massachusetts stirred within him, and so, joining in the conversation, said, "excuse me, Dr. Ball, but I am interested in whatever is said about New England, for my early home was on her soil, and I love her, and believe in her too; for she believes with John Robinson, that more light is yet to break forth from God's Word. If that is heterodoxy, then you will have to count me a heretic. And as to new measures, in my profession we don't care a fig whether they are new or old, if only they meet the disease. This was said with gentlemanly deference, albeit with something of Dr. Bancroft's directness and pith.

Dr. Ball, too, was one of those who declared himself a believer in the "divine institution of slavery." At the spring meeting of the scattered churches, he had taken occasion to read the young Bro. Goldwin and several others a lecture. It was somewhat of an honor to be chosen to represent the local organization in the national body. Mr. Goldwin had been associated with these pastors and churches for six or seven years, and it was quite generally believed by the brethren that it was due him that he should be elected to represent them in the national convocation. But, as afterward appeared, Dr. Ball had been quietly manipulating some of the brethren, declaring to them that it was of paramount importance that strong champions of the "standards," and of strict denominationalism, should be sent to represent the West in the national meeting, and that these New England men were altogether too liberal and undenominational. "The Great West," said he, wants the "true blue;" we must beware of wolves, etc. All this, of course, implied, as it was designed it should; "I, Dr. Ball, am your man; send me."

But to the surprise of no one of the ministers, perhaps, except Dr. Ball, Mr. Goldwin was elected with only one dissenting vote, to be their representative. Dr. Ball, unable to conceal his disappointment and chagrin, at once arose, and launched out on a presentation of the beauties of the patriarchial institution, and on the providential wisdom which ordained that the children of Ham should serve the sons of Shem, and declared woe upon those who refused what the Almighty had so clearly foreordained. Then waxing warm, he fiercely howled against loose doctrine, and vowed that the Bible was enough for him, and it declared that our children go astray as soon as they be born, speaking lies. One brother interjected right here that his children were not so precocious as that; but Dr. Ball did not deign to notice him. Another remarked that the words which the Doctor had quoted, were from the poetry of David, and must not be interpreted in prosaic literalism. To this, Dr. Ball replied, "I must take this Bible as it reads. To this came the rejoinder, "Our Saviour said, 'Unless ye eat the flesh of the Son of Man, ye have no life in you.' Take it literally do you, Dr. Ball?"

Dr. Ball delivered the dedication sermon; occupied the pulpit both Sabbath morning and evening; but failed to receive the fulsome adulation on which his vanity loved to feed, and rode out of Riverton less inflated than when he rode in. Mortimer and Geo. Tupper irreverently agreed that "he talked as though he was private secretary to the Almighty." Refined Mrs. Martyn thought "It was a thousand pities that the new walls should be discolored with so much fire and brimstone. Dr. Bancroft, always quoting Shakespeare, sniffed and said, "Full of sound and fury, signifying nothing;" and dear Mr. and Mrs. Goldwin hung their heads in mute disappointment. Poor Col. Grande was provoked enough, because he found nothing to remind him of Henry Clay. Nevertheless, the next Sunday, Mr. Goldwin preached in review of the history of the little church, and so full of tender pathos, so bright with faith and hope, so warm with re-creating love was the sermon, that Pierpont and Mrs. Drake expressed the universal sentiment when they said, "Now, our church is dedicated."

But let us not come down too heavily on Dr. Ball. His mind was cast in a narrow mould; his imagination was exceedingly scant; so that in forming his sentiments and judgments, he seemed unable to put himself in the place of the "other fellow." His politics and theology were his, not by personal investigation, but by inheritance. Intellectually he lived in the house his forefathers built, and carefully excluded from it every modern discovery and invention. He dwelt in the light of other days. He fell heir to a family tree of inveterate prejudices; which tree he faithfully watered and fertilized. What man is free from prejudice? Let him who is without it cast the first stone.

If Doctor Ball and Mr Goldwin differed somewhat in phrasing their theology they differed more in the spirit in which they held it. One would have his "pound of flesh," because it was "so nominated in the bond," perfectly heartless of consequences. The other, while baiting naught from rectitude, nor one jot from the doctrines of the

Bible, entreated and patiently lured to the door of Mercy which the Pierced Hands held wide open.

Mr. and Mrs. Goldwin were as two musical instruments which were exceedingly unlike and yet in perfect accord. They looked with their own eyes, but in the same blessed light, and animated by the same motive. Their love for each other was not blind, not idolatry; more choice, more discerning far. Mr. Goldwin's hearers had become accustomed to expect from him something to think about, something to carry away which sent warmth into their hearts all the week. No make-believe, nothing thin or vapid could satisfy Mr. Goldwin ,and he always brought his best to his people. He poured out his soul without stint. Hence his preaching was very exhausting to him.

Mrs. Goldwin was a discerning listener, and a critic affectionate and appreciative, while faithful and acute. Their life was a study and practice of the art of presenting the truth so that others would receive it and obey it. Woman's bright intuition and heart-sensing form the complement of men's logic and reasoning. The ancient mouse in the corner of the parson's study, or the garrulous cricket on the hearth, enjoyed rare privileges.

Margaret soon discovered that a certain button on her husband's coats, even on those which were almost new, was torn off, and on observing closely, saw that while "thinking on his legs" before an audience, his mental twisting sought relief in twisting his button, and that when that button was off, his thoughts were apt to be somewhat off like the learned and eloquent Neander, who could not get on in his lecture, unless he had meanwhile a quill in his hand to tear to pieces.

Margaret realized too, that, as with most men, her husband's better thinking, ordinarily at least, was attained only with elaborate use of the pen; and that in speaking from brief notes or from none, he was liable to be unnecessarily repititious, and to be thrown off his track by unexpected circumstances. In fine, she encouraged him to write many of his sermons and deliver them from manuscript.

He always read naturally and effectively, and the majority of his hearers came to prefer his written discourses. Indeed, he generally so enlisted attention to his sermon that the fact of its being written or unwritten was hardly considered.

Margaret, also, with her acute ear, was ever on the alert to strangle that little imp, "the preacher tone," which so often steals into the preacher's throat. "Solemncholy tone," the wags fitly call it. "Preach," said she, "in the inflections and cadences of earnest and absorbing conversation."

No one more readily and thoroughly

responded to Mr. Goldwin's high and uplifting, thinking and spiritual discerning than did Margaret, and they ministered rare comfort and assurance to each other. Margaret's appreciation, above all others, went straight to the heart of her husband, and lifted him over many a discouragement. He, also, although knowing little of the minutiae of household affairs, had a keen and kindly appreciation of the patience and good cheer with which she met the thousand little cares and annoyances which will enter the daily domestic round of every well ordered home.

CHAPTER XXII.

The last bell is striking, and the last feet are hurrying to "Morning Chapel." A moment, and the little call bell on the principal's desk rings one vigorous note; and the accurate little teacher on the left of the principal, record book and long pencil in hand, in tones quick and sharp as the bell, calls the roll which she is correcting and perfecting for the new school year. One hundred names of young lady pupils; down the alphabet amid the Browns and the Clarks, and Johnsons and Joneses, into the large family of Smiths. Now she is in the "T's;" Tabor, Talcott, Thomas, Tupper, "Sibyl Tupper!" "Present." Ho, ho! we do know that name and that voice. It is hardly necessary to say that we are in a ladies' seminary, and it is among the hills of New England. But by what fortune is Sibyl Tupper found so far from home? We'll turn back to Riverton and see.

Majestic and bland Edward Mortimer careers over that town. Its people, for whom he professes so much esteem, are to him of no more concern than so many lost pins. Possibly that same people are shrewder than he supposes. Wit and wisdom are the monopoly of no clime or cloth. Mortimer does not perceive—and if he did, little would he care,—that Rachel Drake detects the base metal under the thin gold wash. He says, "She's too pious; as for the Dale girls, they are too common dust. Col. Grande's daughter is too willing. But the Tuppers, yes the Tuppers! there's blood there. Isabel; she's a chilly subject; but Sibyl, ah! Sibyl! she's my prize."

First music opens the gate. How often evil is set to music. Some half a dozen persons stop after church, to run over a new sacred song. Sibyl sings alto and Mortimer sings bass, and so they naturally sit together, and sometimes have to sing from the same book. Some strains in the tune the have just sung remind Mortimer of a very pretty duet; he hums the air to Sibyl; she would like so much to learn it. He thinks he has the music at his room; has played it on his flute. "O, Mr. Mortimer, do you play the flute? Come to our house and bring your flute. Do." In vain he protests that he only plays a little for his own amusement. "Do come; you must come. It'll be perfectly elegant." The flute player calls at the Tuppers. They admire him. Before long he comes again. This time Miss Isabel has a dreadful headache, and does not appear, so, exactly as he would have it, he spends the evening with Sibyl.

It is to us the refinement of cruelty for a

man like Mortimer, so low in his ideals, so impure in his intentions, deliberately to set to work to gain the affections of a noble, immaculate girl, such as is Sibyl. Yet, in plain prose, this is what some men lay themselves out to accomplish. Like unto street boys who have no apreciation of flowers, but go around and beg them, so that they may pull them to pieces! One would almost expect heaven would straightway interpose to prevent such diabolical plots. And yet, often it seems as though the Fates conspire with the villain. Everything seemed to throw Mortimer and Sibyl together. Did she go out for a walk, or did she step down the street, by some chance he would fall in with her. Always so courteous, gallant, and exquisitely deferential, while gradually and tentatively exhibiting a tenderness and warmth, he steadily wrought his way into that unsuspecting heart.

Was seriousness the word? None more serious, penitential, and religious than he. Hear him declare that he adores Mr. Goldwin and knows that he is just the one to do him good; but he does wonder why he should be so beset and harrassed and tormented with mysteries and dark things. And, subtle reader of the heart, he bemoaned himself the more, because thus he drew upon himself Sibyl's sympathies and prayers and yearnings. How it drew her whole soul to him, to hear him say in well feigned grief, that, "He did not seem organized so that he could believe."

Sibyl gave him the love of her ardent and untarnished nature. The thrill of pleasure which shot through her being, as she sat in church and knew by the rich voice in song, that Mortimer was sitting behind her!

One evening Mortimer seemed unusually affectionate and tender. He fell into a pathetically reminiscent vein. He had often held Sibyl spell bound with his graphic descriptions of foreign lands, and especially of London; of Windsor Castle with its service of silver and gold, valued at more than ten million dollars; of the peacock of precious stones; of Kensington Gardens, and the parks and cathedrals and the wonderful music; and of his uncle's palace and grounds which were in the very cream of position in the West End.

Sibyl at such times seemed borne away to Enchanted Land. On this evening to which we have alluded, his voice softened as he spoke of his blessed mother sleeping in Kensel Green Cemetery. He could say no more, and he and Sibyl wept. Then in the silence he plead, "Dearest Sibyl, may I show you all these sacred scenes? O, go with me. Let me guide you, cherish you, adore you forever." She laid her head fondly upon his shoulder, and he pressed her to his bosom.

Mortimer passed the following winter at

Indianapolis. The legislature was in session, and that little city was all motion and mirth. The social luminaries were at their zenith. Mortimer danced attendance upon the belles of the season, and entered with a free hand into the fashionable dissipation and vice. Dora Preston, "the Kentucky Star," was in the ascendancy, and grave senators and judges crowded in her train. Mortimer and his hail-fellows would come stumbling and yawning into the Capitol Restaurant at nine or ten in the morning, and languidly sip their coffee or champagne, and discuss the fine points of the social brilliants of the hour.

Meanwhile the crafty Mortimer was saying to himself, "I must keep the lines well secured around my Riverton sweetheart." Letters, now and then a choice roll of music, accompanied by neat little notes, full of the tender passion, come to Sibyl.

Now, more than once Gen, Tupper has asked himself, "Who is this Edward Mortimer?" Nor does he gain any very satisfactory answer. Indeed, there seems to be no authority on this question, aside from the man himself; so far prepossessing enough. About this time, in conversation with Judge Bernis, of Indianapolis, upon the mention of Mortimer's name, the sage judge ominously shook his head. "No good; English prodigal; in a far country and on the road to the swine. Too much Paris has spoiled him. My opinion, he's mortgaged to the devil."

Gen. Tupper made no reply to this legal opinion, given in rather unjuridical terms; but he did considerable thinking; likewise did Mrs. Tupper. The solons of the legislature return home. Mortimer returns to Riverton, and is more devoted than ever to Sibyl. Parental protests vex the waters but do not check them. Something must be done. The result is, after conferring with Mr. and Mrs. Goldwin, and, while Mortimer is away for a few days at the Capitol finishing up a gambling schedule which he has on hand, Sibyl, her father's pet, and the sunbeam of her mother, is whisked off a thousand miles to a boarding school. She has had many a hard crying spell; says "Mortimer is perfectly elegant," and declares papa will think so some day. She's very sure she will never love anyone else as she does him. Nevertheless, for poor dear Mama's sake, she has dropped all correspondence with him.

CHAPTER XXIII.

By law, Riverton was the hub of the county; by location it was the hub of several counties. With unbounded faith in the future, or as visitors from Boston said, with accustomed Western effrontery, it was already a chartered city. Riverton was like the boy who dons his father's garments. They are, it is true, much in advance of his proportions; but then he is gaining the better of that fault every day.

An event which made the boy-city swell with pride was the opening of the canal diagonally across the state. This connected Riverton with Toledo and the East, and with Vincennes and the Southern Gulf. Traveling by canal-packets at the rate of seven miles an hour, stowed in cramped and confined quarters; flies, fleas and mosquitoes within; forests, water-fowl, fish, frogs and fens without, was considered luxurious.

The two rivers, Poconock and Rappilee, and the canal helped to develop the country, and developed, also, malaria; that name by which we appear to understand something which we do not understand; unseen and yet universally believed in; a reality which only he that feels it knows. Aboriginal fields, large water courses, sunless shades, dark glades and silent swamps, may live handsomely in poetry and in song. Thousands and thousands and tons of thousands of little imps, dripping with vegetable and animal feculence, poison peddlers, man-eaters—microbes and bacilli we call them now; —come like a thief in the night, and encamp everywhere in "chills and fever;" everywhere on the just and the unjust.

Mr. Goldwin had many a shake with this bane of the new settlement. Quinine and calomel were the medical panacea; poison fought poison, and a good constitution at length came out of the battle victorious, although a costly victory it was.

But an enemy far worse than any miasma or malaria was ravaging Riverton. With the increase of trade and traders, intemperance was increasing. Both gay and festive drinking places and low mud-sill whisky dives were springing up as if by magic. The canal brought not only water but whisky; not perhaps the much "doctored" whisky of today, yet full of devils and death.

Mr. Goldwin warned and entreated, and his soul was sore with grief. His was no doubtful utterance. An equivocal position he disdained. He dealt in no glittering generalities, nor yet in angering personalities, but he called a spade a spade, and his naked facts blistered. The whisky men understood him, hated him, while compelled to respect him for his courage and honesty. In his contact with the liquor curse, Mr. Goldwin had some always reliable coadjutors. The ability and legal learning of Pierpont not all the whisky power of the globe could retain, much less subsidize, or silence; and Dr. Bancroft, by far the most prominent and skilled healer in Riverton, as we have already seen, was not one of those who sell liquor under the guise of medicine. Nothing delighted him better than to come down with his battle-axe on rum casks and drink doctrines.

We have already seen that several years antecedent to this date, O'Flannigan, the pioneer rum seller, had forbidden his daughter to attend church, and he never wearied of inveighing bitterly before his comrades and his drunken sons against "Priest Goldwin," who, he said, led the people of Riverton around by the nose. Therein O'Flannigan came nearer the truth than was customary with him. If he had changed one word, said "led the people around by their reason," he would have been unusually accurate. Mr. Goldwin had gained many signatures to the total abstinence pledge, and snatched some from the toils of the liquor venders, and although many times acting through others, was really the leader in organized effort to close the liquor shops. Yes, close them. For he began at this early date in the temperance work to see that so long as strong drink was freely sold, reform the drinkers as fast as they could, it was only pulling men out below the dam, while money and greed and appetite were chucking them in above the dam.

A city election was approaching, and the advocates of temperance, while seeking to manufacture and focalize healthy public sentiment, called a mass meeting, a grand citizens' rally. As the hour came, in they came; patricians and plebians, clean and unclean, "mongrel whelp and hound and cur of low degree." A number of ladies in attendance, helped very much to redeem the character of the audience. They were seated in the vicinity of the speaker's stand, while the whisky patrons and peddlers, diffusing the familiar odor, were packed into the rear seats. It appeared rather as though the goats outnumbered the sheep.

Col. Grande was passing in and out, exchanging a word with everybody, escorting the ladies to eligible seats, and finally pulling out his ruddy handkerchief and rendering some Jericho salutes, seated himself near the platform and occupied himself in his customary endeavor to twist his frowsy locks across his bald and barren pate. The "Presidential Bee" was buzzing in his ears. He aspired to preside over this meeting, and, in this instance, hs aspiration was gratified. He was called to the chair.

A few preliminaries, appointment of secretaries, and then the speeches began. Mr. Goldwin made, by way of introducing the subject for all to discuss, a plain dispassionate statement of what was, and what might be, and what ought to be, closing with a vivid picture of the advantages and superior possibilities, the brilliant future which belonged to Riverton, if temperate and pure.

Then somebody started the call for Hawkins, and he arose. He praised the people; flung the stars and stripes to the breeze; lugged in all the Latin he knew; vox populi vox Dei; said he, was jealous of the people's rights; believed in temperance and moral suasion; despised a drunkard; did not believe in any legislation or restriction concerning what a man should or should not eat or drink; temperance was a good thing, and would come sometime, but Rome was not built in a day, and vinegar never caught flies. This speech seemed to harmonize well with the back seats.

Then Mr. Pierpont arose. He began very calmly, but it was apparent that the volcano was only slumbering. He spoke with the seriousness of one who had felt the relentless hoofs of the sateless monster, Drink. There was indeed a chapter in his boyhood of which he never spoke. How he had sat with his mother and sister watching and waiting into the late hours for father to return, and how they all trembled when they heard his footsteps; of this Pierpont was silent. But is it strange that he early learned to hate liquor, and swore eternal war against it? A kind, well informed and capable father lost for days in debauch, followed always by shame and confusion and the solemn promise that this should be the last; and this vow only to be succeeded by temptation and persuasion and yielding and fall, until at last he fell into a drunkard's grave,—this Pierpont had seen, and wrung the anguish out of it to the last drop.

He made a very clear lawyer-like argument, showing that the remedy for every public evil was in the hands of the people, and that not to rise in their might against this confessedly mammoth evil was craven and cowardly and criminal. Pierpont's logic no pleader for whisky was rash enough to touch. His words plowed deep. Evidently the goats were a little quieted or momentarily awed.

Then, Col. Grande, after taking a huge pinch of snuff, suggested that they would be happy to hear from their distinguished friend, Hon. Edward Mortimer.

Mortimer arose, slowly and with well-feigned reluctance; played the part of the very "humble individual;" strewed compliments "thick as leaves of Valambrosa" around the honorable chairman and the orators of the evening, and over Riverton, not omitting the superior attractions of its ladies. He did not see how any rational person could be otherwise than a friend of temperance. Moderation in all things was the law of the wise. He despised anyone who had not the manhood to practice self-control. His experience had taught him that each man must stand or fall for himself. Indeed, the whole of this Englishman's homily might be summed up in the text of Cain, "Am I my brother's keeper?" He opined, also, that what was poison for one was often bread for another; that this, which he was proud to call his adopted country, rejoiced in extending the largest liberty to the individual; that we must not allow our noblest moral convictions to carry us beyond sweet charity, or into even the semblance of encroachment upon personal liberty. Then he said something must be pardoned to his early education, and to the social customs of "Merrie old England." This subject of temperance, it should be remembered, was very large and very important, and must be considered in all its bearings. He had thought upon it a great deol. He believed thoroughly in reforms, and in every measure which was for the betterment of man. But we must not put new cloth into old garments, lest the rent should be made worse, and, like our blessed divine Lord, we must have long patience, remembering that it is written "He that believeth shall not make haste." Here it was interesting to notice the derisive grin which played around the corners of the mouths of certain hearears who knew Mortimer thoroughly. Mortimer expounding Scripture! The devil turned saint!

Still further, in the speaker's opinion, the greatest enemies of reform were hobby-riders and fanatics, and he could not forget that our adorable Saviour turned water into wine for the wedding guests, and that the chiefest of apostles said, "Take a little wine for thy stomach's sake." Thus did Mortimer state small fractions of fact and truth, carefully eliding that which would make them complete and truthful; artful in the most dangerous form of lying, which consists in telling only a part, as though it were the whole. Thus did he, while professing to embrace temperance, secretly stab it. Finally he said that, like his unsophisticated friend, Hawkins, he believed in the people, and to their wisdom he would humbly submit the whole question.

This speech was framed and uttered in the most plausible and bewitching Chesterfieldian manner, and with all the adroitness of Mark Antony. Somehow, it left a very agreeable taste in the mouths of those on the back seats.

It is speaking very mildly to say that Mr. Goldwin was very much disappointed and annoyed with Mr. Mortimer, for to him such hypocrisy was sickening and rasping in the extreme. He, "Priest Goldwin," could see that it might be expedient for him to remain somewhat under cover, and press others to the front, but, politics or not, he would never allow the last speech to be the last, and he was vigorously twisting his coat button, sure prelude to a good speech, when a voice became just audible. Everyone looked up, as if saying, "A strange voice! Who can it be?" It was none other than the boy, Jonas Drake. Absent for a time, attending school, a brief vacation now brought him home. Always interested in temperance, the silent, undemonstrative boy had strolled in with the rest, and settled into a seat, and apparently unobservant and self-enwrapped, he had really heard and weighed every word spoken. The idea of his making a speech was as remote from his mind as from that of those around him. But as he listened, the fire burned until it must break out.

As he arose and caught the eyes of all fixed upon him, some lighted up with deep personal sympathy, and esteem, and some with a sort of amused contempt, for an instant a cloud of constraint passed over his countenance; for an instant only. Almost with his first word, his intense convictions bore him into perfect equipoise, and soon the cloud was livid with lightnings. His soul trod the heights of truth and moral obligation; felt the freedom of that upper air, and, like a mountain flood, quit of all impediment, bore straight on. His form became erect and authoritative, his countenance mobile to every shade, now of pathos, and now of scorn, and now of drollery. The audience, captured by the unexpected, enchained, entranced, leaned forward to catch every word. Now laughter, and now tears, played around his hot logic, like sparks showered from the hot iron under the hammer.

Eloquence is unreportable, and we are not so audacious as to attempt to transfer it to paper. While Jonas seemed to disdain all personalities, in the electric light of truth and charity how flimsy the sophistries, how bald the selfishness and hypocrisies of Hawkins and "the distinguished representative of John Bull." It was like pouring noonday upon midnight.

Mortimer was mortified and chagrined and angered beyond all description. If Mr. Goldwin or Mr. Pierpont had answered him, he would have felt honored; but to be impaled so unsparingly on the lance of this strippling knight, this novice, this raw boy! Humiliation could no farther go; and "our distinguished friend, the Hon. Edward Mortimer," wished that evening had found him in Indianapolis, or anywhere except in a Riverton temperance meeting.

Jonas sat down, and then a pause; an instant of stillness, when the assembly drew a long breath—regained itself, and then explosion, then round after round of applause; ladies waved their handkerchiefs, and some of the men leaped to their feet, shouted, huzzahed and whirled their hats.

Somehow, there was a feeling that the last word had been spoken, and the meeting abruptly adjourned.

Then the crowd separated into little groups all discussing Jonas. Jack Barnett said, "I always knew there were more brains under Jonas' hat than people gave him credit for." Schnapps, the jolly beer seller, seemed as much pleased as any of them. "Py tunder und blitzen," he exclaimed, "dot boy ist vun pig virlvind." Dr. Bancroft, who had just returned from a long professional ride in time to hear Jonas, declared that it was "Simply Patrick Henry risen from the dead," and George Tupper asked triumphantly of Col. Grande, "Where's your Henry Clay now?"

CHAPTER XXIV.

The next Sabbath, a stranger, who gave his name as Rev. Jerod Jordan, of Sparksville, accompanied Mr. Goldwin into the pulpit. Recently three new churches had commenced the struggle for existence in Riverton, but Mr. Jordan was there to raise also his denominational flag, and rally around him those who would lisp his shiboleth.

He had called upon Mr. Goldwin and promptly accepted his hospitality, and offered to relieve Brother Goldwin by preaching for him. The latter was indeed needing relief. A little mite of mortality had made his *debut* into the domestic circle some six weeks previous—a pocket edition of Mr. Goldwin; and his demands were numerous and imperative in inverse ratio with his dimensions. Like the nightingale, his songs were given in the night, and the music had not been a lullaby to the parson, or to his beloved partner. Hence, a Sabbath of rest was welcome to Mr. Goldwin.

Reverend Jordan was evidently desirous of publishing himself favorably, and both his prayers and sermons were designed to be very eloquent. In his prayer, after rolling the large words, like hugh boulders, from the dizzy heights of glory, and, as was natural, perspiring in copious streams, he terminated his oratorical supplications thus: "And when we have concluded our mundane peregrinations on this sublunary sphere, receive us unanimously into the sempiternal felicities of the eternally beatified, and we will shake the walls of the celestial Jericho with immutably reverberating hallelujahs forever and ever more—Amen." Mr. Goldwin looked as if the amen brought him relief;and his discerning hearers exchanged significant glances, while a waggish fellow seated near the door, gave vent to an irreverent "Phew!"

The speaker then announced as his theme, "Man's Soular System."

He occupied the ensuing week in calling on everybody and publishing that he had come to Riverton to "get up a revival," and would open up on the next Sabbath in the City Hall." For three weeks he discoursed every night; perhaps to the edification of some; certainly to the diversion of many. After his sermon, he was accustomed to exhort, "Come for'ard, oh, sinner, and get a blessing; yea beloved, come for'ard and be clothed in the garbage of the saints."

Bro. Jordan advocated Christian Union, and taught that the one and simple way of securing it was for all to join his church. Before many days his preaching seemed narrowed down to recommending the peculiarities of his sect, and indulging in thrusts at other denominations. His holy tone and celestial soaring quite captivated Mother Smile. She drank in the words of this new voice with a countenance which was seraphic. For about three weeks he drew the crowd. Two months longer, and he had almost no following, and he suddenly left town, leaving a memento with Mrs. Smile, an unpaid board bill, and with the community, as souvenirs, a few burnt over relics of the so-called revival. After a few weeks, as Sam Drake said, even a policeman couldn't have found the Rev. Jerod Jordan's converts.

There was also, in those days, Rev. Henry Littleton, shepherd at large over the churches. Once or twice a year he visited Riverton, and always to the gratification of Riverton. Benevolence lighted his countenance and resounded from his clear melodious voice. He was an excellent singer, an earnest and practical preacher, and an adroit guide of all varieties of human nature. Educated at the same theological seminary as was Mr. Goldwin, the two had much in common, and, to them to visit and pray and plan together, was like pitching their tent by the lone fountain in the desert. Mr. Littleton appreciated Mr. and Mrs. Goldwin, and he aided others to appreciate them.

Good Brother Littleton—all the children loved him, and when he addressed the Sunday School, as he loved to do, he never talked too long; he never addressed them as babies nor as adults, but as wide-awake boys and girls, and parents and children were alike interested. Mr. Goldwin aimed to make his Sunday School like a bird's nest, fastened to that which is solid on the earth, but always open toward heaven.

In these untrammeled and hospitable years, the home of the minister was open to peripatetic or equestrian clergymen, and wayside wanderers of divers mind and mould, and seldom was long without guests. Then, there were the Spring and Fall convenings of the ministers and delegates of the scattered churches. Riverton being one of the larger and more central towns, was often the place of these meetings. Entertainments in those days included ministers and delegates and often ministers' wives, and also horse or horses. Much housewifely ingenuity was required in contriving that there should always be bread enough and to spare, and that no bed should have too many bedfellows.

Ah, jolly times those were, when the ministers gathered around the minister's board. Wit was discharged at short range and hit every time. Or, seated in the little "front room," how they discussed, threw in bits of experience, and anecdotes and ha! ha's! Tears, too, were close by—sympathizing tears of sorrow or of joy; and many were the nuggets of personal truth gathered here from the soil which lies between the cradle and the grave;—often a very short path, but often rich in better than gold. Occasionally there was a Mr. Dullard or a Mr. Dryasdust, but, as a rule, divinity of the pioneer or missionary kind abhorred dullness, and when logic failed, achieved by dint of wit. Mirth and merriment bubbled sweet and pure, like sap from the sugar trees in the early spring.

Mrs. Goldwin, a veritable Kohinoor, shone with greatest brilliance when surrounded by clerical lights, and passed around with her tea and coffee many a choice bit of impromptu philosophy, or an intellectual puncture, or a felicitious *bon mot*. The blue devils ran from the twinkle of her eye.

The menu of her table was ever simple, plain and ample, but sometimes it offered some exalted achievement in cuisine which evidently was of foreign origin. Somehow a stuffed and steaming roast, or a basket of tea cakes, or a tray of superfine pastries, some special refection—would mysteriously find its way into her pantry just when the hour came to use it. Mrs. Goldwin said she did not believe in fairies or sprites, but she did believe she had the exceptionalist of good friends and neighbors. Whether it was second sight or mind reading, she did not know, but one thing she did know, that the people of the church always knew exactly when to send and what to send to help out her larder.

The State Meeting was the great churchly

feast of the year. It convened in the autumn, sometimes in Indian summer radiance, sometimes in clouds and fall floods. From the Michigan line on the north, and from the Ohio River on the south, the cavalry and carryalls came. One and then another, sometimes half a dozen, would bring up by nightfall at the ministerial manse and manger, on their way to this meeting. Riverton had the pleasure of opening its new church to this body. For a few days the denizens of this youthful but ambitious city saw preachers to right of them, preachers to left of them. The streets were cloudy with men in black.

At these meetings the Home Missionary boxes and barrels were opened and their contents distributed. Out came socks for giants, and clothing for sons of Anak. Evidently, the eastern donors had large ideas of "growing up with the country." Comfortables also appeared in variety of colors to suit the taste of the gay or the gloomy. For the most part, the contents of these boxes were suitable and serviceable and very welcome, a very great help to the over-worked but never over-paid recipients.

Mrs. Goldwin very much enjoyed attending these ministerial meetings, when her wifely and motherly cares permitted. The Kingdom of God seemed hardly invisible, certainly intensely real to her, and the debating and devising for its universal establishment aroused her whole nature. She was also a skillful decipherer of the cunning palimpsests of the human heart, and as an unobserved spectator at these clerical sittings, she found excellent opportunity for this occult reading.

There was also in those elder days freedom, unconventionality, heartiness and friendship, which are less obvious as starch and prim propriety, and congested wealth increase. Plutocrats were then scarcely known, and multi-millionaires quite unknown. Gigantic monopolies had not then carbuncled our nation.

Henry Ward Beecher, then the youthful but much thronged pastor in Indianapolis, accompanied by Mrs. Beecher, made the journey to Riverton to attend the State meeting, and he kept that sedate body in a roar as he described the tribulations and perils, by sea and land, which he encountered on the road, and then the next moment came one of his inimitable touches, which brought them all to tears.

In these ecclesiastical, as in the political, convocations, the question of slavery was irrepressible, and evolved great heat and sometimes dire conflagration. Some never conformed to the march of truth and freedom, and had to be dragged along behind the procession. Some reared and plunged like wild animals at the bare mention of the word abolition, and the Union was dissolved times incredible. However, the majority of the brethren kept serenely on their way, and never flinched or budged when the menagerie broke cage.

About this time, a guest whom we have met arrived at Mr. Goldwin's. It will be remembered that John Goldwin left behind him in Vermont his mother and brothers, Arthur and Thomas. The mother, about a year previous to the date of this chapter, had suddenly sickened and died. She had lived to see her sons educated, and ripened to noble manhood and to usefulness; had seen the last wishes of her lamented husband fulfilled, and then, with a heart abiding in heavenly peace, she had "languished into life."

Thomas Goldwin had accepted a professorship in a nascent college in Illinois. Arthur Goldwin found an implacable foe in the wintry winds of New England, and yielding to the peremptory order of his physician, broke away from the theological seminary, and fled to a southern climate. After teaching for a time in Georgia, and beholding his hopes of recovery stealthily one by one disappear, his heart turned instinctively and tenaciously toward the home of his brother John in Riverton.

The latter, informed though he had been of the feebleness of Arthur, was not prepared for the reality, and the immediate sight of the sunken cheek and emaciated form, so ill contrasting with the bounding, redundant vitality of his brother when last he saw him in Vermont, smote him to the heart. For an instant he was disarmed, and Arthur, though he could but see his brother's dismay, apparently unobserving, extended his hand and gleamed with the old winsome smile.

Arthur's prayer had been answered, and he was permitted to lie down beneath a brother's roof. A travel worn and exhausted invalid, he wept in thankfulness upon his pillow, and amid visions of boyhood, mother and home, and of one dear woman who for more than a twelve month had filled his heart, quaffed with fevered haste from the rivulet of rest.

Meanwhile John and Margaret passed a wakeful night, and no darkness could cover from their eyes that death smitten face. More than once the anxious John stole on tiptoe to the sick man's chamber to assure himself that his wants were supplied. The first sound of the morning was that hollow and ominous cough. As the days passed, sometimes hope borrowed a little strength. Now and then affection almost fancied the disease was retreating. It was only in ambuscade.

As the morning sun grew high and warm, Margaret was accustomed to place a comfortable chair by the open west door, and there Arthur loved to sit. The world was to him so beautiful; never more attractive.

Never did the birds sing sweeter; the wood, the distant river and the blue sky were never dearer companions.

As John passed in and out, the embodiment of vitality and cheer, or joyously wrapped in study or in thought of his dear people, Arthur was made so keenly mindful of what he had chosen and reached after with all his desire; and now, the life plan almost realizing, the prize almost in his hands, lo, his hands have suddenly lost their cunning; his knees tremble, and his feet refuse his bidding. His heart said, "Life is sweet. That tender rose slip"—Margaret's fingers had planted it—"is pouring its gladness into its forming bud. That little bird, its tiny frame is vibrant with song. Those sporting calves and lambs say life is so sweet. To youthful manhood, to me, life is sweet. Is my cup filled only to be dashed from my hand?"

Strange? In sooth it was. New and yet old mystery! Old as man and the secret things of God. So richly endowed he was by nature and by culture and acquirement, and, crown of all, dowered with the love of a rare woman whom he had sought and won while he was college tutor,—the very woman of all the world, as it seemed, who was divinely designed to complete his preparation and furnishing for his life work. So well equipped was he to bear Jehovah's message, so ripe to win, inspire, and lure into light and love. Nevertheless, Arthur had great satisfaction in saying "The Lord thinketh upon me," and his thoughts and emotions underwent a spiritual moulting, and came forth in unique and royal plumage. His heart panted to help his brother man. Who knoweth that this, his desire, is ungratified?

Now, day by day, his hour drew near. Silently he was fighting the final battle. The great "Decisive Battles" are silent and unseen. The foe, step by step, was closing in. But he was not alone. A voice sweeter than any human spoke to his soul: "I am come that thou mightest have life, and that thou mightest have it more abundantly." That word sung in Arthur's heart, and he felt the throb of victory. The bud was not suddenly closing. It was opening for the King's own eternal garden.

Arthur had said, "John, would that these eyes might look upon the place where you preach." So, on a clear, bright morning when the sick brother was feeling his best, John helped him into a carriage, and with little four-year-old Max between them, they drove to the church. Arthur walked slowly in, seeing and marking everything. Then he ascended the platform and sat down, playfully saying, "Who dare say that I have not occupied your pulpit?" Then pausing a moment, with his own inimitable tenderness and affection, he exclaimed, "John, I covet your privilege; I hunger for your opportunity. Oh, if I could only preach to everybody my dear Saviour.". John appeared to busy himself arranging some of the books, and for a moment sought in vain to conceal his long pent up grief. Recovering himself, however, he turned his earnest gaze on Arthur and said, "Arthur, you have helped me to preach; you are preaching."

"Am I? Am I?" said Arthur, with a light in his face from his Lord. "Thank you, my brother, a thousand times thank you for that thought." Then rising and adding, "Thou, Lord, knowest best," he leaned on his brother, and as they walked away, Arthur, putting his hand on the head of little Max, said, "Max, dear, you will preach in Uncle Arthur's place, wont you?"

The following morning Arthur had hobbled to his accustomed chair by the door. Silently, and with something akin to affection, he fixed his eyes upon the little rose slip. When Margaret placed it there, how little did she dream of the kind offices which should be given it. It had for Arthur, feelings, thoughts "too deep for tears."

Mrs. Goldwin was noiselessly moving in and out, anticipating every want, and occasionally speaking a word in her sweet silver voice. "Margaret," said Arthur, "I feel as though that rose bush was sent especially for me." "Yes, Arthur," she replied, "it is yours."

He was plainly growing weaker, yet, with characteristic and pathetic persistence of life, insisted upon rising every morning and maintaining the routine. But soon came a night when the long wrestle with disease was evidently almost over. By his side sat John and Margaret, silently watching for the coming of the Angel of Release. The sufferer lay with closed eyes and scarcely seemed to breathe. Now and then the wind shook the lattice, and moaned like a departed spirit. Margaret leaned with both hands on John's shoulder, and they communed with thoughts too deep for words.

Once Arthur opened his eyes upon them with a sweet smile which said, "I realize it all."

"Love never faileth," said John.

At this word, "love," rallying with almost preternatural energy, Arthur slowly and with labored breath repeated:

O, could I speak the matchless worth,
O, could I sound the glories forth,"

when, his strength failing, Margaret coming to his aid, added: "Which in my Saviour shine."

The long strange night was at last beginning to wane. The first of morning was beginning to creep under the curtain of the window. Once more the pallid lips just broke the silence. John, bending over, caught the words, "Life—more—abundantly," and the spirit passed into the Eternal Morning.

A few hours later, as the earthly form was lying in its last repose, a serene joy lingered in the dead face, like the glory which tarries at sunset, and between the fingers was that one fresh bloomed rose. Love, Birth, Death, and that home was triunely consecrated.

Great beyond expression were the sorrow and disappointment of Thomas, when, hastening in his buggy night and day, over prairies and through sloughs and storms and rivers, he arrived in Riverton only to learn that his brother Arthur had been in his grave seven days. Bitterly he lamented that he could no more see his face until the resurrection morn.

CHAPTER XXV.

Mr. Goldwin had erected a small barn and had added to his belongings a horse, a cow, and a "Democrat," or a stout open buggy, well adapted to encounter the rough, stumpy country roads. On Sabbath afternoon he was accustomed to drive out to neighboring school houses and preach. In this way he multiplied his labors and usefulness, and began what afterward matured into several country churches. Margaret delighted when the skies and the earth were propitious, to accompany her husband to his out appointments. Sometimes the minister found it quite enough for heart and flesh, to keep his appointments alone and on horseback.

The county of which Riverton was the center had increased rapidly in population and resources. On its list of officers appeared now the name of Christian Stubbs, who had been elected sheriff. Col. Grande aspired to that office. When was he not aspiring to some office in the gift of the "dear people?" But amid the strife of hungry candidates, at the right moment, some one sprung the name of Christian Stubbs upon the convention, and forthwith, "Honest Chris" was nominated by acclamation.

Another event of some importance to Stubbs: he and Deborah Dale were married and settled in a little cottage across the way from Mr. Goldwin; and so, two pairs of strong hands, and two heads full of common sense, and one heart, started on that companion voyage so old and yet always new.

Stubbs, a half breed, emphatically of the people, a child of the soil, as the electioneering phrase went, and a product of Riverton, had earned a well deserved popularity. Kind, neighborly, observant and open to light, reliable as the sun, having his own thoughts, and able upon occasion to keep them,—it was interesting, not to say anomalous,—the progress he had made. The tavern and stable boy that greeted Mr. Goldwin upon his first alighting upon Riverton, would scarcely recognize the present sheriff of Coon county. For all this, thanks in large measure to Mr. Goldwin, sculptor for eternity. It is needless to say that a warm attachment,—more—an indissoluble Christian bond, united these two men.

It happened about this time,—a clear winter night,—the stars all coldly gleaming on "the midnight still,"—that Stubbs was returning from a long and belating official trip into the country. A light snow lay in its virgin whiteness, and his horse trotted to the music of sleigh bells, and evidently, as he gained the environs of the city, with livelier remembrance of his manger. The supperless driver was in full sympathy with his horse. The lights of heaven never were brighter, but the lights of earth were extinguished: and even to the prosaic Stubbs, there was a consciousness of the mistery of night and a slumbering city. As he caught sight of a lone beam from his own home, he easily fancied himself sitting under its cheer.

As the sheriff drove to his barn, Deb, who had been napping in her chair caught the jingle of the bells, and it was but the work of a moment to place the light in the window where it would send a shining path into the stable, and to throw a shawl over her head, and trip out and pat "Nobby's" handsome neck.

"What's that? Fire! Fire!" shouted Chris, "I do declare, Mr. Goldwin's stable!" and away he ran, his mighty voice ringing out on the midnight those dread words, fire! fire!

Mr. Goldwin came flying out, but the flames seemed to leap at once to the roof, and he and Chris scarce had rescued the horse and conveyance, before the hay mow was one great blaze, and the victorious fire fiend shot columns of triumph straight skyward, in grinning mockery of man.

Standing as the barn did on an eminence, when compared with the large part of the town, this expensive bonfire commanded the view for a long distance; and soon the whole town was aroused to witness it. Fortunately it was one of those very still atmospheres;

not a ripple of air to turn aside the flames from their upward course.

Margaret shuddered as she realized that with an unfavorable wind, nothing could have saved their dear little home, and she lifted a thankful heart to Him who tempers the wind.

And now the question on every tongue was, "How came the fire?" Queries and surmises arose on every hand, agreeing at last only in this, that it could not be accidental. But then, what possible inducement could anyone have for applying the torch to the little barn of the minister? The mystery remained a mystery, and the fire had its day of town talk.

Dr. Bancroft, who said less and did more, headed a subscription, and soon had a purse made up for rebuilding Mr. Goldwin's stable. In a few weeks it was replaced, and the ill-boding event had disappeared from common thought.

But in the meantime, Stubbs had not forgotten it. He recalled an incident, which had it not been for the fire, he would probably never have dwelt upon again. A few moments before reaching home, and so a few moments before the fire, Stubbs had heard footsteps on the crispy snow, and looking in the direction of the sound he had seen O'Flannigan, the whisky seller, hurrying away, "across lots," toward his home. Chris remembered having asked himself at that time, "What can call Patrick out at this hour?" He had indeed fancied that the liquor dealer avoided him, and would have preferred to be unobserved.

Stubbs immediately had a private conference with Pierpont, and this incident which gave him as he thought a clew to the origin of the fire, he divulged to no one except Pierpont. Meanwhile Chris moved about, just as usual, among all classes of citizens, with eyes and ears open.

At length he heard one of O'Flannigan's patrons who had that day had a quarrel with the liquor dealer, drop certain ominous words, hints that he knew a thing or two about that barn burning. It was not long until, under pledge of protection and reward, Jake Peters, so he was called, made a statement under oath in the presence of Pierpont and Stubbs and Mr. Goldwin, to the effect that he had frequently heard O'Flannigan utter dark threats against "Priest Goldwin," who, he declared, with many cursings, would never keep his mouth shut, nor mind his own business; that he, the said O'Flannigan, never could speak of the minister but in terms of the vilest abuse; and finally, that on the night before the fire, after drinking heavily, O'Flannigan, with a wink and a mysterious air, informed his comrades, of whom Jake was one, that before many nights had passed, the priest's premises would be in ashes, and the priest would have the warmest time he ever had.

Then it should here be stated that Stubbs and Mr. Goldwin had discovered on the morning subsequent to the fire, a heap of combustibles suspiciously placed at one corner of Mr. Goldwin's dwelling house, and exactly where Mr. and Mrs. Goldwin and the sweet children were sleeping. The shavings were charred a little—evidently had been ignited, but for some mysterious reason had refused to serve a purpose so malicious.

It is unnecessary to particularize farther. Let it suffice to say that witnesses and evidence ample had been obtained, and every day the secret coil was tightening about Patrick O'Flannigan.

However Pierpont, and especially Mr. Goldwin, who had the good of the whisky dealers' family greatly at heart, urged that it would be wiser not to press matters to a criminal prosecution. So Stubbs quietly took means to apprise O'Flannigan that it was becoming very dangerous for him to remain in Riverton, and between two days the cowardly villain disappeared. His property proved to be very heavily encumbered with debts, and not long after was closed out at sheriff's sale. By Stubbs' adroit management, a little sum was saved from the wreck to the wife and daughter; both of whom before the year closed, Mr. Goldwin had the pleasure of welcoming to membership in the church.

It should be said here that the O'Flannigan stock of liquors was, agreeably to the desire of the mother and daughter, purchased at private sale, and for a nominal price, and then emptied into the canal,—alas for the finny tribe—while the roomy drinking place, which of course was located down amid "the madding crowd," was converted into a Methodist church; as Margaret said, "a very sound conversion." O'Flannigan himself was afterward fatally shot in a drunken broil in New Orleans. Thus ingloriously did his "star grow dim and disappear."

CHAPTER XXVI.

The second home-letter of Sibyl, the boarding school girl, was written to Isabel. We give here some extracts from it:

"Last night is the first time since coming here that I have gone to sleep on a dry pillow. Miss Furness, the teacher who has special scrutiny over us juniors, dignifies my homesickness with the name *nostalgia*, a common disease, not alarming she says. She is cold and stony hearted, and I cordially dislike her already."

"Yesterday Miss Dean, the principal, met me in the hall, and when she put her motherly arms around me, it warmed me all through. I just adore her, and I fairly bubbled over with happiness all day. And then, too, she is from Vermont, and knows, and praises the Goldwins."

"My room-mate, Sarah somebody, is a tall, lank, consumptive looking individual, and she has the cruelest black eyes that dart through and through me. She has butternut colored hair lying in deep waves or curves, and ending in stiff stubby curls; and if it were not for her eyes, she would seem more like a figure cut in stone than like anything which breathes. Lucy says if I had been a better girl, they wouldn't have put me with such a sphinx! Sarah is very religious though, and I s'pose she must be good, and I ought to be."

"I passed well in my examinations, excepting mathematics. I hate mathematics and always shall. In Latin I was away up, almost to the seniors, thanks to Mr. Goldwin. My Latin teacher praises me right before the class, and I go to my room nearly every day swelling with pride."

"For my first composition, I wrote a little description of the very funny time I had in getting here. And, just for greens, I put it in rhyme, and you ought to see how it took. Sarah glowered and called me frivolous, but Miss Marshall says she's proud of me, and calls me 'Sybil the poet.' But I say again, thanks to Mr. Goldwin for compelling me to write my thoughts, my very own, even though I did scowl at him. Tell John and Waxie to stand by their books and Mr. Goldwin."

"I take my walks with Lucy Darrow. She is so jolly—just bubbling over with fun. And now, for fear you'll think Lucy isn't the proper companion for me, I will tell you of Miss Marshall. She is a senior, and daughter of a missionary in India, and Lucy says she is to be married to a young man as soon as she graduates, and go with him as a missionary to India."

"The other afternoon, it being recreation

day, she met me in the hall, and seeing my eyes were red and swollen, she took my hand so tenderly and said, "Come down to my room. I am all alone this afternoon, and should be very much delighted with your good company."

"I forgot all about my promise to Lucy, and stalked right along to Miss Marshall's room, and never left it till the supper bell. In the pleasantest way imaginable, she drew from me exactly what I like to talk about, my own home people, and I told her everything except about Edward Mortimer. She told me all about her life in India, and the wretched people there, and the missionaries, and I almost felt as though I could be good enough to be a missionary, if Miss Marshall would take me with her, and let me stay with her."

"O, I must tell you of the gloomiest thing which happened when I had been here about a week. One morning at Chapel prayers, Miss Dean, after talking us all into tears, asked us all to rise. Then, that they might know better how to do us the most good, she asked those who were Christians to stand at the side of the room, and those who were not to be seated. Then Miss Furness and Miss Strong took down our names. For a moment I felt as if I was shot dead, and almost went with the goats. But no, dear Mama, I couldn't quite do that. I wasn't alone in these queer feelings. Dill Harkness, my dearest classmate, told me that if the earth had opened to swallow her up, she could not have felt more completely lost for this world and the next, than she did at that moment. Bless her dear heart. I do believe she is all right now."

"I hope our dear Mama's cough is better. If it isn't, don't tell me, for I sometimes feel as if I should never see her again. The dreadful study hour bell is ringing; so good bye my loved ones."

"Your Own Sibyl."

Our school girl naturally fell into the habit of writing, pen-talking as she called it, a few moments at a time, on almost every day. Every week or so she would gather up these journalistic pages and send them to the "dear, dear home people."

A school girl's letters are often accused of being frivolous and vapid. But no one ever laid that charge to Sibyl. Everybody in the home, the General, Mama, Isabel, George and John, and sometimes Mrs. Goldwin, as she happened in, or Mrs. Drake, warmed at once to anything from Sibyl. Here are a few paragraphs from a journal letter of later date:

"Feb. 3rd. Mama, my ears burned yesterday, for I know you were all thinking about me on my twentieth birthday. I cried a little over it, and before my eyes wer fairly dry, I went to Miss Marshall's room, and she moth-

me, and I spend two hours every Wednesday afternoon with her; and she entertains me so delightfully with the things she knows about India."

"I wish George, my dear absurd brother, could hear her, and he would never again say those stupid things about the "noble men and women" made so through their heathen religions. To be sure, there are noble men and women amongst the heathen, but then, bless me! they are so in spite of the false teachings of their religion. Even modern educated Hindoos, with few exceptions, have no real knowledge of the books of their own faith. Even their prayers taken from the ancient writings, which they repeat so devoutly, they do not understand, any more than our Stubbs understands Greek. Why, the people's gods are the biggest villains, so foul that Miss Marshall said she couldn't speak of them to me in plain English. And, Oh, the poor trodden upon women and widows! The father celebrates when a son is born, but the birth of a daughter sets him to wailing and cursing. Better be Waxie's dog, Mixer, than to be a Hindoo girl, if she must be left where the Hindoo religion puts her."

"I asked Miss Marshall whether she didn't think the Hindoo religion could be made over. 'Yes,' she replied, 'in a very restricted sense this could be done, by retaining the little in it that is Christ-like, dropping out all the rest, and in its place substituting pure Christianity.' Still, as she said, this would be like putting new cloth into an old garment."

"If these people can be brought to receive the simple gospel of Christ, the good seed will be in the soil, and the perfected tree is sure to come in good time.. Always when I leave Miss Marshall's room I feel as though there was a good deal to be done in my own heart."

"Feb 9th. Last Sunday our missionary collection was taken, and I wanted to give every cent of my money, and I did give five dollars, and I can just as well do without that new gown which you said I must have before going to New York for the summer vacation. Lucy says I look well in everything I put on, and the Pierponts are not so very 'uppish,' are they? Do thank Mr. Pierpont for getting me this invitation to visit his mother and sister."

"Speaking of clothes, I am reminded of Frank Mansfield, a girl from the city, who came here at the beginning of the year with trunks full of gowns, all in latest cut; and to see her parade them at supper and on recreation days and Sundays, you would think this a gay watering place, instead of a modest, sober minded school, nested amid river and hill scenery. For the first few weeks Frank had a cluster of admiring, not to say envious satellites about her, but one by one they faded away, as they found that she was all gowns and ribbons and jewels and no brains, and not a bit of that application to books which grows brains.

They insist here on neatness, and on good sense in dress, but display doesn't count for much. An unkempt, shabby girl hears from it. The girl that counts here is the one who studies, and who is trying to make of herself an all around useful woman, ready to fill a big niche, somewhere and sometime. Now, my dear pattern sister, you will smile to see that your infant sister, Sibyl, is getting rid of some of her nonsense. Anyway, if I don't make a hit somewhere or some time, it won't be because I don't try."

"Feb. 17th. I have kept my promise, Mama dear, and have never written a line to Mr. Mortimer, but I do love him, and feel so sure that you and father are entirely mistaken about his character. O, I can never promise to forget him."

"March 1st. Mother dear, I do hope I may never have the "big head," but I can just feel my brain growing every day. What a great world this is—oceans to do and to learn. Do you know, I so often think of Mr. Goldwin and his sermons. He always made God so big and so good, and our duty so large. I thought when I heard him I saw it all, but I didn't begin to. I see it now, and ever so many times I am reminded of things he said. Bless him, too, for suggesting this school to

Papa. Our principal, Miss Deane, is just wonderful."

Sibyl was an especial delight to Dr. Bancroft. Her buoyancy, vivacity and crystal sincerity exactly suited him, and as he discovered signs that her fellowship with Mortimer was ended, his heart warmed with delight. The longer he knew Mortimer, the more certain his conviction that Mortimer was a villain masquerading as a gentleman.

Mrs. Tupper, whose ill-turns had made frequent demands upon the professional skill of Dr. Bancroft, with difficulty could determine which she esteemed most, the physician or the man. As family medical adviser, Dr. Bancroft had been granted the freedom and sacred confidence of General Tupper's delightful home, a trust which he always preserved sacredly inviolate.

The Doctor had sometimes taken possession of Mr. Goldwin of a Monday morning, and tossed him about with him in his gig over the rough and often roadless country, until sermons and Sundays and parish problems were completely jolted out of his brain. Sometimes, while Dr. Bancroft stopped to dole out pills and powders, Mr. Goldwin scoured an adjacent grove or hazel patch for nuts. Sometimes he and the Doctor attempted some philosophical or theological nuts. Sometimes he called with the Doctor and sought to administer for a disease deeper and more invererate than any physical malady.

Once or twice Dr. Bancroft had picked up Jonas, the college boy, and pressed him, *nolens volens,* into a ten mile trip. Nothing suited this disciple of Esculapius better than to pump the college boy, unless it was to deal out to this same youth alopathic doses of wisdom in his own curt and oracular style.

But, on the afternoon now to be spoken of, Dr. Bancroft pursued an, if not more original, certainly more romantic course. He asked Miss Isabel Tupper to ride with him on his afternoon round of visits and be his hitching post. This invitation may appear to us to be somewhat abrupt, but not so to the parties most intimately concerned. The preliminary steps which led to this advance by the Doctor it is unnecessary that we should trace. It is enough to know that they had been taken. Such an invitation to ride coming from some persons would not have been heeded by Isabel, but Dr. Bancroft she believed in.

Dr. Bancroft knew "Bucephalus"—'Buce' is the name the steed knew—that he would stand in his tracks by the hour looking and listening for his master, and that when he said "Go," Buce would go. Not the slightest need of anyone to serve as hitching post. No one knew this so well as did the Doctor and the lady. How many innocnt pretexts there are in the world.

Its a two-wheeled affair—the vehicle. But why describe it further than to say that it is a Doctor's rig, and designed for two when desirable, and for hard service always. It has a boot,—the Doctor's special contrivance, ampler far than the ordinary, to enfold him from tip to toe when he has to face the warring elements.

Now a long hill to climb. Buce knows it and does himself proud. See him stretch his royal neck and plant his foot so decidedly. His master allows no cruel check rein on Buce.

Yonder in the hollow is a small cabin. Across lots, over pastures and stubble fields, through gullies and over roots and hummocks and knolls they go straight for that house. Once the Doctor has to let down the rails of a fence, but he sometimes enjoys making his own roads, and also quietly enjoys introducing Isabel to some of his roughest paths.

Here we are, dogs and all; dogs of all shades of yellow and of all ages; the poor man's usual canine comforts. There's a sick woman here. She's yellower than the dogs; been pining nearly a year. Three small children are playnig on the rattling, bare board floor. The Doctor's brusque cheer does her good, but despair dwells under her ribs. Early home comforts and refinements she left a thousand miles away, and she and her

Philip lit down here in the woods and commenced the struggle for life.

The Doctor's great heart inwardly groans. He knows medicine will never heal her; knows, too, that he'll never get one red cent for his pains, and yet that does not enter his thought.

Philip, dear man, comes in bringing tied up in his old torn handkerchief three little speckled green bird's eggs taken from a deserted nest, for his wife Mollie. Sometimes he ploughs up a family of young rabbits, and then he brings her one of the soft, round-eyed bunnies. Sometimes he brings a sweet scented twig or flower. She's always in his thoughts. He always brings a smile and a happy word; sometimes brings a bright smile to her wan cheek in return; but not always; often melancholy and suffering iron out the smiles. Philip plows, ponders, puzzles, sometimes prays; turns his back to the poor sufferer and weeps on his pillow in the darkness. There's one thing in that home which luxury and splendor often seek in vain,—one deep, strong, constant bliss. Philip and Mollie love each other. Such love, even when it passes to be only a memory is untold measures better than never to have loved. Somewhere, sometime, enriched and blossomed out, the two loves will be one flower.

The Doctor returns to the awaiting Isabel, and drives into the woods, and by a lonely narrow way, crosses over to another farm house. Here is old Mr. Barker leaning on his crooked staff. He is in one of his dismal moods, and in truth, it would be hard to say when he was in any other mood. Complaining was habitual with him, if not constitutional. "Grunting as usual," the neighbors said of him.

He regales you with one and the same tale; that nobody cares for him; he has outlived his usefulness; ought to have died twenty years ago; everybody has been against him all his life. In such a minor key Mr. Barker was always singing the same doleful song. He was always laying heavy blame upon his best friends, attributing all his failures to their interference. Even his very excellent wife, Prudence, who worked and worried and schemed and economized herself into the grave ten years ago, and who really supported herself and her four children, and her husband into the bargain; never received anything from him in return but grumbling and fault-finding.

The truth was, when left to follow his own plans, he was a timorous, bungling, blundering, belated performer, sure to end in wreckage. Visionary, irresolute, conceited old fellow, and born grumbler! His boys, fortunately embodied the mother's thrift and energy, and genius for affairs, and as they could ill brook the father's chronic whining and inefficiency, early in life pushed out into the world, and were making for themselves a very creditable record. Doctor Bancroft gives this patient a little flattery and a dose of bread pills and he's in high spirits.

Then the Doctor and Isabel drove four miles farther, passing but two houses on the road. Here was a sick woman, young Mrs. Armitage. She had been tenderly brought up in sight of Bunker Hill. Married somewhat against the wishes of her friends, and now settled away out here in the woods; an entire stranger and the nearest nighbor a Dutchman, a mile farther on! Often she saw not a human face for weeks, except that of her husband, Peter Armitage. This woman, this tender social flower, torn up and thrown out into this desert, was dying for want of society. Her unfeeling relatives in the East did not write to her oftener than once a year. Her rootlets seemed forced to feed on self. Who can wonder that mind as well as body became unhealthy?

Dr. Bancroft's cheerful face was better for her than all the medicine. What could he do for such a case? She needed a change; a complete change; something to set the wheels of mind and body going in a new track. And above all she needed an interchange of sympathies, a social reciprocity, a journey clear out of self into the lot of others, and of the great world.

Her husband, Peter, good natured soul, had what he could eat and drink and wear, slept well and could work all day and not feel tired the next day. He was happy, as were his fat horses. Why shouldn't he be? His horizon was bounded by his farm. He really understood the nature of his brindle cow much better than he did that of his wife. "Oh, ill-matched pair," said the Doctor.

During these professional pauses, Isabel sat behind Bucephalus and talked to him, got out and rubbed his nose and petted him, watched the birds and studied the bugs, and read her book and the clouds, and mused.

Her heart ached as the Doctor gave her briefly the sad condition of several of his patients, and her kind soul began to devise, as only a woman can, to send little delicacies and bright books and papers to Mollie and to Mrs. Armitage. Tears moistened Philip's eyes as he met Isabel a month afterward and tried to thank her.

A child was the Doctor's next care; a fine rollicking boy, who had been very sick. But now the Doctor was merry with delight, as he declared that Davie was fast coming up. Nature and wise treatment were winning the day, and the boy's face lighted beautifully when he saw the good Doctor.

Meanwhile, Isabel was quite absorbed in watching a beetle tugging away at a round lump of dirt twice his own size.

"What a parody on humanity," exclaimed the Doctor, as he saw the laboring insect.

"In the comparison I'm not sure but the bug has the best of it," said Isabel. He seems in his place and contented and happy; that is bug-happy."

"When it comes to mankind," observed the Doctor, "it does seem as though all were in the 'winter of their discontent,' and I might add, each expecting it to be made glorious summer by the coming of some sun of York."

"Well, Doctor, is that a parody on Shakespeare or on humanity? I rather think it is both."

"But," said the Doctor, who had been visiting disappointed people, and was still under the shadow, "it does seem as though the great majority of men never get beyond discontent and long expectancy—one long winter. Their glorious summer tarries—so far as human vision can see, never comes. If their sun of York comes, he doesn't bring summer."

"Oh, Doctor Bancroft, you are in a cavern. Come! Here's a sun which does bring summer. Come out into the sunlight. There are more people reasonably well and happy, than there are sick or discontented. Doesn't one of our poet singers teach that, 'take the whole year round, there's no more night than day?'"

"Averaging the world, Isabel, what you say may be true; averaging my patients, I fear it is not true. Who has the truth?

Who sees correctly? Who is clear of all prejudice? These farmers, for instance, think the carpenter with his regular working hours better off than they; and the carpenter thinks the farmer with his standing by and seeing things grow is better off than he; and half Riverton, I dare say, envies me my supposed leisure and irresponsible don't-care life. Little they dream what I see and what I carry."

"That's it, Doctor, everyone looks through his own little gimlet hole. But, what's the remedy? What's to cure all this prejudice? Isn't it in one word, love? Love opens the eyes, clears the vision, sweeps away dark obstructing walls. Faith, hope, love, but the greatest of these is love."

The Doctor, who in reality did not altogether adopt his own reasoning, was silent for a moment. He was admiring the wisdom and sunlight of Isabel's thoughts. Then he said, "You are right, Isabel, profoundly right; and I always in my speculations have to come to this: the One Divine Physician, who was love incarnate, saw without prejudice; saw all the disappointment, all the sorrow, yet He permitted it. He did not extinguish it. He simply showed us love. This way lies liberty, this way light, this way life."

"And now for the last call of this trip," said the Doctor, "and then I can throw off till—till—"

"Till the next summons," rejoined Isabel.
"That's about it," he replied. . "Isabel, how would you like to be a physician?"

"Never! Never that for me, Doctor."

They are out on the old "Michigan road," smooth wheeling; "Come Buce," and away they whirl. Now they are in the outskirts of the town, and at Uncle Billy Newman's door.

He's a battered and worn out piece of furniture, loose and creaking at every joint. Life has gone with him but roughly. Wife and children are gone save one elderly daughter, Cordelia, who dutifully cares for her father's comfort. For years he was Tim the blacksmith's best help, right hand man, main dependence. But now for a year he has been shut in, and much of the time bed-ridden. Rheumatism has pinched and corded him up.

As the Doctor softly opens the door, Uncle Billy is singing to himself:

"A charge to keep I have,
A God to glorify."

"Good morning, Doctor. I was just looking for you. The rheumatism gave me a hard twist last night, but let up a little toward morning."

"Yes, Uncle Billy, I heard you humming the good old hymn; I see that joy cometh in the morning."

"O, yes, Doctor, the morning's coming; bless the Lord for that, but meanwhile, he gives me songs in the night, too."

Everybody liked Uncle Billy Newman. Hawkins and Tim, sneer as they always would, and pretend to see some selfish motive in everybody, never had a word to say against Uncle Billy.

"How far that little candle shines," said the Doctor almost involuntarily, as he looked admiringly upon his patient.

"Doctor," said Uncle Billy, the bright twinkle in his eye, "I was a thinking last night that the Lord was a snuffin' my poor candle."

"So that it might give better light," rejoined the Doctor. "Like David, you sing of the Lord that lighteth your candle."

"Doctor, Cordelia's just been a reading to me the precious words of Jesus: 'Neither pray I for these alone, but for them also which shall believe on me through their word.' O, to think that the blessed Lord has prayed for poor twisted up Billy Newman."

The Doctor said, as he rose to go; "Billy, you always have the true medicine close by you."

"Meat and drink, Doctor; meat and drink. Bread of which if a man eat, he shall never hunger."

Doctor Bancroft told Isabel he always felt in this house that things were reversed. He was the patient, and Uncle Billy the physician, "and," said he, "he always helps me."

The afternoon has gone and they are come to the brow of the hill north of Riverton and overlooking town, rivers and country wide. There's the new court house with its image of Justice poising the scales in serene majesty on its dome. There are several churches and school buildings, bridges, mills, warehouses, several blocks devoted to merchandise and traffic, homes of thrift, comfort and competence; and away to the eastern limit of the growing city, on a handsome knoll, conspicuous are the rising walls of what is to be the county seminary; the joy and care of Mr. Goldwin. Intersecting or surrounding all are field and forest and stream, and all shimmering in the light of the setting sun.

Here they paused, and Doctor Bancroft said, "Such scenes are blessed sermons to me. When I reach this point at edge of evening, I always stop and look into the sunset."

After a moment of silence, the Doctor turned his clear blue eyes full upon Isabel, and said, "So, you are sure you do not wish to be a doctor?"

"Very sure," was the reply.

"Well, Isabel, will you be the next thing to that, a doctor's wife?"

Isabel paused and blushed like the sunset, but she did not say "no."

Nearly a week went by, and, with General Tupper's family carriage, and Isabel at his side, Doctor Bancroft repeated his round of calling upon his chronic invalids, dispensing everywhere the fitting remedy with abundance of good cheer.

With woman's tact and invention, Isabel overcame the protests of Mrs. Armitage and her irresponsive husband, and the slender little invalid was most comfortably robed, and with the Doctor's tender and gentle assistance and the strong rough aid of the inwardly protesting husband, she was lifted to a half reclining position on the back seat of the Tupper carriage. "We'll bring her back with roses on her cheeks," said the Doctor, as they waved a good bye.

A week at Mrs. Tupper's, another with Mrs. Drake, and a third with Mrs. Goldwin, and sure enough there were roses on the once pale face of Mrs. Armitage, and the bloodless lips became like buds of promise, and the limp attenuated hands took on color and vitality, and it seemed as though a new soul looked out of her eyes; as indeed there did. For these three weeks of rest, social cheer and quiet thinking, brought not only physical but spiritual renewal, and Mrs. Armitage ceased to quarrel with what had seemed a frowning Providence, and saw behind the cloud the smiling face of her loving Father. This very world but yesterday thought so cramped and drear, was now to her like a native clime and not a foreign land.

When Mrs. Armitage returned to her husband it was with a package of congenial books in one hand, and a root from Mrs. Goldwin's white moss rose bush in the other. But, better still, she brought home on her cheeks the pink roses of girlhood.

Nor, indeed, had the three weeks of lonely life been lost upon the husband. The brief separation had moved him to reflection, stirred his mind and softened his heart. When the wife returned there was an unwonted warmth in their embrace. They looked into each other's eyes with a completer and sweeter understanding of each other than ever before.

We do not mean to say that in every respect the two were one. This could not be. A fiddle of but one string cannot vibrate with all the music of a well strung harp. Before long husband and wife were regularly seen on the Sabbath in Riverton church. Books, flowers and the year round bloom of kind thoughtfulness and loving deference, each to the tastes and especial prefernces of the other, and more, an open and obeyed Bible, transformed this home which had been a prison into the "House Beautiful."

Miss Isabel was often seen now sharing with Doctor Bancroft his rides, and her loving and timely ministries often brought the very cup of healing which was life. Now abideth Faith, Hope and Love. But the greatest of these is Love.

CHAPTER XXVII.

Five years later, look again within the home of Robert and Julia Armitage. You'll find there a pair of four year old twin boys, Bruce and Brace. It is early morning and the mother has left them sleeping in their trundle bed, and stolen softly out to start the domestic wheels for the day. Robert is already out feeding the stock and milking Shiny and Brindle.

Breakfast over, and the good housewife soon has her hands in the dough; and Robert is sent to inquire into a disturbance in the trundle bed. Somehow the morning nap of the twins is much abbreviated, and to his dismay he discovers them jumping up and down and playing horse on the parental bed. One fat boy jumping on a bed is too many, but two are worse than Bedlam. It is a strange physical or psychological fact, that what one of the twins does, the other must always help him do. The father picks them up, one in each arm, and chucks them down pretty decidedly on the lounge, with strict orders to sit still till Mama comes.

But he has hardly turned his back, before the irrepressibles are dancing on the lounge, trying the springs..

Soon Bruce is ominously still. What is he doing? Brace makes it his immediate business to find out. Ah! the young hopeful has found a little hole in the plastering and he's very busy making it larger. As Bruce prefers to monopolize this employment, Brace feels injured, deprived of his rights, yells out "Mama," at the top of his voice, and runs and kicks and pounds the door till he brings Mama. Bruce well knows that he's a law-breaker and runs away to the farthest corner of the room.

With many devices of motherly ingenuity and story telling, the effervescing pair are finally dressed, both with clean faces and clean pinafores, and covered with mother's kisses. After a big bowl each, of creamy country bread and milk, the mother and boys indulge in one of the richest feasts of the day. Although Mrs. Armitage's house work was never at an end, yet she felt that some things could wait, but that her growing boys could not wait. So, she took them every morning, before she sent them out to play, for a little visit, as she expressed it. She told them of the dear Jesus, who loved little children, and whose kind eye followed them all day as they played; and she planted many a good seed in those tender hearts. Meanwhile, they hug and kiss "pretty Mama," pull down her hair and rub their fat hands all over her face,—hands so white and plump that they look like biscuits with pegs stuck in them. She gives to each a "tookie," and says, "Going to be good all day?" "Yes, dood all day," they both echo, and out the innocent mischiefs run.

Brace spies a little switch which he would like to use on old Towser. So, he drops his nibbled cookie for a moment to pick up the little whip. Bruce, whose cookie has gone the way of most cookies, snatches up the dropped sweet meat and makes off with it. Brace armed with justice and his switch, pursues the little peculator, determined to reclaim his stolen property, and chastise Bruce instead of Towser. "Thrice armed is he who has his quarrel just." Bruce ran well for a time, but there's many a slip. Some luckless stick or stone trips him, and he falls, and Brace on top of him. They indulged in a lively set to. Brace comes off first best with the first round, and is ready to fight to the finish, but Bruce ignominously takes to his heels, and leaves his antagonist master of the ring.

Brace, quite elated, looks about him for more worlds to conquer, and thinking it would be fine fun to paddle in the water trough, climbs by a block of wood and reaches with his chubby hands the edge of the trough, when over it tips, and Brace enjoys—hardly enjoys—receives a cold shower bath,—water and more water in his face and down his body. First a chilling pause, then an outcry, loud and louder. "What under the sun!

my child, my child! For pity's sake! What have you done?" exclaims the terrified mother, as she snatches up the drenched youngster, and rushes him into the house. She soon has him stripped and rubbed down, and put to bed in disgrace. This irrepressible seems at this moment so submissive and penitent, and the wages of transgression have beeen paid so amply and promptly, that the mother does not find it in her heart to give the scolding she has ready.

And now Mrs. Armitage straightened up, drew a long breath, smoothed down her somewhat disturbed hair, and repaired once more to the kitchen. "Pooty, pooty, Mama!" were the first words which greeted her in that direction, and there was Bruce standing in a chair by the kitchen table, with both hands in the tomato basket, making pomace, and squeezing and squirting the juice in all directions. His clean pinafore! Alas! Alas! "I declare! If this isn't too much for anything!" broke out the tired mother. First she wanted to scold, and then she wanted to cry, and then she wanted to laugh.

These children, it was to be observed, though so similar, were nevertheless quite dissimilar, as added years evinced. Brace was always tumbling headlong into something, and always bawling and crying. Bruce was more cautious, and if he fell into trouble did very little crying. Brace wanted you to pet him. Bruce did not thank you for the petting. Brace would fall down and then cry for somebody to pick him up. Bruce would cry and kick if anybody picked him up. Brace told everything which ever went through his mind. Bruce seldom told others his mind or his plans.

"Here it is almost noon. Dear me! How shall I ever get on?" But the blessed woman did get on, and grew in saintliness by many a lesson in patience and self mastery, and by many a comforting and reassuring word from Robert.

The day is done. Evening veils this world and unveils the worlds above. The steam engine twins at last are still. Mama has heard them repeat in concert, "Now I lay me," for if she has them repeat it singly, before the first would finish, the other would be asleep. Side by side now in their little bed fast asleep!

Mrs. Armitage has dropped down in the rocking chair by the open front door—almost the first easy moment she has had during the day. Robert, the last chores done, sits down on the door step at his Julia's feet. How he laughs as she gives him some of the day's exploits of the twins. A few moments for loving thoughts and words, and two tired mortals follow their children to bed.

"Julia," says Robert, as he looks at the sleeping cherubs, "We're poor enough, the Lord knows, but there isn't gold enough in all the round world to buy those boys."

We have taken a peep five years in advance into the Armitage home. We shall have more than our hands full if we essay to take up all the evidence of enlargement, increase and progress in these Riverton households.

He who should really write the daily history of a home, of its thoughts, its hopes, its fears, its struggles, its sacrifices, its battles with temptation, its prayers, its defeats, its victories, its life-framing, its sculpturing for eternity,—he who could really tell us the real story of a single home for a year, much more for a lifetime, would never want for reader or audience. His story would far outrival the most wondrous fiction.

Men talk and write and sing about the "decisive battles of the world;" always some Marathon or Waterloo or Gettysburg. They forget that the greatest Thermopylaes and Rubicons witnessed on earth are those not witnessed save by the One All Seeing—such as John Wesley's mother alone on her knees in prayer, or David Livingstone kneeling at midnight in his tent in the jungles of Africa, or the youth, Abraham Lincoln, prostrate and weeping the lone night away by his mother's grave, or the battle of many a mighty soul, the secret conflict at the parting of the ways, between eternal right and wrong.

We see and mark the marshalling and pomp and pageant, and hear the clash and clangor, chronicle whatever is "full of sound and fury," but the decisive battles of time, of eternity, occur behind all this outward, far behind the stage where the god Appearances is the throned and worshipped. We men count that cause which is only effect; place the monument on the wrong field, and the crown on the wrong head. We transscribe history! Outlines, merest sketches, ill proportioned, absurdly arranged and without perspective; as like the real as the Chinese doll is like a living soul! He who should really give us the record of the experience-life of a single home for a generation; say rather he who could give it; he would well be called the historian. His volume would always be in market.

In this, our sketching of a life story, naught so presumptuous do we attempt. But we must tarry here a moment within the open door of the home of Mr. and Mrs. Goldwin. At the date to which we have for a moment advanced, this home is enlivened by two auburn-haired boys. The younger of the two, Alton, has a classical face, and long curls, and eyes where roguery ambuscades. Perpetual motions these boys are, mind and body; incessantly prying into the philosophy of things.

Across the way, in Sheriff Stubb's happy home, are two bouncing children; two first class specimens of healthy, hearty baby beauty, "and not too bright and good for human nature's daily food." Do you recognize Deb, the jolly off-hand never worrying Deb, now that she is the wary care-taking planning mother? She and Chris. are waxing manly and womanly every day, and don't know it.

Stubbs is in almost every day at Mr. Goldwin's, and the boys are always climbing on his boots or his shoulders for a ride. The oldest one, Max, rattles off his primer to Chris. like a fanning mill; knows the story under each picture, repeats it word for word, and just as well with the pages upside down.

The other day Alton was, wonderful to relate, all at once invisible and very still. Search was instituted and his mother who knew he must be in mischief, found him sitting on the floor behind the door with the scissors clipping off his handsome curls, for the poor youngster thought "curly head" was a term of opprobrium. This innocent sacrifice of beauty threw the household into mourning.

Dr. Bancroft happened in today, and set down a basket of large ripe tomatoes for Mrs. Goldwin. Little curly head watched his opportunity and fell to examining the contents of the basket, pitching the tomatoes on the floor. Presently he called out "peachers, peachers!" and his eyes opened like saucers; and sure enough, one of Dr. Bancroft's jokes, a basket of splendid peaches, with a few tomatoes to conceal them.

This boy Alton, boy No. 2, little curly head, precocious little explorer, could shed the curls, but there was a deal of brain hidden away under them, and, as after years disclose him, he is scholarly, of keen and correct literary discernment, and a studious and devoted champion of truth.

While we are considering the younger Goldwins, let us take a leap of several years, and again step into the home of the Riverton minister. How Max and Alton have grown —grown physically, mentally and morally. They are fairly sprouting with arithmetic and Latin and high ideals. And how patriarchal they have become: for there are now three who are younger than they; two boys, hair of a chestnut brown, Alex and Earnest by name, and, most precious of all the family jewels, little Sister Miriam.

These Goldwin children are decidedly unlike, each after his own kind; no goody, goody about them; nothing angelic; large installments of Adam and Eve in them. The father often playfully said to the mother, "Margaret, I must preach all that I ever expect to on family government, while the children are young, yes, very young."

"Not quite all John, dear," said Margaret, "you are likely to have opportunity to do a little experience preaching, and that's the kind of preaching which takes effect, you know."

To characterize the young Goldwins, we

must somewhat blend child and adult life. Alex, alert of mind and body, struck while the iron was hot, and always kept the fires burning, and to a sacred purpose. Every feature of his mobile face beamed forth the intelligence and graciousness which lighted mind and heart. Buoyant and enkindling, he was his mother over again. Eager he was, ambitious, magnetic, tactful, a friend to everybody and everybody's friend.

Ernest was deliberate, weighty, stable, encyclopaedic; thoughtfully, conscientiously taking his position, he was not easily dislodged. He was good humored, ready at repartee, open as the day, hungering to serve the lowest and neediest, and the very stuff to make a cheerful martyr to principle.

Miriam was the special pet, and for her the chivalrous brothers were ever ready to take up arms. She seemed to come right up; took her place, even with her brothers, and kept it. What others labored for, she arrived at by swift intuition; studied the same branches as her brothers, and soon mounted to be equal to any position; just the one she was for any emergency; all her life the staff which never breaks whatever may lean on it. Versatile, well poised, rich in gleanings from the broad fields of letters, of wide charity and large grasp, she came gracefully to fill the measure of the all-around woman.

Here the young Goldwins are, turning the dining room into a play room. Ernest plays preacher, mounts a chair, and in stunning tones reads the hymn; while his undevout audience mimic or criticize, applaud or scold, as the mood inclines. Soon all are engaged at the top of their lungs, each determined to be heard; and then the long suffering Dominie springs out of his study chair, comes to the head of the stairs and stamps, and shouts "Stop, boys, stop, stop!" Suddenly the crescendo becomes diminuendo, and the youthful actors have scampered into the back yard, where there is more room for noise, and the "peaceful war" goes on.

One night Alex. came to his mother with a perplexed countenance, and said, "Mama, it don't seem to me that God always hears us when we pray."

"What makes my boy think that?"

"Why, because, I just beg Him for lots of things, and He never sends them to me."

"Well, dear," said the wary mother, "come, lets talk that over a little. You remember that yesterday you asked me to let you go swimming with Bob Hanchett, and I had to say 'no.' This morning you asked me to let you children have a basket of lunch, and go up to the 'fountains' for the day, and I said 'yes.' So, God sometimes answers 'no,' and sometimes answers 'yes;' just as He sees will be the better for you. Isn't that right, my boy?"

"Yes, Mama; God, I s'pose, knows best, but sometimes I forget to put that into my prayer."

One evening Mr. and Mrs. Goldwin were having a little twilight talk with the children about the Bible. Ernest asked, "Papa, how did God tell the men how to write in the Bible? Did He just holler down out of the sky and tell them?"

"No," spoke up little Miriam, "that wasn't the way. I'll tell you how He did it. He just put it into their thoughts."

"There," quietly remarked Mr. Goldwin. "Miriam, in half a dozen words, has given as good a definition of Biblical inspiration as all the theologians."

It was amusing to hear this group of children talk over everything, sometimes with themselves, sometimes with Papa and Mama; everything from Robinson Crusoe or Arabian Nights or Aesop's Fables in the Latin reader, or Caesar's Commentaries, or Zenophon's Retreat of the Ten Thousand, or Shakespeare; to the last sermon, or Biblical poser or quandary, or lecture, or debate, or political speech. Each youth had an opinion and was not slow to express it, and woe to any bubble of conceit. It was quickly pricked. A rare education it was to be a member of this family.

A few years more, and the Goldwin children were singing, "We are seven;" and and while it was not "And two are gone to sea," it was, and two are gone to college, that is Max and Alton, and two more, a boy and girl, have come to keep up the infant class.

Of these two, the boy, Roswald, was, taking his composite photograph, mercurial, sensitive, now on the heights, now in the depths, generous, affectionate, a knight of the heroic olden time, chivalric, eager to do or die for honor's sake, aspiring, classical, sometimes poetic and electric and eloquent.

The girl, youngest of the seven, was called Lucille, or, briefer and oftener, Lux. "The last still loveliest," she completes and crowns the whole. God filled her soul so full of His blessed sunshine, that it wove its skeins of gold through and through her waving hair, and danced in her starry eyes. Elastic, suasive, uplifting, prevailing, she was enough to put hope under the ribs of cold despair. Self-forgetful, self-sacrificing, she grew to move through this hospital world almost with the magic touch of a Florence Nightingale. "Loving herself last," she was from first to last, loved of all who knew her.

It grew to be unwritten law in this Goldwin home, that each child should read the Bible through before reaching the age of seven years, and then receive on his seventh birthday a handsome Bible. Sometimes sitting beside the mother while she was working, sometimes beside an older brother, the little ones daily read their "chapters." Many were the knotty questions awakened by the readings,—some to be answered, and some to be passed on to a later day.

Industrious and nobly emulous, college

was one of the hill tops toward which these brothers, and sisters too, set their faces. Eagerly they gathered and saved their little earnings, and "college" was written on them all.

Happy home, where good works abounded, and where they must needs be mixed with much faith, for many times the wherewithal for educating the children was not in sight, and present only to the strongest faith. In securing an education, some of the children literally worked their own way. All of them encountered many an "iron gate," but when they had pushed clean up to it, somehow it opened to them.

One of these times of emergency, when the iron gate seemed bolted against every human ingenuity or resource, Mr. Goldwin received a letter from a gentleman in Brooklyn, N. Y., containing this question, "Are you the John Goldwin who graduated from Andover Theological Seminary in 1829? If you are, I should like to communicate with you on a matter which to me is of great importance."

This letter seemed very strange, mysterious; and out of the flood of recollections it called up, Mr. Goldwin could fasten on nothing which solved the mystery. But he replied to the letter writer promptly that he was doubtless the John Goldwin whom he wanted to find. Back came a reply and a draft for Mr. Goldwin calling for $150, and the following explanation, "You will perhaps remember losing a sum of money, about the time you graduated from Andover Seminary. You probably do not know how you lost it. I do know. You laid your purse, containing $19.00, on the counter in the book store, and you never saw it again. I am the guilty man. I stole your purse. The money I enclose is, I believe, the principal and the interest for these many years. In all this time, I have never thought of my wicked part in this transaction without some twinges of conscience. But not until now has the enormity of my guilt driven me to confession and reparation. God knows that I am a penitent man, and I think he has forgiven me. Will you forgive me?"

Now, this conscience money came to Mr. Goldwin's pocket, at the very time when Lucille ought to return for a second year of study at the Seminary. So, prayer and providence by a strange way opened this gate as they did also many others in the history of the Goldwins.

After all, it was not so much the formal teaching as it was the living pervading spirit, the pure, spiritual air of this home of the Riverton minister, which made it so blsesed. Everything about it seemed to say, "It is our greatest privilege, not as it is called to rise in the world, but to better the world." Happy home where the temptations and tears are chased away by patience, prayer, heavenly vision and divine cheer, and where love hangs a rainbow on every cloud. In that home beautifully, beneficiently grows and opens the fragrant calyx of character.

CHAPTER XXVIII.

At the Female Seminary, vacation was about to give the hard taxed brain cells that change which is rest, when Miss Dean rapped at Sibyl's door. Hardly had the latter time to wonder what she had done to require a personal visit from the principal, before Miss Dean exclaimed, "I have news for you, Sibyl, straight from home; a note from your father, introducing the bearer, Mr. Mortimer, and requesting that he be permitted to escort you to New York."

For an instant Sibyl threw up both hands in mute amazement. She was white and then she was crimson. Then she broke out, "Mr. Mortimer! A letter from Papa! What, Miss Dean! you don't mean it.!"

"I do mean precisely that," replied Miss Dean, her eyes twinkling with amusement, as she held up a neatly folded letter.

"Dear blessed old Papa! Isn't that just perfectly lovely!" Then, her eyes glowing with a thousand lights, "Where is Mr. Mortimer?"

"In the East Parlor."

Sibyl did not ask to look at the letter, but away two feet bounded to find Mr. Mortimer.

He was pained to say that his time was

extremely limited. Only two days until Saturday, and then he must take passage for London; just received word; pressing business; must go. But oh! he must see his darling Sibyl once more, and her good father had so kindly granted him the opportunity.

Two hours later and the overjoyed, rapturous girl and her ardent suitor were on their way to New York. Then, by degrees, Mr. Mortimer began adroitly to unfold to her his wish, his plan. This was a very sudden summons. He must go by the first steamship; and could not tell when he could return. Perhaps not for six months; perhaps not for a year. A year without seeing the angel of his life! Cruel thought. He could not endure it. Before leaving Riverton he said he had had a long talk with her father and mother, and everything was perfectly adjusted now. They had come to see eye to eye. Both your father and mother, he said, have so unreservedly and lovingly given you to me. We belong to each other now, dear Sibyl. God meant us for each other. Sibyl's heart was so full she could not utter a word.

Then Mr. Mortimer suggested the question, why should not Sibyl go with him to England? He was sure that her father, generous soul, if he was here, where he could know all, would instantly give his approval. They would write to him and explain the whole matter. And as for the school, the Seminary, a few months of travel in the Old World, with him as pilot, would be worth to her a thousand seminary educations.

Poor bewildered, enchanted Sibyl! What could she say? Under his magnetic spell, she seemed to acquiesce. Such a lovely plan—how could she reject it? But she would think it over and decide when they reach New York. Perhaps Mrs. Pierpont would know exactly how to advise her.

Arrived in the crowded Gotham, and about taking carriage to the hotel, Sibyl observed a lady standing near and eyeing them closely. Everything about her carried the impression of intelligence, refinement and elegance. Apparently, as she was about to step into her close carriage, her attention had been arrested and fastened upon Mortimer and Sibyl. An exclamation, evidently, was upon her lips, and scarcely could be suppressed. Such a look as she riveted upon them! So full of surprise, sorrow and indignation! Sibyl could but mark it.

However, she would the next moment have forgotten it, had she not observed that Mortimer no sooner saw the lady, than disturbed, confused, almost black in the face, he siezed Sibyl's arm and hurried her away, and handed, almost pushed her, into the nearest cab, thrust himself in and shut the door with a heavy bang, as though he was shutting out Apollyon himself. This done, Mortimer, greatly relieved, wiped his forehead and muttered something about being always glad to escape from the insolent hotel runners and hackmen.

That evening Mortimer devoted himself to Sibyl; and lavished on her all his subtle art. Never did he seem more fascinating. He was in the high flush of success, and sentiment and fancy obeyed his slightest bidding. Sibyl seemed to be in a delicious dream. From him an influence emanated which exhilerated, and yet held her like a pleasant intoxication; like an atmosphere rolling in gentle waves from some elysian island, and steeped in aroma of elect spices and aromatics of eternal summer-land. The hours stole softly by in velvet sandals.

"Tomorrow, my precious darling, we will step across the avenue into the Rev. Dr. Winchester's church; he is an old acquaintance of mine; and he will formally and sacredly seal the union in which our hearts now and forever live. This vision of soul, this discovered harmony, this blessed mystery of love! Infinite Benevolence fills the cup and presents it to our lips. This sacrament of our hearts—refuse it? Madness! Revolt against Heaven! Tomorrow night, my love, we'll bound o'er the billows for 'Merrie old England.' So saying, he bent over Sibyl and kissed her, and bade her good night.

Did the vision of that sweet trustful face follow him with uncomfortable suggestions?

Did it arouse an accusing voice? Self absorbed, he paced up and down the corridor. As he paused under the lights his face betrayed the secret debate; soon dismissed, however.

He said within himself that unquestionably he was really doing the best thing for Sibyl. Indeed, he was giving her rare opportunity. Riverton! That dull frontier, backwoods town! Or the prim propriety, the bondage of a boarding school! He chuckled as he told himself how he was about to emancipate this rare bird. He was opening the cage and giving her the freedom of the world, and he fairly patted and caressed himself in admiration of his perfect scheme. He had discovered the diamond. He could give it its fit setting. He would make the world bow down before it.

Did he dream that an eye was at that moment glowering upon him out of the shadows of the farther end of the corridor? Truth to say, he did once fancy a form dread and strangely intrusive, flitting yonder in the shadow. "I did see her," he exclaimed almost aloud, and stared with bated breath.

"Ha! ha! These spectres of the mind!" he said; and shook himself and flung out his arms, as though tossing aside an unwelcome dream. As a prop to his self-complacency over his "philanthropic scheme," and as a means of Beelzebub casting out Beelzebub, he walked back into the wine and billiard rooms.

Sibyl was still seated where Mortimer left
 cious cloud-enswathement should break, and
lest the angel almoners of this ethereal bliss
should be affrighted. She shrank from return to common "garish day."

But at length, as she came down to where
she felt her feet still touch the dull, cold
earth, a fever of thoughts and emotions oppressed her. She arose, straightened herself
to her full height, pressed both hands to her
forehead, as if recalling herself to the unvarnished real, and approached the window,
opened it, and stepped upon the balcony.
The air blowing up the harbor and ladened
with the strength of the sea, fanned and
relieved her hot temples. She gazed upon
the lights skirting the long, long street, till
in the distance they seemed at last to mingle
and blend with the lamps of the sky. She
keenly reflected that she was alone in that
great Babel which resteth neither night nor
day; one lone drop among the countless.
She seemed feeling about like one arousing
from a dream, and grasping after the link
between the strange present and the past.
She wandered back—it seemed a long distance back—to the little room in the seminary. She almost listened for the retiring
bell. But swift thought could not tarry
there. Those mute passionless stars! She
had grown to know them and love
their fidelity as they watched above her fath-

er's and mother's door.' O, if she could only fly this moment to mother's door, mother's arms. "Mama, dear, dear, Mama! Let me bury my face in your lap once more and tell you all!" and her eyes were blind with tears.

Sibyl had been walking quite unconsciously till she had reached almost the end of the long balcony, when she suddenly paused arrested by the sound of loud and boisterous vociferations. Evidently they proceeded from the gaily lighted billiard rooms beneath. Above the clink of glasses and the click of balls, arose, along with fumes of liquor and cigars, the hilarious ejaculations and unseemly expletives of a voice which instantly startled her, and fastened her attention. She leaned on the railing and listened. Yes, she was sure it was the voice of Mortimer. Could it be? The same voice which but an hour ago held her by its bewitching spell, now grated harshest discord to her feelings. No nature could be more foreign than hers to suggestions coarse and grovelling.

Slowly she turned back to her room, closed and fastened her window, drew the curtains and tried to think; dropped upon her couch and buried her face in her hands. Doubts were stealing into her paradise. Suspicion was fastening his venomed fang in her breaking heart. The question, "Am I decieved?" forced itself upon her, and cruelly pierced her. A dreadful sense of solitariness and perplexity crushed her; her frame shook like a leaf in the winter blast, and the tempest of conflicting emotions broke into a pitiless sobbing rain. She was where the ways part, and never was she so alone; so weak, so blind, and no halt; driven to choose and plunge. Was she alone? There was one outlet, one refuge; there always is.

She cried, "O, God, I am thy child. Lead me. Lead me."

Suddenly there was a rap at her door. The servant brought Sibyl a note. She turned up her light and read:

"Dear Madam: Permit a stranger this word. I am no stranger to him who accompanies you. Edward Mortimer is my husband; Married Apr. ———, 183—. As fortune—rather, Divine Providence, would have it, I saw you as you first set foot in New York, and as you hastened into the cab. Nor did Mr. Mortimer escape seeing me. As confirmation strong, look at the hotel register. He has reported his name as 'Mort Edwards and sister.' Thin disguise! Praying that no one may be so deceived as I have been, nor innocently suffer as I have suffered, and hoping it is not too late to save you from my fate, I am

"Elizabeth Olmstead Mortimer."

"Married! Mortimer married!" shrieked Sibyl, and unable to read another word, blinded, almost stunned, fell into a chair as if struck down by a deadly blow. Then, suddenly, and with all the resoluteness of the noble woman that she was, she sprang to her feet and almost fiercely snatched up the little bit of paper and read, and read again; and then, passing her hand across her forehead as one coming out of a horrid dream, slowly read and weighed each sentence—each word. Her mind flashed. She saw all—understood all. That seemingly inexplicable confusion of Mortimer; that precipitate plunge into the carriage; that woman's gaze upon them of cloud and fire; here was the key to all this; Mortimer's wife! "He such a deceiver! Arch deceiver! O, that cannot be; it cannot be. And yet—" she suddenly arose, drew her wrap about her, and firmly descending the marble stairs to the office, consulted the hotel register. There it was, midway on the page, his writing; she knew it only too well:

Mort Edwards, Room 39
And Sister, Room 18

The clerk looking up unconcernedly from his desk as Sibyl moved away, could but mark the indignation which burned in that face of rare loveliness, and appeared in every movement of that agile form.

With the first promise of daylight, a closely muffled lady was to be seen giving directions to a coachman to drive her to No. 28 W. Fortieth street, a location which at that time was at the extreme northern limit of the city. "How far?" she asked. "Better'n a mile, Ma'm." "Very well, take me there as quickly as you can."

"What a face," thought the coachman, "Never saw a prettier in my born days; but there's trouble there;—ah, trouble's in the like of them faces;" and the philosophical driver cracked his whip.

Sibyl sank into her seat and sobbed piteously. For hours she had not shed a tear. Indignation tossed her on its topmost sea. But now, once free—the toils broken and she escaped; alone; no Robinson Crusoe ever felt more alone; and now forced to seek an asylum among strangers, tears seemed her only resort.

Daniel Pierpont's mother, for it was to her Sibyl was going, was a plain, unpretending, modest woman, with not a few legends of hard experience written on her brow and around her honest eyes; and across her storm beaten features sympathy and benevolence played, like sunshine over the ridges of the somber cliff.

To say that she was not surprised at Sibyl's early arrival, and did not mark her eyes swollen with weeping, would be manifestly untrue; but to say that with womanly wisdom and tact, she veiled her surprise and gave a motherly welcome to her Daniel's pet friend, the lonely home-starving school girl, would accord with exact fact. Nor was she long in fancying that some grief deeper than home sickness wounded the poor girl's heart.

That evening, as Sibyl and Mrs. Pierpont sat alone in the gloaming by the warm grate, the sore soul refused longer attempt to conceal its wound. Sibyl told it all, and dear Mrs. Pierpont could not refrain from tears, mingled with anger, nor from fervent words of gratitude to God, as she realized how the dear girl hung as by a hair over the precipice, and by some timely and unexpected intervention had escaped. The mother heart quickly reflected, too, "What if it had been my own sweet Mabel?" Taking Sibyl's hand in hers they sat in blessed fellowship and the silence of overwrought hearts.

Immediately the dutiful and affectionate Sibyl wrote to her father and mother, and with childlike and characteristic frankness, told them everything. The return letter from Gen. Tupper, of course confirmed what she had begun to suspect, that the letter which Mortimer presented to Miss Dean at the Seminary was a base and cruel forgery. Deciever, liar, jesuitical hypocrite, every day seemed to open to Sibyl and her friends a yet lower deep of baseness in the polished and adroit villain.

There were two younger inmates of Mrs. Pierpont's home, a son and daughter, Arlington and Mabel. The former was a determined and resolute fellow—not a genius, except so far as genius is capacity for hard work. Work Arlington Pierpont would and did, and his intense ambition fed and directed his zeal. But what fed his ambition? When we know this, we will know Arlington Pierpont. While carrying an almost fierce will power, it was veiled under a quiet well poised demeanor, and aided by a generous and genial nature which won him favor everywhere. While not a sport, he was sportive and athletic. Very few city-bred young men had his muscle.

"If I reach my pinnacle," Arlington reasoned, "and I am bound to get there,—I shall need tough fibre. Mother quotes to me, 'Seek ye first the Kingdom of God and His righteousness, and all these things shall be added to you," but secretly I paraphrase it thus, 'Seek ye first the kingdom of gold and its glory, and all the world shall be at your feet.' Time enough in the future to take up the old version of dear puritanic mother's text. College, well its a solid stepping stone for me, and I came off with *eclat* there. And now, three years of Blackstone and Kent have magnificently augmented the gray matter in my brain. Judge Phillips Wentworth thinks he has read me through and judicially sized me up, and tomorrow it will be 'Wentworth & Pierpont, Attorneys and Counsellors at Law.' Now for the climb. The Vanderveres, the Astrals and Belfontes will now open their gilded palaces, and the hearts of their fair maidens to the much talked about and rising young attorney. Then, there's this bright and bewitching

Sibyl, this pet of Daniel's, this transparent, lustrous gem of the 'Golden West,' that has just dropped into our home. She's enough to dissolve the cold calculating opaque heart of even this sinner."

Arlington loved to play sentimental airs upon the harp, and often Mabel, and Sibyl by her side, accompanied him with their soft and sympathetic voices, while the mother by the window sewing, listened with a deep though tranquil joy, occasionally looking out of the window with that absent and yet expectant look, blind to immediate objects, and pensively ruminating the past.

But the cup of pleasure overflowed to all in the house, when Daniel Pierpont and Emily Sherburne, now Mrs. Pierpont, arrived. And now, in the first surprise and merriment, and while all are talking at once, and laugh and serious and jesting remarks come in wholly unreportable style, we will just take occasion to say that after a lively correspondence and most harmonious adjustment, and an engagement and some waiting and various delays, and after the death of Emily's father, the way opened for their marriage. Ruth, still in the old home on Church Hill, was now Mrs. Harry Burnham, and dear Jamie's weary heart had ceased to beat, and he had gone to his mother and his Saviour.

This visit of Mr. Pierpont and his bride at his maternal home, coinciding so happily with Sibyl's vacation—who could tell the gratification it brought? Of this not the least was the enjoyment realized when Emily at the piano was the center of the admiring and affctionate group.

She touched the keys as with a caress. Added to long study, and to accuracy in execution, Emily had that musical intuition which constituted her a choice interpreter of the great master composers. Her refined and finished renderings captivated those about her, and held them as by a magic spell.

Then, too, her voice in song was pure, chaste and sympathetic, and went straight to the heart. She seemed to carry in her nature something of the sunny and mellow air of her delightful southern home.

Do you wonder that Daniel Pierpont, as he thought of the long years of uncertainty and steadfast waiting, and of the rich fruitage they had at last brought him, felt that the half could never be told.

Sabbath morning that was a happy group, the Pierponts, seated together at church; and who but a mother can fully understand that mother's emotions? Was it accident, or was the aptness itself an illustration of the text, when the minister presented these words, "And He led them forth by the right way?" The Lord led them—the children of Israel,—by a proverbially crooked path through the wilderness, and yet, as now everybody can see, it was by God's straight way.

More than one in that large audience felt that the Lord had led the pastor to exactly the heavenly manna for them. Sibyl thought she was a personal commentary on the minister's text, and something gathered in her throat as she tried to join in the hymn:

"Thus far the Lord has led me on."

CHAPTER XXIX.

Sibyl's vacation passed all too swiftly. She and Mabel took delight in traversing the great city together, and sometimes, to their great pleasure, Mrs. Pierpont brought her experience to bear as their chaperone. To our western girl, every day brought some discovery or adventure, every day novelty, exhiliration and rest, and not only more complete acquaintance, but riper, more retentive friendship.

What with counseling clients, many of whom Judge Wentworth was only too glad to place in the hands of his junior partner, and with arguing cases in the court; what with office work and with consulting heavy sheep bound volumes of law, and with the growing demands of his club rooms, and the increasing calls into coveted social circles, Arlington had small leisure to devote to home guests.

Yet Sibyl and Arlington met every day, and occasionally he would give with her a half day to some excursion—a sail in the harbor, or a run into the country, or through parks, libraries and museums; or now and then an evening at some choice concert or "lecture."

More than one of Arlington's fair lady admirers in the concert room, leveled her glass upon this queenly stranger who sat beside the coveted attorney; "Such eyes; such an intelligent and illuminated face; nothing rustic there surely. But who is she?"

Together with the Pierponts, Sibyl, with all her characteristic zest, rejoiced in the auspicious omens which were bestudding the sky above Arlington. None understood better than she the keen joy which comes in the flush of fresh blossoming success, and she found herself delighting in it somewhat as with a personal interest. Who can witness the launching of a ship, and not feel stirred somewhat as though himself identified with it?

Nor was it strange that Arlington, much as he prized his home, was coming to think of it as possessing a peculiar attraction, now that he could feel sure of meeting Sibyl there. His thought was, "Let me have Sibyl in the society of the affluent and fashion-leading. She is quick to see and learn. She'll soon be as perfect in social flavor as any of the *beau monde*, and far more original and brilliant. She's like Judge Wentworth's French wines which smack of the purple clusters on the sun-clad hills. She's of the timber which will polish and preserve the inimitable native grain." This young barrister was a skillful, and, in this case, certainly, a correct reasoner.

Life at school was doing much for Sibyl. It was swinging gates ajar all about her, and she was catching precious glimpses into a boundless world; that of thought, study and the ideal. She flushed with the glow of discovery, and the eagerness of the hungry when finding true bread. The kaleidoscope of life was manifold and ever revolving before her, as well as before Arlington; although the scenes and shading were not his. She enjoyed conversing with him, discussing books and reading and weighing his estimates of men and thngs, and testing his way of looking at everything. Not so well versed and fertile in opinions as he, still, as with her brother George, on many topics she stoutly dissented from Arlington's positions;—a fact which greatly amused and attracted him.

So, on smooth, well oiled axles vacation had rolled by. The school girl's trunk was packed, and hastily she and the Pierponts were taking an early breakfast, expecting the hack to call in a few moments.

It was an unusual hour for Arlington, who loved his morning nap, but this morning he was among the first to arouse the house. At breakfast he was unusually silent and self absorbed; and several times as Sibyl suddenly looked up, she discovered him gazing abstractedly at her.

It was all arranged. Henceforth Sibyl was to consider that the home of the Pierponts was one of her homes. Mabel said they must have her during vacations, and Arlington declared that he should have to institute suit against her if she violated that contract.

As on the September morning, Sibyl began to retrace her steps toward the Seminary, how vividly she contrasted herself with the Sibyl of a few weeks previous. How strange the old hills looked in the light of yesterday. The same route, same scenes, but could it be that she was the same one who so recently looked upon them through such happy dreams? Dreams indeed; was it not all a dream? Could it be reality? Alas, it was the cold and bitter real. He who was but yesterday the trust, the hope of her heart, the center of her love, so suddenly stripped of all disguise. She saw now the studied deceit, the deliberate diabolical plot, which wound like a slimy reptile through, from first to last of her acquaintance with Mortimer. The long, cunning, cruel, crime! She hid her eyes as if trying to hide from view some frightful shape.

The bitter cup was not without its blessing to Sibyl Tupper. Something out of it was wrought into the sweet, noble, strong woman that she was to be. If she entered Seminary Hall with a step a trifle less buoyant, it was more resolute and firm, and with no misanthrophy, with her faith in the good stronger than ever.

"I was perilously near the whirlpool," she

said; " my prow already dipping into the mad vortex, when He who answers prayer, in the very nick of time, snatched me, saved me; and surely saved for some good purpose. He must have something for me to do. Whatever it is, I want to do it. Blessed Mama's old word so often was, 'Do the next thing;' and grand, faithful Mr. Goldwin used to say, 'Whatever thy hand findeth to do, do it with thy might.' Now school is the next thing, study the 'whatsoever thy hand findeth,' and I'll do it too. And wherever I go, I'll be a missionary; who knows where? Perhaps in Riverton, perhaps in India."

Sibyl lived on the earth, and yet in a house which touched the heavens. Under such aims and aspirations life had no insipid taste; rather was daily filled with divine nectar.

Vacation brought Sibyl to New York once or twice a year, and during the intervening months communication with the Pierponts was by occasional correspondence. She was ever charmingly frank in expressing her opinions and preferences, and Arlington was equally frank in declaring to her his plans, and picturing his hopes. Indeed, so engrossed was he in his personal schemes, that it was almost impossible for him to avoid communicating them to his friends.

It was the evening before Sibyl's graduation day, and she sat alone in her room. Her simple commencement gown which was spread on the bed by her side, had successfully passed the scrutiny of the feminine artists. Her graduating essay, tied with dainty blue ribbon by Lucy Darrow's deft fingers was on the table before her, and she had sportingly dubbed it her "Rubicon." She was reflecting, "There must be some Rome for me to conquer. Wonder where it is. But I shall surely know that, when I am commissioned."

Presently two letters were handed in to Sibyl. Both of them were superscribed in a manly hand which she had occasionally seen before. She opened the one from Arlington first; a breezy letter, containing an account of a dinner he had just given at the "Hamiltonian."

"Plates," he wrote, "were laid for a hundred guests. Tip top fellows they were, every one of them; socially and politically the very cream of New York. Rich and rising men, they represent piles of money. Many of them are party bosses. They run the political mill. And I mean to make them do some pretty substantial grinding for me this Fall. I am laying the track for the office of prosecuting attorney; a fat office when you take in all the perquisites; and I shall come steaming in on election day. My friends are going *en masse* for me, and say they will 'stampede the convention,' but what they will have me nominated. This office, however, is only a stepping stone. I am bound for Congress, and who knows what next? My campaign speeches are ready on tap. I'll play most musically on the patriotic chord, if Sam Johnson did say that 'Patriotism was the last resort of scoundrels.' Its all a game anyway, and I may as well take a hand in it as anybody. As they say out in your Hoosier State, 'The longest pole knocks the persimmons.'"

"The dinner cost a deal of money, but it was great, and the wine was simply superb. After dinner wit scintillated and coruscated, and the host was covered all over with compliments and glory. Then there was more wine and more demonstration, and then the carriages rolled away. Now you, my unworldly friend, Sibyl, are shaking your head at what I have written, but some day you will be proud of me.

"Last and most important, and for which in fact I am writing this letter, my congratulations on your successful and flattering completion of your seminary course. And now for the wide wide world."

In this connection we will say that Arlington Pierpont omitted saying in his letter to Sibyl, that some of the after dinner speeches showed more wine than wit. Such maudlin, slobbering, vulgar stuff was too sickening to chronicle. Drunken hands hurled glasses of wine against the beautifully frescoed walls; carpets and furniture carried indelible marks of the midnight revel. Even the host himself all but lost himself. And the men of the company who were temperate and self-trolled, and in justice it can be said that they were in the majority, left for their homes with small ceremony. The fact is Arlington Pierpont was already launched on the sea of temptation, and was boldly wantoning with its billows.

The other letter brought to Sibyl by that same mail, was from Jonas Drake, one of her early acquaintances at Riverton; a note bearing congratulations and friendly wishes from the college boy to the college girl. Like that received from the city lawyer, it breathed of ardent hopes and endeavors, but how different from those of Arlington; in implied purpose and preference as widely sundered from him as the poles. Jonas was resolved on preaching the gospel, and his present objective point was the theological seminary. The modesty of Jonas, coupled with manliness and a beautiful enthusiasm for pure ideals, impressed Sibyl. "The contrast," she thought, "Arlington living for this world only, and Jonas for both worlds."

The next year Sibyl spent at home in post graduate work along several divergent lines. An hour of the morning was, as she said, devoted to a cooking school, with her mother as instructor. For another hour or more she was home secretary to her father. An hour of the afternoon was spent in English classics, with Mr. Goldwin as teacher. Also few days closed without visits to the lowliest and neediest.

In process of time came a visit of Arlington Pierpont to his brother Daniel in Riverton, which was as unexpected as it was significant. The tall, handsome, brilliant attorney of New York, was a conspicuous and distinguished figure on the streets of Riverton. His evenings were sedulously spent at General Tuppers.

One morning Arlington announced to Daniel and Emily that time was up; that he must be off; that duck and deer hunts on these preserves must be postponed; that legal business was pressing; could not wait another day. As he flitted into Riverton so he flitted out.

At this time George Tupper, fresh from West Point, was at home on a short leave of absence. He and Arlington were soon on friendliest terms, jolly, jocund, and facetious.

Scarcely had Arlington so suddenly turned his back upon Riverton, when George hastened to the room of his idolized sister, Sibyl. To his surprise she was as cool and undisturbed as though matches and marriages were the veriest trifles, to be had at any moment for the asking.

In high glee George caught her up in his arms and kissed her profusely, and planted her in an easy chair by the window, and himself in front of her.

"Sib. you're a diamond!" Then rather repelled by her deliberate manner, he added; "Take it deuced cool, don't you?"

Sibyl turning on him a half reproving look, asked, "George what do you mean? Pray explain yourself."

"Now Sibyl, no playing off. Do you suppose we are blind? Just come down from your high mightiness. Tell a fellow, when is the wedding to be? I'm to be the best man, you now, so I hope you'll call off the affair when I can get a furlough."

"Furloughs enough, if you wait for my bridal day," said Sibyl indifferently.

An instant's pause, and leaping from his chair as though a thunder bolt had struck him, he shouted: "Sibyl Tupper! What! You don't mean to say—you don't mean to say—that you have refused Arlington Pierpont?"

"I mean exactly that, George, dear."

"Sibyl! Sibyl Tupper! You're the confoundedest idiot the sun shines upon;" and away he stalked out of the room.

Sibyl caught up her garden hat and following her impulsive and irate brother, softened down his ruffled temper with her sweet sisterly tact, as she knew so well how to do, and then, arm in arm, brother and sister strolled down by the river bank, which had long been the family trysting place, and sat down for a talk.

"This spot is romantic, George; it is historic. Don't you remember that Daniel Pierpont and Cousin Emily were sitting in this very spot, in the moonlight, on that June evening so long ago, when that base savage shot his arrow into the flesh of poor Pierpont?"

"Yes, and if I'm not mistaken, that was the night that Cupid's arrow pierced Emily's heart."

"And there, George, is the very old log on which we sat that bright summer day when you opened to me your soldier boy aspirations."

"So it is, Sib., so it is. How little I knew then for what I was asking."

And so in a sort of reminiscent mood they chatted on for some time, bringing up odds and ends of their good old times; but studiously avoiding the subject, which, for both of them, filled all the near horizon, until George abruptly said: "Tell me, Sibyl, why you don't marry Arlington Pierpont. Time enough yet to recall your hasty decision, for he adores you. Don't you like him?

"I see much to admire in him, George, but I don't love him. I can't love him. It did me a world of good when dear Mama folded me in her arms and said, 'In this matter follow your reason and your heart, my darling; follow your reason and your heart.'"

"Yes, but I don't see why he don't take your heart. He's wondrous clever; bound to reach the top. Ten years more, and he'll be in Congress."

"Congressman, President or King; that

could make no difference. I could never marry him. You can call it moonshine, or 'piosity,' or whatever you please, George; but the truth is you and Arlington live in a different world from mine. And, much as I know you wish to, you cannot understand my feelings and motives in this thing. Arlington Pierpont does not fill my ideal."

"Hang your ideals. Shades of Moses, Sib! Stop your pious romancing. Don't live in the next world till you get there. You are throwing away the chance of a lifetime. You may grow fantastic and priggish and live in sack cloth and ashes till you wither up, and then draw a blank; but love without glory or money makes a poor outfit."

Sibyl grew pale and flushed, by turns, as she silently prayed for just the convincing word. Then with quivering lips she said: "George, I can't look at life solely or even primarily from a commercial view; and ought you to? There's the way of the world and the way of the Christian, and you and I with our training, ought to know which of these ways to take. Marriage is no mere bargain. Mind you, I don't despise money, but I do despise these all 'hire and salary' estimates. Arlington Pierpont has ability and application; is determined and resolute; has position; has rare opportunity, but, George, I fear he is going to miss his opportunity. Moreover, if Arlington had every other quali-

:ation, I should not dare to marry a man who sports with the wine cup."

"Well, Sibyl, all I can say is, you are hopelessly, provokingly old fashioned."

For a few moments brother and sister were silent, and George was breaking up dead twigs and tossing them, one by one, into the river, and looking meanwhile as though his ambitions for Sibyl, one by one, were floating out to sea.

"Let me read you this," said Sibyl, as she drew a slip of paper from her pocket. It is a part of Mr. Goldwin's words at the wedding of Susie Barton, the other day. They went straight to my heart and I came home and wrote them down while they were fresh in my mind: 'Beloved friends, you stand here under the eyes of these kind observers to confirm a union already established in your hearts; one which has God as its founder, God as its protector. Sealed in purity and cemented in the love of the heart, it is the most precious of earthly bonds; and while it brings new duties, brings also new and higher joys. May this union now about to be consummated, be sweetened and hallowed by your mutual consecration to our common Lord and Redeemer.'"

"Now, George, these words from Mr. Goldwin exactly comport with my idea of a true marriage. More could not be asked of mortals, yet I could not be satisfied with less. Could I, George? Could I? Do you really want me to be satisfied with less?" And with her glorious eyes she looked straight into his.

George grew thoughtful and subdued, and for a few moments was silent, and sat looking abstractedly at the little island in midriver, where the birds were billing and cooing and nesting with such delicious *abandon* and with none of the perplexities and disappointments which torment us human kind. Ambitious and worldly though he was, at heart there was something in him responsive to higher and nobler things, and through Sibyl he often caught a glimpse of them and realized his own lack. His sister's rejection of Arlington Pierpont amazed and angered and disappointed him, and then gained his respectful toleration, and then his approval. "After all," he reflected, "the girl may be the wisest in the thing. Time will tell."

Rising, he said, "Forgive me, Sibyl. I've raved at you like a bear. I suppose you are right; from your standpoint you must be; you always were right,—you and Mr. Goldwin. Buss me, Sib., and let's go home."

Drawing near the house, Sibyl tripped off, George after her and dropped down on the velvety moss under the old basswood tree, now completely grown over by a wild grape vine. How the climber had intertwined and infolded the tree, overtopping it and trailing down on all sides.

"George, this vine has improved the time

since we sat here three years ago,—or is it four?"

"That's it, Sib. Gain to the vine, but loss to the tree, for you see the tree has surrendered, and simply exists for something else to lean upon, and coil about, and absorb its life. See, it is dying at the core, growing hollow, branches are dead. Some day in some storm the tree will collapse, and away goes the vine with it."

"Why, George, you didn't mean it but you've given me exactly the parable I want this very minute;" and her face lighted up with the discovery.

"What's on tap now, my charmer? You can't submerge or shock me again. So open out."

"Since you urge me, George, I will open out and you may fight me if you want to, if you will surrender at the finish. About the vine, I don't mean to be a vine; simply a leaner, a graceful twiner, a parasite, or a trailer. Call me 'strong minded' if you will, but I scout all this dribble about its being masculine, or unwomanly for a woman to have a self-supporting occupation, a calling, a profession, or whatever you may name it. Not a preacher, nor a lawyer for me. Oh, no, no. But what do you say to my being a doctor?"

"A doctor! What trash you are talking, Sibyl. What's got into you lately?"

"Nothing except a little of the old Tupper

independence and be-something spirit, I guess."

"Well, now what's coming next? As soon as a fellow is cooled off from one heat, you bring on another. You are more exasperating than a half-day's drill under a Fourth of July sun;" and his stick ploughed up the moss savagely. "A doctor indeed! I think I see you; hair cut short, parted on the side, pill bag in hand, shingle out:

DOCTOR SIBYL TUPPER, Spinster,
Physician and Surgeon.
Office Hours, 8 to 10 a. m., and 7 to 9 p. m.

"No more good times for me when I come home. My sister a servant of the public; a regular social petrifaction."

At this Sibyl rung out her merry contageous laugh. "Why, George, really the mantle of prophesy has fallen on you. I may never put out my shingle, as you say; but here's Dr. Bancroft, up to date in surgical and medical science, just hungering for such a student as I would mean to be,—one with a 'bent' you see. I am no crank or comeouter or hobbyist, George; but I do mean to study and learn, and fit myself for life in the fullest meaning of that word. And then, a knowledge of medicine would be almost indispensable, if I should be a missionary;— oh, George, don't stare at me so! You frighten me. You must let me think out loud to you. However, as to my particular career, I have no anxiety about that; it will shape itself."

"Well, Sibyl, go and talk your wild vagaries to Mr. and Mrs. Goldwin, and give me a rest. I can't fight any more before dinner, and I won't surrender. Hello! There's the dinner bell. That's music to a hungry fellow. This is the day for Jane's pot pie and apple dumplings. You've given me a glorious appetite, Sib."

CHAPTER XXX.

Three more years have passed over Riverton. A Sabbath softness and tranquil joy are floating on the air, and nature seems an embodiment of worship. It is one of those sweet summer days that lie like islands of enchantment between the waves of heat and cold. It is not the Sabbath, but it is midweek, and yet the Riverton church is open, and the people are flocking to it. The ushers are specially busy, ubiquitous and gracious. And well they may be, for they seldom have a greater opportunity.

The audience room is filling very fast. Today no objections to front seats. Flowers are almost everywhere, and the pulpit is embowered and well nigh buried with them.

"Your voiceless lips, O flowers, are living
    preachers,
Each cup a pulpit, every leaf a book."

Their language goeth everywhere, and they graciously temper the odor of sanctity, harmonizing it with the calm triumphant joy which exhales from all hearts. Flowers fitly garland this day of spiritual espousals.

On the pulpit platform are several clergymen. Among them, and sitting to the right, is the Rev. Dr. Charles Whiting, President of the College from which Jonas Drake was graduated; and to the left is the Rev. Henry Littleton, who has encouraged so many pioneer churches into permanent life. In the center sits the Riverton minister abiding in the fullness of his strength, and carrying no ominous prints of the passing years.

Seated immediately in front of the pulpit is a man with a face as modest and manly as you ever set eyes on. His dark hair shades a fine strong brow, and there are suggestions of unfathomed depths in those large blue eyes.

Do you recognize in this man the boy Jonas with whom Mr. Goldwin once sat on the rocks which fret the swift waters of the Rappilee, and threw out a line to tempt the wary pickerel and bass? What if there were other lines thrown out on that day into deeper depths, and those which will reach into far days and lands.

Jonas Drake has completed his college and theological seminary course, and has been interviewed concerning several of the more attractive and promising pastorates, to any one of which he seems well adapted; but, true to the spirit which he has early imbibed under Mr. Goldwin's ministry, he has promptly turned from them to choose an almost entirely missionary enterprise, in one of the most crowded and neglected districts of the city of New York.

Now that he is to be ordained to the ministry he says, "Where a place so fitting as at home among my old friends and neighbors? And who shall preach the sermon if not Mr. Goldwin?"

The preliminary session for testing and passing upon the candidate has been held. The ministers have aired their pet theories and crucial doctrines in their catechizing of the young recruit; but he has stood fire successfully.

True, old Father Crane screwed about in his seat; a little uneasy because he missed from the answers of the candidate the ancient stereotyped forms, and listened in vain for the hackneyed phrases. Dr. Ball, too, at first eyed Jonas quite askance, and turned his antique guns upon him. But Jonas, as it proved, had looked into the intricacies and dark problems quite as far as had Dr. Ball, and his modest but skillful turns hedged in the Doctor, and indeed several times brought down the house. Mr. and Mrs. Goldwin exchanged glances and smiled inwardly.

One thing became sufficiently evident: Jonas was well acquainted with his Bible, and his doctrinal system and his faith grew not chiefly out of one or two isolated excerpts, but out of the manifest meaning and teaching of the Bible as one book; as a unit; grew out of it as naturally, as gracefully as the branch out of the vine. It is clear, thought the ministers, that this young man knows his Bible and intends to preach it.

But doubtless the most impressive moment came previous to this, when Jonas being asked to give in some detail his religious history and experience, did so in terms simple, tender and really eloquent. His early thoughts and queryings all to himself, his apparently barren but really absorbent and germinant boyhood; how his mother then understood him so well and dealt with him so wisely; how Mr. Goldwin fished with him, won him, and stole into his heart before he knew it; how he led him into the light and love of Christ, and out under the infinite skies of divine thinking and living;—all this was so simple, so touchingly truthful, that the attention and interest became intense. When he said, "Brethren, my Saviour always first, and my mother and my pastor next," there was no dry eye in that audience.

A moment's pause, and Mr. Goldwin asked the candidate to state his views concerning the application of Christianity to life, the life that we are living. Here Jonas was quite at the front.

"As it appears to me," he replied, "immense spaces of human thought and conduct lie as yet untouched by the ten commandments or by Christian love. As ministers, we are appointed of God to lead the way in bringing the gospel of Christ to bear upon politics, the ballot, slavery, marriage, divorce, the liquor business, the gambling den, the impure resort, upon buying and selling, upon the entire use of money; upon the relations of rich and poor, employer and employed, white man and red man, black man and every other man. Since you, brethren, have asked me the question, may I not ask, is it not the fact that we have not yet dreamed of applying Christianity except in spots?" Mr. Goldwin's face was radiant.

"But," said Dr. Ball, "my dear young man, with all this array of side shows, how are you to find time to preach the gospel?"

Promptly came the reply, "Dr. Ball, I do not expect to find time for anything except preaching the gospel. I know of no side shows. There is a system of truth, no doubt; and we, as we hope, have caught glimpses of it, and I mean to preach the truth and nothing but the truth as it is in the Bible, so far as I know it. But I do not live for my system. That is not my object. My system is good for naught, except as, by the help of God, I can make it save men. Lost men are what I am after, and the gospel of Christ, pure, simple and direct, is my instrument for reaching, for rescuing them. Wherever there is a human being who needs Christ, there is my pulpit and my audience." It was evident that with some of the brethren this view of the work of the ministry meant for them, in their thinking and their methods of work, revolution.

The editor of "The Watchman of the Valley" was in Riverton at this time, and for a double purpose. At an early hour in the morning he called together the ministers, and with business directness, sprung upon them two questions, and said that as soon as they were answered, and this blessed young man was dubbed a preacher of the gospel, he must face toward the big city by the Ohio.

He asked, "Do you like The Watchman of the Valley? And what can you do to help me to make the paper better?"

"Of course we like The Watchman of the Valley," answered half a dozen voices. "You know we do," said Bro. Littleton.

"Well then, if you do, why haven't you told a poor despairing editor so before? Without doubt, your wife knows that you love her, but she wants you to tell her of it once a week or so," said the editor. This was pat, and a broad smile went around.

"Your editorial on divorce laws," remarked Dr. Whiting, "was a long step in advance. As you say, 'let the law be placed on the statute book, that no divorced party, except he be divorced, for the scriptural reason which breaks the marriage bond, shall be allowed to marry again until five years subsequent to receiving divorce papers, and nine-tenths of the suits for divorce would be declared off."

Then a good natured free-lance discussion as to how to edit a paper, followed, and after numerous suggestions and endorsements, all cordially agreed with Mr. Goldwin, that it was no easy task to discern the word for each hour, to keep just enough in advance of the people to lead them, and that the editor, like the preacher, needs outlook, needs the vision of the seer; needs, indeed, a sixth sense; a sense of the interesting and the timely, as well as of the useful.

As we have seen, the ministers are now on and about the pulpit platform, the audience is in full attendance, and Mr. Goldwin is preaching the ordination sermon. His special theme is, "Our Saviour's Pulpit." We can only give the merest outlines of the eloquent discourse.

Mr. Goldwin said: "Christ was our model in respect to his pulpit, as well as in respect to everything else. He stepped into a boat and bade his disciples push out a little from the land, and from thence he addressed the multitude.

"His was a floating pulpit, sensitive to every breath of air, every agitation of the elements;—no rock or stone, impassive, irresponsive to the forces around.

Nevertheless, His was an anchored pulpit; —never adrift, never at the mercy of the elements; recognized every movement, but never was ruled by it; always in the deep, never the deep in it.

"His was the pulpit of a large auditorium, —large as all out of doors; addressed Jew and Gentile, Dives and Lazarus, the little children and the hoary patriarch, China and India and all that lies between.

"His was a human pulpit, always in earshot of man; acoustically was perfectly placed; touched every string of the human harp, and with the caressing touch of the sweetly, profoundly human.

"His was a divine pulpit,—always open toward heaven."

Mr. Goldwin's closing words, addressed to Jonas, were "fu tender," hopeful, triumphant; a father to his true and very dear son.

Dr. Whiting then delivered a brief address which was in many ways a gem, apostolic, classic, uplifting. Rev. Bro. Littleton followed with the ordaining prayer.

During the singing of the closing hymn, to the surprise of the congregation, Jonas walked out, and then, as soon as the people were seated, to their still greater surprise, Jonas walked in with Sibyl Tupper at his side, and the two took their places immediately in front of Mr. Goldwin and were married.

Five years and a half have passed since the blessed wedding day of Jonas and Sibyl; years full of work among the lowest in a very neglected quarter of New York City. Many of the coveted pulpits of that city were opened to the gifted young man, but none of them were large enough to tempt him or his

God-sent helper, Sibyl, from his rapidly growing missionary church.

Now we come upon an event which we would gladly spare from these pages. It is a night in January, and bitter cold. The clock in the great tower is solemnly tolling the midnight, and the fevered throb in this congested ganglion of the city is unwontedly subdued. For a moment even the wicked have ceased from troubling, and some of the weary are at rest.

For three days Jonas with a policeman at his side, has been searching for a lost man. Every clew has failed, and in despair he is almost ready to abandon the search, when at last, in a battered and all but roofless hovel, with only the cold stars as sentinels, the lost is found, stiff, frozen and stark dead. Drink has done its worst and Arlington Pierpont is gone.

It is the only too familiar story. Petted and flattered by the rich, solicited with the wine glass from the hands of bewitching loveliness, hobnobbed with the sated scions of wealth and fashion, serving their hour in the brilliance of his entertaining genius; gay salons of women, wit and wine, then the club room and the wine and more wine, then the gambling table and the inevitable drink, then the gilded saloon; power of sustained work gone, clients gone, money gone, political friends and chums of better days gone, ambitions and aspirations gone, self-respect and manhood gone, pleading of mother and brother and sister unavailing;—then at last the low dive.

Not at a leap, did Arlington Pierpont go down, but by gradual descent, and with intervals of repentance, and brief and yet briefer reform, till at last it is almost unbroken debauch, ending in delirium and death.

In the pocket of the dead man was found a note, written a week or more previous to his death, and probably in the last sober moments he ever knew.

"My precious mother: A horrible pit yawns before me, and a thousand demons are at its bottom waiting to welcome me. 'At the last it biteth like a serpent and stingeth like an adder.' You told me so and now I know it to be the truth. I am a slave to drink. I have broken your heart, and this thought will sting me forever.

"Your lost boy,
"Arlington."

Two weeks later, Daniel and Mabel, and Jonas and Sibyl by her bedside, the broken hearted mother passed into the exceeding peace of heaven.

Poor, lonely Mabel! Sibyl, in her simple and resistless way, took the dear girl to herself and her home. They were as one. Mabel always, wherever she might be placed, was forgetting self in doing service and kindness to others, and here in Sibyl's medical dispensary, and in ministry to the friendless and poor she found exactly her work and her happiness.

Beside this, many a day witnessed this sweet, modest, brave girl, medicine case in hand, going among the squalid hovels, climbing the battered and filthy stairs of wretched tenement houses, kneeling by the sick, the sinning and the sinned against, huddled in dark cellars or desolate attics; time after time bringing love, sympathy, and, where it was wise, assistance and pecuniary help, until those hard-faced, imbruted, callous beings began to say, "I really do believe she cares for us;" and many a despondent, heartless recreant began to catch visions and hopes of better possibilities.

CHAPTER XXXI.

Pass now to a date more than forty years after Mr. Goldwin first set foot in Riverton. The forms of many of those with whom we have been familiar, rest now in the silent city of the dead on the eastern slope of that now populous commercial center.

A marble monolith bears the name, "Tupper," and beneath its shadow is gathered all that is mortal of General and Mrs. Tupper. George Tupper fell while gallantly leading his brigade to the charge in the late Civil War. John Tupper studied law with Mr. Pierpont, and in '49 was caught in the tide which swept so many to California.

Here in the practice of his profession, he, at length, to his great surprise, stumbled upon Edward Mortimer. Marked and bent with a weight which was far more than that of years, sin-visaged and unkempt, and passing under several aliases, now and then something of his former courtliness of manner appeared, like the blossom on the nettle. He had at last rendered himslf so odious that prison walls with difficulty protected him from summary justice at the hands of "Judge Lynch." Under this remnant of a man, Tupper, who had not seen him for more than fifteen years, recognized the identical Mortimer, who entirely failed to recognize the boy, John Tupper, in the Judge Tupper, before whom he was arraigned.

To the utter amazement of the criminal, the Judge proceeded to review his whole history, his excellent parentage, whose name he had always dishonored, whose pillow he had filled with thorns; his noble, guileless wife, whom he had coldly, deliberately deceived and deserted; his plots and lewd attempts upon innocence; his dissolute effrontery, insolence, and nauseating hypocrisy; his vagabond and vermined life, a slimy serpent crawling under the fair flowers of earth.

This blot upon creation, this criminal so long a stranger to the blush of purity or honor, so impregnable in his self complacency, so hideously audacious in his villainy, at first stared unconcernedly at the Judge, then, as he listened, surprise became blank amazement; then he seemed suddenly to recall something with a sting. Then athwart his dark visage flashed a light, swift, momentary and lurid as lightning bolts across a cloud—a flash of discovery which said more plainly than words, "Ah, Judge, now I recognize you; see in your features, resemblances which glass before me one whom I beguiled, and but for an interposing God, had forced to be a partner in my infamy and ruin." He seemed to himself to stand uncovered in the revealing fires of the last Day.

In spite of himself, his once superb frame, now shattred and broken, trembled; and his countenance assumed what seemed the pallor of death. The judge impaled him on the javelins of his uncounted crimes, and tortured him until the spectators hung breathless, and almost their indignation had turned to pity.

Then promising the miscreant that if he was ever seen by mortal eye again on that coast, it should be the last of earth to him, and on condition that he should flee the continent before the next sunrise, the Judge dismissed the case. Before an hour had passed, the wretch had engaged as cook on a whaling vessel just putting out, and thus Edward Mortimer dropped forever from public view.

At length, with pockets well lined with shekels, Judge John Tupper returned to Riverton, opened a law office, married the attractive Waxie Drake and installed her to preside at the old Tupper home.

Turn again to that same hillside place of graves. There is a little square plot of ground marked off by an iron fence, and almost filled with hillocks. The bronze plate on the iron gate bears the name of "Perkins." Here are the graves of Mr. and Mrs. Perkins, and of several of their adult sons. The father had been a phenominally successful Indian trader, and was a large land holder. His three daughters were noble women. Several of his sons ran as swiftly as intemperance and vice could carry them, to the grave.

One of them, amid great *eclat*, was married to Kate Grande. Mrs. Col. Grande plumed herself vastly on bringing about so "splendid a match." But the bridegroom was hardly sober when the solemn words were said, and in less than a twelve month the foul debauchee was borne with much pomp to a really dishonorable grave. Alas! How many funerals of this kind Mr. Goldwin could recount.

A few steps, and we are on the gravel walk which leads to Samuel Drake's hospitable door. How the trees have reached out and up; have grown venerable and majestic. The honeysuckle still curtains and garlands that window where we last saw Mrs. Drake, her sewing in her lap, and sweet thoughts which might have graced a seraph's lyre, working into the stitching. Occasionally as she lifted her eyes to the far away "blue," she sent thoughts swifter than the lark and sweeter than fragrant honeysuckle, straight to the Great White Throne.

Dear, good Mrs. Drake, divinely guided counselor, consoler, friend. The King had need of her. She's close by her Lord now. Her monument? Look around, in her home; in her church; in the secret place of hearts she had cheered and enriched. Mr. and Mrs. Goldwin said when she ascended, that earth had lost something which could never come to them again, this side of Heaven.

But there is Mr. Barnett; call him Jack

and he'll not resent it. His Vermont wife passed away years ago, and now he is married to Rachel Drake, that beautiful composite of father and mother, and they affectionately cling to the old Drake fireside.

We'll follow Mr. Barnett through the familiar house. Ah! Sure enough, there's Samuel Drake just out the back door, on the bench under the apple tree,—and the kind eyes of the old dog look up at his master, as if he wanted to say, "We are growing old together."

Sam and his dog, "Mixer No. 3." The veteran pioneer doesn't spring to his feet as promptly as when we saw him last. "Rheumatiz" stiffens his limbs. But he's still plain homespun, honest, contemplative Sam Drake. Rachel rests her hand on his shoulder and caressingly smoothes the gray locks over his temples. How her tender love soothes his bereft soul.

But if you want to see the old time lustre in his eye, speak the word, "Jonas." He'll not be long in telling you of his boy's great work in New York City. And Jonas' children; ah ,the children! some of them nearly grown. Well, you may as well sit down, for Sam won't let you off now until he has gone them all over; given you their names, ages, and their several kinks and specialties.

And Sibyl? Sam Drake thinks she's the flower of the world. And, in truth, Sam. is about right. Sibyl is the same wonderful woman, only maturer, and, if possible, of more manifold beauty. She mingles in blessed unity the every day natural, and the ideal and the spiritual.

As for Jonas, eloquent and devoted minister, he says that those who are always pitying him because his work lies among the poor and neglected, are wasting their breath. Said he, "I would rather preach the gospel to the poor, than to be President of the United States;" and he is always maintaining that it is Mr. Goldwin more than any other man who speaks through him.

We miss from the streets of Riverton the tall soldierly form of Col. Grande. Surviving Mrs. Grande by several years, one day he was suddenly siezed with a violent fever, and in the ravings of delirium, he was announcing himself as candidate, now for Justice of the Peace, now for City Clerk, and now for Constable of the third ward, and finally, before sinking into a comatose state, from which he never rallied, he was muttering something about Henry Clay.

Dr. Bancroft, brusque and benevolent as ever, still practices his profession among a select circle of old friends, who will not consent that he should surrender them to any other physician. Long ago he built himself a house on the street just back of Mr. Goldwin, and Mrs. Bancroft we are pleased to remember as the even, kindly and discerning Isabel Tupper.

Over against Dr. Bancroft is a spacious dwelling. Read the door plate—"Daniel Pierpont." Ah! There he is on the piazza. His iron gray hair, and his happy sons and daughters about him, recall us to a realization of the lapse of years. United States Senator he is now, and indeed, has been for several terms.

Emily, matronly and winsome, stands beside him on the piazza. Beside him she has been all these years, filling and adorning her station, alike in Riverton or in Washington.

Daniel Pierpont, not impatient for promotion, unselfish, incorruptible, serenely beheld whole generations of upstarts dash by him into momentary notice—irridescent bubbles. But when times of peril called for a man, a statesman, and one not for sale, all eyes fastened on Daniel Pierpont, and his promotion came like the dawn, normal and resistless as the march of the sun.

But here we are before Mr. Goldwin's home. How the hill has been cut away in order to bring the street to uniform grade. We'll climb the steps to the first terrace. The house has grown, has a wing now on the west side. One was planned for the east side, but as Jack Barnett would say, "did not realize;" an aborted organ, arrested growth. A kitchen "lean to" has developed until now it carries a second story.

With the house the household has grown. The city has grown, and now wears the *toga virilis* with abundant self-consciousness. The canal, the Wabash and Erie, no longer is—has run its day. Its channel through the city has been built into a street. Four or five railway lines now hub at Riverton. Business crept up town, absorbed the old church building, and sent the congregation four blocks away into a symmetric sanctuary built of stone.

But, now we have regained our breath and taken our bearings, let us climb to the second terrace and pull the door bell to Mr. Goldwin's home. A daughter answers it, the youngest, Lucille by name—Lux., they call her. You would know her by the sparkle in her eyes. We catch glimpses, too, of half a dozen others, nascent editions—some enlarged editions—of the original volume.

We count ourselves peculiarly fortunate, for we have happened on a family reunion, and they are all at home—five sons and two daughters—perfect number of Scripture. "The boys," as the mother calls them, are called men on election day, and are ordained ministers, save one, and he is hard on the way. Foreordained ministers, some call them; but the boys themselves stoutly maintain, that they are examples as well as exponents of freedom of the will. Will enough they all have, the mother says. Yesterday was Sunday, and four of them were in the pulpit together. People remarked that the pulpit was "filled."

This hour at the Goldwin home, however, is no Sunday hour. We are on the edge of the dark. The parlor lamp is bright, but the eyes are brighter. The family have drifted into the parlor. Father and mother are side by side in their arm chairs. The light reflects from their faces which time has chiseled and beautified, but recognition is instant,—it is still John and Margaret.

This, however, is the "children's hour." They are all talking, and all talking at once; and the venerable moderator of assemblies in vain calls to order; Margaret laughs and tells him this is an interlocutory session, and the parents gracefully subside, and unremonstrantly enjoy.

As father and mother were laying their heads on their pillows for the night, Margaret whispered, "New broom still?" "Aye, aye," said John, "always new," and he drew her to his lips.

How tenderly, reverently, everyone speaks of Father Goldwin. Dr. Goldwin, as some address him, for his Alma Mater, years ago, honored herself as well as him in conferring the doctorate on him. Even wicked men eagerly take to themselves the credit of recognizing this modern saint. He is bowed with his years and physical infirmities, and has resigned the work in Riverton to stronger shoulders; but he still carries the gospel to what he calls his country parishes. For ten years or more after resigning his pastorate in Riverton, he continues these "out appointments" irrespective of seasons or weather..

Of the love which grew between the people of these rural churches and Father Goldwin, it is impossible to convey adequate idea in words. It was beautiful and wonderful; and children's children in that vicinage, to this day point to his benign face looking down upon them from the wall, and rehearse his good works with moistened eye.

They tell of that last Sabbath,—communion Sabbath—when the white haired saint, too feeble to stand, and voice weakened to a whisper, sat in his chair, while they all gathered close about him, breathless to catch every word.

After this last public ministration, he continued to go about his home, and to take his accustomed daily walk, and with keen eye to mark the daily movement of events in the wide world, until, one morning it was whispered on the streets, "Father Goldwin is gone," and Riverton was silent and in mourning.

"Now there was leaning on Jesus' bosom one of his disciples whom Jesus loved." These fit words prefaced the funeral discourse.

Today a memorial window sheds its opal and crimson and sapphire lights on the hallowed spot where this Riverton minister for so long a time preached; and bears in illuminated text the words:

"REV. JOHN GOLDWIN, D. D.
He walked with God, and he was not; for God took him.'."